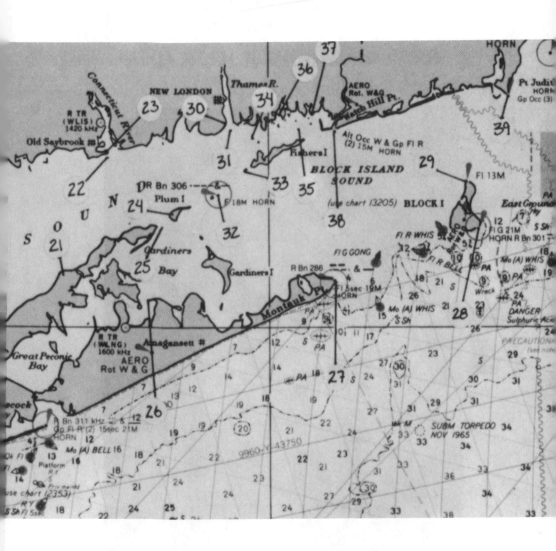

Author Harlan Hamilton

LIGHTS & LEGENDS

A HISTORICAL GUIDE TO LIGHTHOUSES

OF

LONG ISLAND SOUND, FISHERS ISLAND SOUND
AND BLOCK ISLAND SOUND

by   Harlan Hamilton

Edited by Julius M. Wilensky

All photos by the author unless otherwise noted

Library of Congress Card No. 87-50764
ISBN No. 0-918752-08-6
SAN No. 210-5810

Dedication

For the Keepers of the Light,
Past and Present

There is nothing that moves the imagination like a lighthouse.

Samuel Adams Drake
15th Century Historian

TABLE OF CONTENTS

3

Part II - Lighthouse Technology and Definitions

EDITOR'S PREFACE

When Hal Hamilton first approached us with his idea for a lighthouse book, we were astounded to learn that none existed for Long Island Sound and Block Island Sound. I've been admiring the variety of lighthouses on the Sound for the 50 years that I've been cruising these waters, and with other sailors, have wondered about their history. Most sailors know the legend of Execution Light, but there are stories associated with all these lights, whether appropos to their names or not. We discussed the scope of the book together, sailed to Sheffield Lighthouse together, and agreed on what the book should be. We have covered all the lighthouses still standing in this area, whether or not they still function as lighthouses.

There may be more history than you want in here, but scholars and lighthouse aficionados will appreciate Hal's thorough research. These histories and stories have fragile lives, as keepers and other sources of information pass away. It was none too soon for the stories of these lighthouses to be collected.

While each of the 39 lighthouse chapters is complete in itself, we think you'll find them more fun to read if you'll first go through the section titled "Development of Lighthouse Construction" just before these 39 chapters. Technical information is included in the last three chapters. For instance, Hal refers to third order or fourth order lenses throughout these 39 chapters. Chapter 41 explains the order of lenses, and much other technical information is included in Chapters 40, 41, and 42.

As the title *Lights and Legends* would indicate, Hal has humanized the history of these lighthouses. Though nearly all are unattended now, the history of the lighthouses is inextricably interwoven with that of their keepers, and that of their locales. Hal has also included vivid descriptions of the architecture and construction of each lighthouse, and their architectural significance. If you're at all interested in the lighthouses you pass, you'll find Hal's accounts fascinating reading.

Our author was born in Medford, MA, 1927, and raised in New England. His family first settled in South Berwick, Maine in 1751. After graduating from Boston Latin School in 1946, Harlan Hamilton enlisted in the Navy, then graduated from the University of Colorado with a B.A. in English. Later he received an M.A. from Columbia University, and an Ed. D. from Boston University. Hal is an Associate Professor of English at Jersey City State College in New Jersey. We think he's done splendid research and are proud to present his work to you.

Julius M. Wilensky
Stamford, CT
June, 1987

INTRODUCTION

Frequently people ask me how and when I became interested in lighthouses or why I decided to write a book on lighthouses. In answer to the first query, I usually reply, "I don't know." Perhaps it was my New England upbringing (Maine and Massachusetts) with countless trips to the shore on Sunday drives with my parents, brother and sister. Or perhaps my interest was perked by youthful readings about lighthouses and the families who lived in them. I suspect it was a combination of the two, although I cannot recall the titles of those early books. Then, too, as a young sailor in the United States Navy at the close of World War Two, I must have seen and passed many lighthouses in the various parts of the world we visited. Whatever the source, I have always had an interest in and fascination for lighthouses for as long as I can remember.

Until two years ago, I shared a Triton 28 sloop with a friend, and for ten years we sailed up and down Long Island Sound. I often wondered about the lighthouses we frequently passed (there are 39 of them) on our travels but could find little or no information about them in any of the yachting guides we carried aboard. Finally, in the spring of 1984, I made my first trip to the main branch of the New York Public Library on Forty-Second Street in Manhattan and to the New York Historical Society on Central Park West in search of information on local lighthouses such as Stepping Stones and Execution Rocks. My curiosity and interest aroused, I continued my research that summer in Washington, D.C. at the National Archives (where I read original lighthouse logs written in beautiful script by keepers) and the library at Coast Guard Headquarters at Buzzards Point. One thing led to another and, three years later, this book was born. My hope is that readers will enjoy reading *Lights & Legends* as much as I enjoyed writing it.

Covering more than a century and a half of lighthouse construction, the 39 lighthouses discussed in *Lights & Legends* exhibit considerable variety in function, materials, and structural type. They are all located in the First Coast Guard District. The three oldest lights are: New London (1760), Montauk Point (1797) and Eaton's Neck (1799). These lighthouses once served as landfall lights marking major sea routes. The remaining lights date from the early, middle and late 19th century and the early 20th century. Some of them are built on shore or on small offshore islands. Others are wave-swept or water-bound structures rising up from the shallow waters over dangerous shoals and reefs. They rest on foundations built of granite, iron-plate caissons or reinforced concrete. Superstructures exhibit the same range of materials. The lighthouses vary in style from Gothic Revival to Second Empire. Most of the lights are now unmanned (all were once staffed) and have automatic electric lamps, but several of them retain old if not original Fresnel lenses.

The lighthouses included in this book illustrate the history of lighthouse technology from 1760 to 1912. They represent a major engineering challenge: they are often located on unstable sandy bottoms remote from land and, once built, they must endure extreme conditions of high winds, raging seas, winter ice floes and corrosive salt air. Moreover, their function as aids to navigation demands that they be as reliable as possible. In the period represented by the lighthouses in *Lights & Legends*, these problems were addressed by several advances in lighthouse engineering. Among these were: the introduction of better materials in the form of cast and wrought iron and concrete; the use of cement-filled iron shells for foundations on sandy shoals; innovative construction techniques such as the use of pneumatic caissons; and the increased standardization of design in foundations, superstructures, illuminating apparatus and ornamental elements. Each of the lighthouses described in this book embody one or more of these important developments.

The lighthouses are also significant because of their role in the maritime history of the areas they served. The lights reflect the growth of shipping to and from the principal port of New York City via routes northeast of the city where Long Island Sound meets the East River. Ships approaching New York City from the North Atlantic commonly took (as they do today) advantage of the relatively protected waters of Long Island Sound; the lights at the eastern entrance to the Sound served not only such New York-bound traffic, but also vessels bound for the coasts of Connecticut and Rhode Island.

Because of the extensive involvement of the federal government in improving channels and providing navigation aids, because of the substantial technological problems encountered and solved in such construction, such as at Race Rock, and because of the economic importance of shipping in the New York region, the navigation systems, particularly the lighthouses, of the region possess national historic significance. The lighthouses also relate to the more general history of their individual localities. Especially in the case of eastern Long Island, local people have a long history of participation in seagoing activities, such as fishing and coastal trade.

Technology has provided the means whereby the navigator today goes about his business with a considerable degree of safety. However, at the same time technology has depersonalized the aids to navigation and has taken away virtually all of whatever humanness the aids once possessed. The blue-uniformed, dedicated "wickies" who used to wave at passing vessels from their lighthouses are gone forever. Grand masonry towers like Little Gull Island Light are rarely built now; in fact, the Coast Guard can scarcely find the funds to maintain existing ones. A steel skeleton tower is now considered adequate to get a navigational light to its proper height. One cannot but note these things without feeling a degree of nostalgia and sadness.

There is no question that today's modern lights are far superior to the whale lamps that once lit New London Light, for example, and that it is much easier and less expensive to switch on lights automatically instead of having a keeper do it manually. But the romance is gone. Our minds can easily conjure up the vision of a neat, clean lighthouse and its faithful keeper, dutifully going about his or her lonely work, who, when the occasion demanded it, summoned that extra bit of courage to rescue victims of a storm-aroused sea, despite the danger to his or her own life. It is impossible to summon up any sentiment for an automaton which the lighthouses have become.

The old masonry towers are not disappearing, however; they are still being utilized by the Coast Guard and will continue to be as long as they are safe from the sea, easy to maintain, and at the proper place to warn mariners most effectively. The greatest threat to our lighthouses, however, comes not from nature but from man. Once a lighthouse becomes automated and uninhabited, it becomes a subject to fearful mindless vandalism which threatens to destroy it. Windows are broken, graffiti is scribbled on its walls, empty beer and soda cans are strewn everywhere, structures are broken into and valuable equipment stolen; one historic light was even set on fire. Is this to be the fate of these noble sentinels of the sea?

As these towers become surplus to the needs of the Coast Guard, they are offered to federal, state and local historical agencies for preservation. It seems to be the only way to save them from complete destruction. As a result, many of these old, historic lights survive today in national, county and city parks (as in New Haven and Bridgeport, Connecticut) to be seen and enjoyed by millions of people. Some of these old structures have been restored and refurbished and re-equipped as when they were active aids to navigation. The lighthouse in Stonington, Connecticut is a splendid example.

Lighthouse lenses, tools and other equipment are being preserved in maritime museums along our seaboards. Unfortunately, there is no full-scale aids to navigation museum in the country; to see the various examples of this type of equipment, one has to travel fairly widely. It is unfortunate that more energy and thought are not going into the systematic collecting and preserving of specimens and examples of aids to navigation and related equipment, for, unquestionably, the evolution and technological development of lighthouses played a significant role in the nation's maritime history.

Finally, the reader should note that the story of the lighthouses in this volume is not simply the saga of illuminating devices that changed with the needs of the times. It is, instead, an expression of human effort, courage and sacrifice that went into the making and keeping of the lights so that sailors could safely sail the Sounds. The story of these lights is not just about steel or stone, but about men and women whose courage and devotion to duty in making and keeping the early lights burning demanded more back-breaking labor and greater exposure to danger than it does today. The old-time keepers of the lights were men and women with brine in their blood. To many of them, the most important thing in the world was the lighthouse they stood watch over, year in and year out. *Lights & Legends*, then is really about the keepers who looked after the lights, the engineers and builders who constructed them, and the members of the Lighthouse Board whose wisdom and vision made the aids to navigation system what it is today, one of the finest in the world. The building and maintenance of United States' lighthouses has been a noble and humanitarian work, filled with romance, adventure, loneliness and danger.

Harlan Hamilton
New York City
February 10, 1987

ACKNOWLEDGEMENTS

The author gratefully acknowledges the assistance and support given to him in his research for *Lights & Legends* by the following persons:

Geraad F. Abbott, M.D., New York, NY

Monica Albala, Museum Curator, Nassau County Museum Reference Library, East Meadows, NY

Mrs. Louise S. Anderson, Noank Historical Society, Noank, CT

Heagen Bayles, Sands Point, NY

Mrs. Dorothy W. Benson, Westerly Historical Society, Westerly, RI

Nona Bloomer, Reference Librarian, Guilford Free Library, Guilford, CT

Charles Brilvitch, Laurelton, NY

Colonel John F. Bradshaw, Southampton, NY

John F. Byrnes, Director, Disposal Division, Office of Public Buildings and Real Property, General Services Administration, Boston, MA

Jerry J. Callis, Director, Plum Island Animal Disease Center, Plum Island, NY

Ralph E. Carpentier, Director/Curator, Town Marine Museum, East Hampton Historical Society, Amagansett, NY

Thomas L. Cheney, Counselor-at-Law, Mystic, CT

Brenda B. Conradi, Museum Archives Assistant, Mystic Seaport Museum, CT

Mrs. Lois Tyte DeWall, Research Assistant, Suffolk County Historical Society Museum, Library and Archives, Riverhead, NY

Ruth Doherty, Librarian, Suffolk Marine Museum, West Sayville, NY

Sarah Gleason, Information and Public Relations Specialist, Rhode Island, Office of Information and Education, Providence, RI

Louise Gudelis, Librarian, Greenwich Library, Greenwich, CT

Gretchen Hammerstein, Librarian, Groton Public Library, Groton, CT

Mrs. Helen Hendricks, Greenwich, CT

C. Wilfred Hunter, Executive Director, Old Saybrook Chamber of Commerce, Old Saybrook, CT

Lauren Kominsky, Curator, The Historical Society of the Town of Greenwich, Inc., Cos Cob, CT

Dorothy T. King, Librarian, East Hampton Free Library, East Hampton, NY

Mrs. Elizabeth Know, Secretary and Curator, New London County Historical Society, New London, CT

Mrs. Eleanor H. Kurz, President, Sands Point Civic Association, Sands Point, NY

John Lee, Senior Assistant Librarian, State University of New York Maritime College, Fort Schulyer, NY

Mrs. R. Ashley Lewis, Old Saybrook, CT

Robert B. MacKay, Curator, Society for the Preservation of Long Island Antiquities, Setauket, NY

Mrs. Laura Bent MacKenzie, Research Volunteer, Fairfield Historical Society, CT

Alexander G. MacLeod, Port Washington Chamber of Commerce, NY

J. Lance Mallamo, Director of Historic Services, City of Suffolk, Division of Cultural and Historical Services, West Sayville, NY

Gregg D. Mecca, Assistant Director, The Stamford Historical Society, Inc., Stamford, CT

Joann Meyer, Reference and Adult Services Librarian, Port Jefferson Free Library, Port Jefferson, NY

Nancy L. Moskowitz, Librarian, The Huntington Historical Society, Huntington, NY

Paul J. O'Perko, Reference Librarian, Mystic Seaport Museum, Mystic, CT

John E. O'Shea, Historian, Town of North Hempstead, NY

Mrs. Giorgina Reid, Montauk Point Erosion Control Project, Inc., NY

Linda Reiser, Secretary, Sag Harbor Chamber of Commerce, Sag Harbor, NY

Elizabeth Anne Reiter, Reference Librarian, Groton Public Library, CT

Mrs. Joan G. Robidaux, Librarian, Lockwood House, Norwalk, CT

Anne L. Simko, East Shore Ranger, Department of Parks, Recreation & Trees, New Haven, CT

Mrs. Mary A. Slavin, Senior Assistant Librarian, Jersey City State College, Jersey City, NJ

Jefferey A. Spendelow, Director, Falkner Island Tern Project, Guilford, CT

Kate Steinway, Curator, Prints & Photographs, The Connecticut Historical Society, Hartford, CT

George D. Wagoner, Director, Southold Historical Society, Southold, NY

Myra Walsh, Secretary, The City Island Historical Society, City Island, NY

Mrs. Shirley Wendroff, Senior Library Assistant, Jersey City State College, Jersey City, NJ

John H. Wheeler, The Old Saybrook Historical Society, Inc., Old Saybrook, CT

George L. Williams, Landmarks Chairman, Cow Neck Peninsular Historical Society, Port Washington, NY

Eugene Wick York, Consultant in Historic Preservation and Building Restoration, Stonington, CT

Dorothy Zaykowski, Librarian, John Jermain Library, Sag Harbor, NY

●

The author also gratefully acknowledges the following members of the United States Coast Guard (the modern Keepers of the Light) who cheerfully and freely gave of their time in various capacities:

Third (now First) Coast Guard District, Governors Island, NY
  Lieutenant Commander (DPA) Marc W. Wolfson
  Lieutenant (j.g.) Spencer Byrum, Aids to Navigation
  Lieutenant Jay Melott, Aids to Navigation
  Lieutenant Paul Reid, Aids to Navigation
  Lieutenant (j.g.) Edward Tupay, Engineering Division
  PO1 Raymon Fuller, Public Affairs Specialist
  SN Robert LeValley, District Public Affairs
  Jay Silberman, Environmental Protection Specialist
  Lewis D. Wunderlich, Environmental Protection Specialist
Fort Totten, NY, Aids to Navigation Team
  BM1 David Foley
  BM1 Ronald J. Kline
  EM3 Bernard Aschendorf
  FN Joseph Martinek
Eaton's Neck Station, NY
  CW0 Richard Marini, Commanding Officer
  MK3 Thomas Leganza, Aids to Navigation Team
  SN Michael Fraumeni, Aids to Navigation Team
  SN Robert Moorehead, Aids to Navigation Team
Montauk Point Station, NY
  BM1 Eugene Hughes, Officer in Charge
Star Island Station, NY
  BM1 John Varner, Executive Petty Officer
  BM2 Michael Dulurry
  MK2 Kenneth Schaefer
  BM3 Joseph Bersick
  BM3 John Marowski
  MK3 Sean Lynch
  MK3 Edward Sanderford
  SN William Carl
  SN Robert Chrysler
  SN Cindy Clark
Block Island Station, RI
  BM1 S.J. Galazzo, Officer in Charge
Station New Haven, CT
  BMC Stephen P. Carlesco, Officer in Charge
  BM1 John Godfrey
  BM3 Thomas Grossi
  BM3 Sean McGarigal
Aids to Navigation Team, New Haven, CT
  MKC Glenn J. Schillumeit, Officer in Charge
  BM! Charles C. Kerr, Executive Petty Officer
  MK2 Theresa Dalton
  EM2 Andy Apenburg
  EM3 Karl Kent
  EM3 Tom Laureyns
Coast Guard Station, New London, CT (Fort Trumbull)
  BMC Bruce Latvis, Operations Officer
  BM1 Richard "Rick" Martin

MK1 John Cadarette
Watch Hill Station, RI
BM1 Rusty Merritt, Officer in Charge
BM1 Tony Methot
Point Judith Station, RI
BM1 Peter Swanson, Officer in Charge
United States Coast Guard Academy, New London, CT
Mary McKenzie, Head of Public Services, The Library
Pamela McNulty, Reference Librarian, The Library
United States Coast Guard Headquarters, Washington, D.C.
Dr. Robert L. Scheina, Historian, Public Affairs Division, Office of Boating, Public and Consumer Affairs

●

The author wishes to thank the following publishers and writers for permission to use material from their publications. A more complete bibliographic entry may be found in the "Reference" section for each lighthouse at the back of *Lights & Legends*.

Charles Brilvitch, Bridgeport CT for use of portions of his *Walking Through History, the Seaport of Black Rock and Southport, 1977.*

Dodd, Mead & Company, Inc., New York, NY. *Famous Lighthouses of New England* and *Famous Lighthouses of America,* by Edmund Rowe Snow, 1945, 1955.

The Jackson Newspapers, New Heven, CT. For articles which appeared in the *New Haven Register* on March 18, 1976 and the *New Haven Evening Register* on May 8, 25, 1949. Reprinted by permission. See references for New Haven Harbor Light and Falkner Island Light.

Howard N. Knowles for material from his monograph *A Lighthouse of Stone.* Northport, NY, 1978.

Long Island Community Newspaper Group, Mineola, NY. For material in the *Port Washington News* and *The Huntington Long Islander* used for Sands Point Light and Lloyd Harbor Light.

Long Island Forum, West Islip, NY. "Noah Mason and Sands Point Lighthouse" by Robert George Kassner, January 1982.

The Middletown Press, Middletown, CT. "In All Weather, the Lights Must Beam," August 16, 1963.

New York Daily News, New York, NY. "Old Lighthouse Blinking Out," March 21, 1971; "A town steeped in tradition" by William Neugebauer, February 25, 1979. Copyright © 1971, 1979. Reprinted by permission.

The New York Times, New York, NY. "Stamford Light, Scene of Murder and Romance, Faces Destruction" by David Anderson, June 16, 1953; "Greenwich Sees the Ghost of 1656" by John W. Stevens, August 1, 1956. Copyright © 1953/56 by The New York Times Company. Reprinted by permission.

Providence Journal Company, Providence, RI. *The Providence Sunday Journal,* "A century on Guard," January 2, 1916; "Sentinels Along the Shore," November 10, 1963.

Random House, Inc., New York, NY. *The South Fork* by Everett Rattray, 1979. Mary Rattray Kanovitz and David G Rattray for permission to use portions of

Jeanette Rattray's book *Ship Ashore*, 1955.

Mrs. Giorgina Reid, Montauk Erosion Control Project, Montauk, NY for permission to use material about her erosion control project at Montauk Point.

Soundings, Essex, CT. "Focus, Eaton's Neck Station, U.S. Coast Guard" by Peter Barlow, June 1964; "Coast Guard Begins Restoring Orient Point Light" by Barbara Dorman, November 1973. Additional articles noted in "References" at back of this book.

Staten Island Advance, Staten Island, NY. For their excellent coverage of the sinking of the "Celtic" and "Cape Race" in their November and December 1984 editions. See Norwalk Island Light, Chapter10.

The Suffolk Times, Greenport, NY. "Original Light Returning to Horton's Point" by Francis Wagner, July 14, 1977; "P.I. Light to Go Dark" by Diane Plows, March 23, 1978. Reprinted with permission.

George L. Williams and Jacqueline K. Bahn for quotes from their *Sketchbook of Historic Homes on Cow Neck Peninsula.* Port Washington, NY 1982.

United States Lighthouse Society, San Francisco, CA. Wayne Wheeler, "The Fresnel Lens," *The Keeper's Log*, Winter 1985.

Yankee Magazine, Dublin, NH. "High Bid Wins It," May 1984.

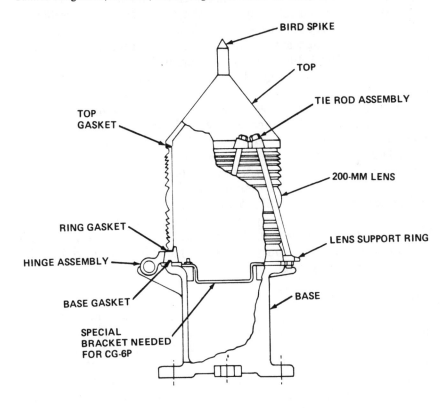

Sketch of assembly of 200 mm Lantern.
Used at Peck Ledge Light Chapter 9. See also page 254

Courtesy U.S. Coast Guard

13

DEVELOPMENT OF LIGHTHOUSE CONSTRUCTION

Early History

In Colonial times, the individual colonies built and administered aids to navigation with no centralized planning. The lights for this period were generally of the "landfall" variety, signalling the approach to a major harbor. Their construction followed no overall pattern of structure and design. A typical colonial light is New London Light (1760). It is octagonal in plan with thick brick walls and few windows. Its construction, while hardly resembling the typical colonial house, was nevertheless well within the capabilities of the 18th century builder relying on traditional masonry techniques.

The newly constitued United States Government assumed responsibility for aids to navigation in August 1789 under the ninth law passed by the Congress which marked the first provision for federal public works. While the act enabled the Government to establish and maintain lighthouses and other aides to navigation, it included no clean delineation of administrative responsibility; nor did the Executive Branch settle the matter. In fact, early administrative problems often remained unresolved until reaching the highest levels of office. In several instances, the President ruled on remarkably small items, such as Washington's opinion on the purchase of illuminating oil, or Jefferson's on the hiring of a lightkeeper.

The Treasury Department received responsibility eventually, and the job was delegated to the Commissioner of Revenue, who in turn designated the custom collectors at the ports to oversee lighthouses in their areas. This system, with no central control, resulted in uneven performance among the various areas, leading to the consolidation of management in 1820 under the Fifth Auditor's Office of the Treasury Department, where it remained until 1851. The lighthouses of the early national period resembled very closely those from colonial times. Lighthouses built at Montauk Point in 1797, Eatons Neck in 1799 and New Haven in 1804, for instance, are masonry towers, octagonal in plan, much like New London Light built in 1760.

Increasing Need

Before 1850, the aids to navigation multiplied several times over, from just a handful of lights in 1789 to 55 in 1820, to 210 in 1838, and to 325 in 1845. Among the important factors that accounted for this increase were the rise in shipping and the changes in navigation needs attending new ship construction and propulsion technology. The first half of the 19th century saw a tremendous rise in ship-borne commerce, particularly in the approaches to northeastern cities such as New York, one of the nation's busiest ports. Like other metropolises of the northeast, New York's population was growing as migrants from both nearby rural areas and foreign countries came to the city. Population growth encouraged commercial expansion and a consequent rise in shipping in all approaches to the city.

The changes in shipbuilding affected aids to navigation in several ways. In the early national years, all maritime traffic was wind-powered, but by 1850 steam engines drove about 15% of the commercial vessels serving ports in the United States. Steamships made greater speeds in protected waters, requiring more and more reliable aids to navigation in the busy channels. Also, commercial vessels were generally being built longer, with greater drafts, and therefore were vulnerable in heretofore safe waters over shoals and reefs. Besides the expansion of demand for lighthouses required by more traffic and larger vessels, many previously unknown hazards were located through improvements in hydrographic surveying techniques. Some shoals were located through extreme application of empirical proof: vessels ran aground on unanticipated hazards. Ship John Shoal Light in Delaware Bay gained its name from one such unfortunate occurrence.

Masonry Construction

Lighthouse technology benefited from scant professional direction until after 1850. The Corps of Topographical Engineers (precursor to the Army Corps of Engineers) advised on siting, but vernacular building technology continued as the primary structural influence. Even when professional architects or engineers participated in lighthouse design, the structures followed the vernacular, masonry techniques of long-established use. The tower built in 1848 at Execution Rocks, for example, was designed by the influential architect Alexander Parris. Nevertheless, the structure closely resembles the lighthouse of the colonial and early national periods. Built of stone blocks, Execution Rocks Light has a circular plan, whereas the earlier lights were octagonal. However, the overall convergence in structure and appearance outweighs the differences between Execution Rocks and earlier towers. The lighthouse built in 1868 on Little Gull Island in eastern Long Island Sound also displays masonry construction similar to towers from the 18th and early 19th centuries.

Lightships

A more intractable structural problem was encountered with the marking of water-covered shoals and reefs. The first means for signalling such sites was the lightship, a vessel moored to the hazard and fitted with a beacon. The earliest United States lightship was placed off Sandy Hook, New Jersey in 1823. Lightships, however, offered low reliability, because they were subject to the same winds and seas as the passing vessels which required the beacons. Thus, the lightships were most likely to break from their moorings, or otherwise fail, at the time of greatest need. Even in times of relative calm, the lightships rocked with the waves and therefore presented wavering beacons. American technology provided no alternatives for marking shoals due to the difficulty of securing structures in the soft, muddy bottoms on these locations.

Lenses

Poor performance of optical devices also compromised the United States lighthouse system. Standard equipment was the parabolic reflector, a concave fixture, located behind the lamp and coated with a silver-based compound. The reflectors projected the lamps' light over a useful distance, but their performance declined over a very short period, because the government-issued powder that the keepers used to polish the reflectors abraded the silver coating. Reflectors continued in use even after they were made obsolete by the Fresnel lens, invented in 1822 by French physicist Augustin Fresnel.

The Fresnel lens resembles an upright cylinder with slightly tapered ends and comprises a central spherical-sector lens with concentric rings of prisms mounted above and below. The central lens refracts the light, and the prisms both refract and reflect, the latter function causing the intensification of the beam. The Fresnel lens was not used in United States lighthouses at first, because the holder of the patent for the parabolic reflector, Winslow Lewis, lobbied vigorously to protect his interest. Lewis benefited from his personal relationships with officials in the Fifth Auditor's Office, and successfully forestalled deployment of the superior illumination technique until Congress acted in 1851 and ordered Fresnel lenses installed in all lights.

The Congressional Act of 1851 culminated a period of civilian discontent with and government investigation of the lighthouse system. In the 1840s, problems stemming from the jerry-rigged administrative set-up had affected operations and prompted complaints from mercantile and shipping interests. The Fifth Auditor's Office had other responsibilities than lighthouses, and the local administration of the lights benefited from little central administrative organization or technical standards. In 1845, Secretary of the Navy George Bancroft appointed two naval officers, Lieutenants George M. Bache and Thornton Jenkins, to study the nation's aids to navigation to "procure information which might tend to the improvement of the lighthouse system."

Bache and Jenkins traveled extensively to observe operations and conditions. They traveled also to Europe to examine lighthouse technology there. Their principal recommendations, formalized by Congress in 1851, was administrative: establish a national Planning Board to make detailed operations reports and guide legislation, and assign in each district Army engineers to superintend construction and maintenance. The report also provided the basis for improved technology, with a recommendation to adopt the Fresnel lens, which was mandated subsequently by the Congress. The United States relied upon lens-makers from France and Germany to supply the Fresnel lenses; the late adoption of the lens created a lag in United States capability in this area that was never made up. As late as 1913, the United States Lighthouse Service had to purchase Fresnel lenses from European firms.

Screw-pile Construction

Bache and Jenkins saw in England a means to secure structures upon shoals, the screw-pile. The structure rested on wrought-iron columns with cast-iron screws attached to their bottoms. By rotating them, the columns were literally screwed into the shoal bottom, much like a screw entering wood. This technique enabled the placement of solid structures on shoals, this replacing lightships. The first American screw-pile lighthouse was completed in 1850 at Brandywine Shoal in Delaware Bay. The Lighthouse Board, the new administrative agency·created by the 1851 Act of Congress, deployed 50 screw-pile lighthouses in the decade following their introduction, mostly in the Carolina Sounds and Chesapeake Bay. However, the spindly-looking structures were of little use in the strong currents of eastern Long Island Sound or in waters subject to ice floes as found in New York Harbor. The ultimate technological significance of the screw-pile, for the New York area at least, lay in its introduction of iron as a structural material for lighthouses.

Throughout the mid-1870s, massive masonry construction provided the only alternative to screw-pile structures for water-bound sites. Stepping Stones Light and Race Rock Light used masonry foundations with some success. They exemplify also the increased stylization of lighthouse structures in the late 1860s and early 1870s. The construction of Race Rock Light illustrates the difficulties associated with such masonry lighthouse foundations. The foundation consists of fitted stones, each weighing from three to five tons, with a total weight of about 10,000 tons. Temporary piers were built for the unloading of materials, which were ferried out at considerable inconvenience and expense. An inclined trough some 75 feet long was built to conduct materials from the landing piers to the work site, where extensive underwater labor was required to lay the stones. The project lasted five years and cost more than one quarter of a million dollars.

Iron-Caisson Construction

The alternative to these costly and dangerous endeavors came in the form of the iron-caisson foundation: a hollow cast-iron shell filled with sand, rock or concrete. Usually measuring about 30 feet in diameter and 35 feet in height, these cylinders could be put in place while empty, then filled, offering relative ease of installation as well as final weight in the hundreds of tons. Their adoption depended largely upon the growth of the nation's iron industry, which by the 1870s had reached not only high levels of output but also a high degree of specialization. The Government could issue plans for the curved, cast-iron caisson plates, with flanges for bolting them together, and reasonably expect at least several competitive bids for their supply.

Cast-iron Superstructures

The earliest caisson-based aid to navigation in the Third Coast Guard District is the 1877 Ship John Shoal Light in Delaware Bay. Not only was Ship John's foundation made of iron, but the lighthouse superstructure also consisted of cast-iron plates bolted together by means of inward-projecting flanges, cast integrally with the plates. This cast-iron superstructure followed the Second-Empire style. The use of such designs did not last into the 1880s, however, as the Lighthouse Board standardized the format for cast-iron lighthouse superstructures. The standard took the form of circular-plan towers with tapering walls, surmounted by a watch deck and lantern, or a lantern alone. Essentially functional, the standard design incorporated some Victorian details, usually in the form of cast-iron brackets supporting projecting galleries, or cast-iron hoodmolds for windows and entries. While such elements assure a relatively minor role in the overall utilitarian appearance of the standardized iron towers, they do nonetheless contribute to the sense of temporal origins of such towers, placing them firmly in the late 19th century.

In the 30 years after 1880, standardized iron towers or iron caissons proliferated in the waters of the northeastern United States, with at least three dozen erected in that period. Examples included in this book are Latimer Reef Light (1884) and Orient Point Light (1899). Compared to the extensive construction projects for masonry-based aids such as Race Rock (1878), building a caisson-based aid was significantly less difficult and costly. The plates were prefabricated and then assembled in place. The Lighthouse Board even produced pre-printed construction specifications to send out for bid. The structural specifications underwent some updating and adaption to local conditions, but these emendations were minor, such as slightly altering the diameter of the watch deck or specifying a trumpet-shaped top for a caisson. Thus, the iron towers resulted in a significant savings in design effort.

Pneumatic Caissons

One notable variation in the building of iron-based aids was sinking the foundation into shoals by means of pneumatic caissons. The foundation shell was assembled and filled, leaving open a vertical shaft through the center and a chamber in the bottom. The shaft formed an air-lock through which workers descended into the chamber where they dug out the bottom-sand, which enabled the caisson to penetrate into the shoal. When the caisson was embedded to the specified depth, usually less than 20 feet, the shaft and chamber were filled. West Bank Light in New York Harbor was placed in this manner. Other caisson-based aids on shoals simply rested on piles driven into the bottom. On reefs, the caissons rested on a leveled bed cut into the rock. Construction of masonry lights was anachronistic by the early 20th century, because the technique of prefabricated iron-plate construction had been adapted to land-based aids at an early stage.

Reinforced Concrete

Just as the use of iron in the building technology of the late 19th century had revolutionized lighthouse design, so did the increasing acceptance of reinforced concrete in the early 20th century cause a major shift in lighthouse construction. Spurred by the plans and patents of such innovators as C.A.P. Turner, reinforced concrete found many new applications. The Lighthouse Board, which was to become the Bureau of Lighthouses (or the Lighthouse Service) in 1910, built its first reinforced concrete lighthouse in 1908 at Point Arena, California, about 100 miles north of San Francisco. Several more reinforced concrete towers were erected in the next few years, all in the West. In 1912, the first eastern lighthouse of this material was erected at Lloyd Harbor, New York. Two years later, the Lighthouse Service placed a reinforced concrete structure at Brandywine Shoal in Delaware Bay, replacing the wholly deteriorated screw-pile structure which still rests beside it.

Reinforced concrete lighthouses are relatively rare in the northeastern states today, but not because they were insufficient. On the contrary, the low cost, high strength and relatively maintenance-free character of the material made it most suitable for lighthouses. Their rarity (which is why Lloyd Harbor Light should be preserved), instead, can be traced to the high rate of survival for the iron towers which to this day remain, for the most part, sound. Furthermore, the rate of new lighthouse construction in the northeast decreased, since by 1920, virtually all the ranges, hazards and landfalls were well-marked. Lights built after 1920, mostly on the West Coast and in the Pacific, primarily used reinforced concrete construction.

•

In summary, the lighthouses discussed in *Lights & Legends* illustrate the full range of lighthouse technology from 1760 to 1912: early stone lights; iron towers on caissons; the standardization of iron towers in the late 19th century; and the introduction of reinforced concrete structures. The lighthouses discussed herein also stand in testament to the commercial importance of shipping in the greater New York area. The lighthouses in and around the city illustrate the ongoing effort to facilitate shipping to and from the most important port in the northeast.

Finally, many of the lights, notably Lloyd Harbor and Montauk Point, form important elements in the historical awareness of people in those localities. The needs of shipborne commerce created a demand for aids to navigation which always passed and sometimes exceeded the technological capacity of the United States Lighthouse Service. The imposing structures which stand today are not only a sign of the Lighthouse Service's success at building in the most extreme environmental conditions, but are also parts of the maritime heritage of their area and the nation.

CHAPTER 1

THROGS NECK LIGHT, Fort Schuyler NY (1827)

Old Light List No.: 471 (Obsolete)
Location: Latitude 40° 48′ N
Longitude 73° 48′ W
Height: 36′ (HAW 69′)
Range: l2 miles, Fixed White Bell
Lens: Fourth Order Classical, 490 candlepower
Rebuilt: 1906
Discontinued: 1934

In the 19th century Throgs Neck Lighthouse served as a leading light for vessels after leaving Hart Island (to the north and east) or Rikers Island (to the west). From about 1827-1852, the light consisted of "eleven fish oil lamps, with spherical reflectors, arranged around two horizontal tables." The original lighthouse was a wooden tower on the northeast face of Fort Schuyler, was 61 feet high, showed a fixed white light of the fifth order, and was visible for 11 nautical miles. The keeper's dwelling was an old, two-story frame farmhouse. The lighthouse and keeper's house were rebuilt in 1906 with a $10,000 appropriation from Congress, A red-brick conical tower replaced the wooden one apparently. This tower was replaced in 1934 with a skeleton tower, which was replaced in 1986 with a 60-ft. grey pine tower with a range of 11 miles (LLN 20560). Today, the keeper's house continues to serve as a home for a Coast Guard family.

When the station was first built, the Lighthouse Establishment was merely an appendage of the Revenue Service, the commissioner of which was the general superintendent of lights. Collectors of customs were the superintendents of districts. With such a system, many of the light keepers and their families indulged in license if not lawlessness. They lighted the lamp at night, put it out in the morning, gave the station a superficial cleaning, called "a Scotch lick," and, after that, did what they wanted to do. Some of them farmed, others went hunting or fishing, and some followed their old avocations. A large proportion of them sold rum on the premises.

The first keeper of Throgs Neck Light was a man named Young, and his successor was a Jeth Bayles. They kept a bar on the first floor of the keeper's house which became the favorite resort of sportsmen and the half-way house for the hunters of New York City who went to Eastchester to shoot ducks. Since the Neck was a natural peninsula between Long Island Sound and the East River, it was no stranger to soldiers or sailors on leave. Evidently there were no reports of violence caused by excessive drinking at the Light, since that trade was carried on surreptitiously, and any reports of violence would have closed it.

The name of the peninsula honors John Throgmorton (or

Throgs Neck Light, Fort Schuyler, NY

Throckmorton) who arrived here with a band of followers in 1643 only to be chased out by the Indians. In the 19th century, the wealthy, including Collis P. Huntington who made his fortune in railroads and H.O.Havemeyer who did likewise in sugar, had summer homes here. In the 1872 *List of Light-Houses*, it is spelled "Throgg's Neck," and its number is 170.

Throgs Neck today is the site of the New York State Maritime College. The main classrooom building is the massive grey stone pentagon at the tip of the point, Fort Schuyler, named after General Philip Schuyler who kept a warehouse of stores here for a possible invasion of Canada which never took place. The fort (1834-38, I.L. Smith, architect) dates from the period between the War of 1812 and the Civil War. Fort Schuyler, paired with Fort Totten on Willets Point in Queens, New York, was designed to rake the lower part of Long Island Sound with cross fire. However, the fort never saw action and was abandoned in 1870 to lie empty until the Works Project Administration restored it in 1934 and converted it to the Maritime College. It is considered one of the finest existing examples of Napoleonic military architecture. The Pentagon in Washington, D.C. is modeled after it. Tours of the fort are conducted by appointment only by calling (212) 409-7200.

●

Moon Cussers

One of the reasons that progress in lighthouse building was slow in the early days of our Republic was that safeguarding ships would have seriously damaged the wrecking business. In those days, the otherwise solid citizens of certain coastal communities had a rather peculiar attitude toward disaster at sea. Clearly, maritime accidents were a God-given gift to wreckers. Whoever got to the wreckage first deserved the spoils, so their thinking went. If nature did not do her best to wreck a ship, they helped her out.

Armed with broomstick handles and lanterns, the "moon cussers" (moonlit nights were bad for business) lured many a ship to destruction on the reefs with false lights and beacons. The story is told of how a so-called preacher, whose main business was wrecking, once interrupted a passionate revival meeting, told the congregation to bow its head in meditation, and sneaked out the back door. He had just received a message that a ship had been wrecked, and he wanted to be the first one to make a deal with the skipper floating her. Early rescue stations and lighthouses were not accepted in all communities, because the moon cussers saw them as threat to their "business." In some instances, the government had to wait years to establish a proper aid to navigation because of local indignation toward it.

CHAPTER 2

STEPPING STONES LIGHT, Great Neck, NY (1877)

Light List No.: 20545
Location: Latitude 40° 49'.5 N
Longitude: 73° 46.5' W
Height: 46'
Range: 12 miles, Fixed Green, Horn
Lens: Fourth Order, Classical Fresnel (1889)
with 1000 watt lamp

Description of the Light

Stepping Stones Light is a square, red brick tower with a mansard roof and dwelling on a granite ashlar round platform that rests on a riprap foundation. It lies about 1600 yards offshore and is listed in the National Register of Historic Places. Its primary power is provided by subcable. The light marks a major hazard in western Long Island Sound and is used as a primary navigational aid. It guards the approach to New York City's East River and warns shipping of an extensive shoal and series of rocks which occasionally break the surface of the water and extend northward from the shore near Kings Point, Long Island. The lighthouse, situated on the northernmost reef, takes its name from these rocks.

There is an inner passage along the Kings Point shore marked by nuns which is safe enough for nine-ft. draft if you pay attention to what you are doing, but if you go anywhere between Stepping Stones Light and the nuns, you are asking for trouble. People run aground by the score.

First money for a lighthouse in the area was appropriated in June 1874. Plans called for an erection of a day beacon on the Stepping Stones and a lighthouse near the end of Hart Island, about 1¼ miles north. apparently the government had difficulty in obtaining title to the land on Hart Island, and in its annual report for 1874, the Lighthouse Board decided to change the location of the light to Stepping Stones.

Work on the lighthouse began late in 1875. A. D. Cook was the contractor. A total of 900 tons of encroachment boulders were required in addition to the riprap for the foundation. The encroachment boulders were delivered at intervals between 1875 and the spring of 1878. The dwelling was completed in January 1877, even though the date 1876 is carved on the granite panel on the front of the tower, and the light was first exhibited on the night of March 1, 1877. The lighthouse was modified in 1944, updated and furnished with more modern equipment. It was automated in October 1966.

The foundation of Stepping Stones Light was built directly over a large rock which barely broke the surface at low water. A large circle of riprap was placed to enclose it, then the center of the riprap was leveled to receive the foundation. The outer foundation wall consists of large, rough-faced granite blocks laid in courses. Its wall tapers inward slightly from a base diameter of 48 feet, and it has a height of about 30 feet. Concrete fills the granite rings of the foundation, except for a rectangular space in the foundation's top which was left open to create a basement for the lighthouse. In the brick-lined basement there is a large (approximately 5-ft. in diameter) wooden cistern that stored fresh drinking water for the keepers.

An early (1889) Fresnel lens remains in the lantern. The lens consists of glass prism rings mounted in brass retainers. It is drum-shaped, sending light in every direction. The lens originally intensified the light from an oil-fired incandescent mantle, but today an electric lamp furnishes illumination. This old Fresnel lens is the most important functional aspect of the lighthouse.

Significance of the Light

Stepping Stones Light is significant as an admirable representative example of brick-and-stone Second Empire style dwelling, a style that was supplanted in the 1880s by the use of prefabricated cast-iron plate construction. It is also significant in the history of the New York City region, because it formed a principal component in the aids-to-navigation system serving the approaches to the city from Long Island Sound. The 1870s saw a doubling in the value of ship-borne commerce in New York City, imports alone rising from $281 million in 1870 to $459 million in 1880. The passage northeast of the city, where Long Island Sound meets the East River, accounted for a substantial portion of this increase in water-borne commerce.

The hazards in the area are, for the most part, either marked or well-known, but no system signaled a continuous channel. When completed in 1877, Stepping Stones Lighthouse worked together with two older lights, Great Captain Island (1829, see Chapter 5) near Greenwich, Connecticut and Execution Rocks (1850, see Chapter 3) near Sands Point, New York, to define such a clear water channel. Ships bound for the city from the Sound stayed south of the other two lights and then north of Stepping Stones. Upon rounding Stepping Stones, the ships followed the land-based aids to piers in the Bronx, Manhattan or Brooklyn. Stepping Stones Light thus played a pivotal role in New York City's water-borne commerce.

The lighthouse (architect/builder unknown) represents the last period of 19th century brick-and-masonry Second Empire lighthouse construction, as noted earlier. These materials dominated lighthouse building from the colonial period through the 1870s, offering the only means to assure stability for the heights required in lighthouses. Before the 1850s, lighthouses generally incorporated scant stylistic intent, simply fulfilling their utilitarian purposes. In the 1850s, however, the highly decentralized government offices responsible for lighthouse construction and operation were reorganized under the Lighthouse Board, the first federal agency with sole responsibility for aids to navigation. In the decades following

Stepping Stones Light, Great Neck, NY

this reorganization, centralized planning and design enabled the Board to promote a certain degree of architectural content beyond the functional, thus promoting pride within the Board and respect from others.

Interestingly, the Second Empire style carried over into the first generation of iron lighthouse construction, which followed very closely after Stepping Stones. The 1877 Ship John Shoal Lighthouse in Delaware Bay, for instance, is built of cast-iron plates, but it also takes the form of a Second Empire-style dwelling. Stepping Stones, then, typifies the very last period of brick-and-stone lighthouse construction. It also illustrates the trend toward stylization in lighthouses which continued to affect their character even after building technology underwent total change. By the mid 1880s the conical iron tower (see, for example: Greens Ledge Light, Chapter 8; Stratford Point Light, Chapter 17; Peck Ledge Light, Chapter 9, Saybrook Breakwater Light, Chapter 22; Orient Point Light, Chapter 25; and Latimer Reef Light, Chapter35) had become standard, signaling the end of the brief period when lighthouses were built as architectural, rather than technological aids to navigation.

How Stepping Stones got its Name

An old Indian legend has it that Habbamoko (a), the Evil Spirit, and the Indians of Connecticut (or the Siwanoy Indians of New Rochelle, New York) fought for possession of that territory. The battle was close, but slowly and surely the Indians, fortified with their own potions and wizardry, pushed the Evil One back along the shore of the Sound toward City Island and Throgs Neck. The future looked bleak for Habbamoko (a) until he spied between Long Island and Throgs Neck a chain of rocks laid bare either by low tide or by one of his demonic associates. He quickly stepped across these rocks and escaped from his pursuers. Safe on the Long Island shore, he took his revenge by heaving at Connecticut (or New Rochelle) all the boulders he could lay his hands on. His aim wasn't too accurate, and many of his boulders went as far as Maine, thus littering the New England states with rock formations.

In colonial times Long Island Sound was known as the Devil's Belt due to the sudden storms and destructive nor-easters that raged there as well as to a strong belief in the Devil shared by the inhabitants of the region. On early maps the Sound is noted as the "Devil's Belt" and Stepping Stones as the "Devil's Stepping Stones"—a cluster of mussel-covered reefs within sight of City Island. The name "Devil's Stepping Stones" persisted into the latter part of the 19th century, but it proved too cumbersome for mariners' charts when the lighthouse was erected on the northernmost part of the reef in 1877. However, the name lived on in local usage for a number of years. Fish peddlers landed their boats on the Throgs Neck beaches, blew their horns to summon the housewives, and shouted, "Fresh fish—right from the Devil's Stepping Stones!"

CHAPTER 3

EXECUTION ROCKS LIGHT, Sands Point, NY (1850)

Light List No.: 20485
Location: Latitude 40° 52.7' N
Longitude 73° 44.3' W
Height: 42' (HAW 62')
Range: 16 miles, Flashing White every 10 seconds, Horn
Lens: DCB-10, 500 watt lamp
Automated: 1979
Radio Beacon: 3I6 kHz; XR (__ . . __   . __ .) I, IV, 20 miles

Description of the Light

Execution Rocks Lighthouse sits in 37 feet of water, 1690 yards north of Sands Point, Long Island, New York, at the western end of Long Island Sound. The granite tower is painted white with a brown band around the center. The lighthouse was placed in operation in 1850, and was reconstructed in 1868. According to the 1878 report of the Lighthouse Board, the natural rock on which the lighthouse stood was reinforced by additional rock due to damage by severe gales during the autumn and winter of 1877-78. The original fourth order classical lens was flashing white with a flashing red sector between NE ¼ N and E by N. The interval between flashes was ten seconds.

The radio beacon of the light has distance finding capability which can be used in this area in conjunction with WCBS-WNBC on High Isalnd (northeast of City Island). Execution Rocks is by far the most powerful light in the western end of Long Island Sound. It is listed in the National Register of Historic Places.

Two of the last keepers before the light became automated in 1979 were Tom Buckridge, who was keeper of the Montauk Light for 20 years before he came to Execution Rocks, and George Clark, who was born during a terrifying gale in the lighthouse on Little Gull Island and spent his childhood at the light.

Besides the 1850 lighthouse, the site includes an attached granite keeper's dwelling erected in 1867 (the house's construction date is carved in raised letters on the lintel above the door), and a concrete-walled oil house erected between 1910 and 1920. A large, roughly circular mass of riprap provides an artificial island for the lighthouse, and a riprap jetty with a concrete dock extends westward from the main portion of the site.

The lighthouse tower takes the shape of a squat, truncated cone with a pronounced taper to the walls. The 42-ft. tall tower is about 26 ft. diameter at its base, and about 13 feet at its top. Its walls consist of granite blocks laid in coursed ashlar. The octagonal lantern is glazed on all sides and has a pyramided roof topped by a ventilator ball with a lightning rod. The original fourth order beacon rotated by means of a weight-driven gear train. The lantern is bereft of historic illuminating equipment, since a modern rotating electric beacon replaced the Fresnel prisms in 1979.

Inside the tower, the first story is lined with brick, while the masonry walls of the upper four levels are not covered. The floors have been modified, consisting now of open gratings on I-beams set into the masonry walls. Structurally, the lighthouse tower retains all of its original fabric except the interior floor plates. The interior of the keeper's dwelling still exhibits the original wall, ceiling and trim, including a handsome stairway with its curved cherry-wood railing.

Significance

Execution Rocks Lighthouse retains a high degree of historic integrity and as such is significant as a representative example of American masonry lighthouse technology, an example that is heightened in importance, because it was designed by the noted American architect Alexander Parris (1780-1852). The masonry construction of the 1850 tower is typical of virtually every major light erected before the 1870s when iron replaced stone as the principal structural material for lighthouses. The keeper's dwelling, which dates from 1867, illustrates stone-based lighthouse technology just on the eve of its eclipse by iron.

Execution Rocks Lighthouse is also significant in the maritime history of New York City, one of the nation's most important centers of shipping in the 19th and 20th centuries. In addition to the lights of Great Captain Island and Stepping Stones, the Execution Rocks beacon signals the approach to New York City from the northeast where Long Island Sound joins the East River.

Until the introduction of iron in the mid-1870s, American lighthouses relied almost exclusively upon masonry construction. Wood presented the only alternative, but the requirements of stability and height, as well as the stringent conditions of the salt water environment, eliminated wood as a practical material for lighthouses. For the most part, pre-1860 masonry lighthouses had little decorative or stylish intent, with their essentially utilitarian format mitigated, if at all, only by carved hoodmolds or perhaps a fancy railing. Execution Rocks presents an important example of the functional approach to lighthouses.

Born in Maine, architect Alexander Parris moved to Boston, Massachusetts in 1812. His work included many notable Neo-Classical designs such as Boston's St. Paul's Cathedral and private homes on Beacon Hill. He also executed commissions for the federal government, such as the U.S. arsenal at Watertown, Massachusetts, the drydocks at Boston Navy Yard, and other harbor installations. During Parris' career, neither architecture nor engineering existed as discrete professions, and Parris provides an excellent example of the lack of clear distinction between the two. While fully capable of rendering stylish plans, such as for the Cathedral, he also addressed projects of almost completely practical content, such as drydocks.

28

Execution Rocks Light, Sands Point, NY

Parris obviously interpreted his commission for Execution Rocks Lighthouse as one to be fulfilled from the practical, rather than the aesthetic, end of his capabilities. Indeed, Parris' major concern was with the siting of the tower, a concern which prompted some dispute when the builder and masonry contractor, Thomas Butler, insisted upon a different site on the reef. Butler based his plan upon consultation with pilots and ships' masters, while Parris apparently chose the location offering most economical construction. The government prevailed, and Butler built the tower per Parris' instructions. This dispute emphasizes that Parris' participation was based more upon engineering considerations than upon architectural design and helps to explain why the tower resembles so closely the traditional ante-bellum masonry lighthouses, even though a major architect helped with its planning.

The 1867 keeper's dwelling illustrates the changes in masonry lighthouse design in the 1860s, when the traditional materials were still utilized, but lighthouses and related structures began to assume a more stylish appearance. This evolution can be traced to the formation in 1857 of a national administrative agency responsible for lighthouses. Under the centralized planning of the Lighthouse Board, the nation's aids to navigation become more reflective of prevailing taste, perhaps in an attempt by the Board to express the stability and order it brought to the country's navigation system. With its peaked lintels, semi-elliptical attic lights and deeply molded cornice, the keeper's dwelling presents a Neo-Classical aspect, illustrating the survival of such styling in government-sponsored buildings after its eclipse in the private sector.

The Legend of Execution Rock

There are those who say that Execution Rocks Lighthouse is built on the bones of the real Patriots of the American Revolution. In a sense, this is literally true, because the name of the light is borrowed from barbarous reality. In the early 18th century, the colonial administration was often embarrassed at public executions, because when standing on the gallows or before a firing squad, the condemned often screamed out inflammatory and rebellious defiance of the king. Fearful of the effect on the population, the king's justices around New York decided to kill the colonials in private. Soldiers dug a prison pit deep into the rock reef off Cow Neck (Manhasset Neck) and, at low tide on execution day, a prison boat carried the condemned from Sands Point to the reef.

The prisoners where chained to great rings set in the walls of the pit and drowned as the high tide slowly filled the pit and finally swept over the rocks. The bodies were either left there to become skeletons to drive new batches of the condemned insane before they drowned, or were carted away and buried in unmarked graves when the rings to which they were chained were needed for still more executions.

Even though Execution Pit (as it was called) was out of bounds to the public, its horror became legend in colonial America. Some historians suggest it was the main ispiration for the line in the Declaration of Independence which talks of "the murder they commit on the inhabitants of these United States." Legend has it that the ghosts of those condemned to die in the creeping horrors of a slowly rising tide eventually took their revenge on the king's men. It is said that as George Washington and his ragged army retreated from Manhattan toward nearby White Plains, a shipload of British soldiers sent in pursuit foundered on Execution Rocks, drowning all aboard.

This story may not be true, but the building of Execution Rocks Lighthouse provided proof of just how much it had burned itself into the nation's consciousness. The federal government laid down unique regulations for the operation of the lighthouse. Never again, ruled Congress, would any man feel "chained" to Executions Rocks. Instead of agreeing to serve for a specific time, keepers served there as long as they were willing. If they wanted to move, they could request and get an instant "honourable" transfer "without prejudice."

Another version (among several) of how Execution Rocks got its name is based on historical references to the fact that the original settlers of Manhasset Neck (called Cow Neck) named the rocks, because they were such a dangerous obstacle to ships entering Manhasset Bay (called Cow Bay) and caused so many accidents and injuries. Settlers displayed lanterns from the highest elevations to help vessels navigate along the coast, but there were no regular keepers on duty, so the lanterns could not always be relied upon. Whatever the origin of its name, Execution Rocks remains one of the most interesting lighthouses in Long Island Sound.

•

World's Tallest Lighthouse

One of the world's tallest buildings is also its tallest lighthouse. Located on one of the most populous islands in the world and standing more than 1000 ft. above sea level. New York City's Empire State Building sends a two billion candlepower light a distance of 300 miles by air and 80 miles by land. Also in New York City is, of course, the Statue of Liberty in New York Harbor. Its lighted torch at night is reminiscent of the Pharos in ancient Alexandria, Egypt.

CHAPTER 4

SANDS POINT LIGHT, Sands Point, NY (1809)

Old Light List No.: 483 (Obsolete)
Location: Latitude 40° 51.6' N
Longitude 73° 43.5' W
Height: 51' (HAW 65')
Range: 12 miles, Fixed White
Lens: Fourth Order, 490 Candlepower
Refitted: 1864
Deactivated: December 1922

Although the coasts of Long Island Sound boast many famous lighthouses, certainly one of the most celebrated is Sands Point Light. Although the original lighthouse was closed in December 1922, I included it in this book, since it is one of my favorite lights and is such a prominent landmark to anyone sailing on Long Island Sound. Contrary to rumor, singer Barbara Streisand has never lived at the light, if she knows about it at all.

The United States Lighthouse Commission thought that the old light was too far from the end of the reef to effectively warn vessels to stay clear of it, especially small boats, so it installed a flashing green acetylene beacon (that requires attention only once or twice a year) on a forty-ft. steel skeleton tower on the outer edge of the dangerous rocky reef 325 feet offshore. The new light had a tank house at its base and rested on a pyramidal concrete block on a riprap foundation in the water at the end of the reef. The old light, now privately owned by an old seafaring family, guided mariners for 113 years. Even so, many ships and lives were lost on the rocks protruding into the Sound.

Sands Point Lighthouse was named after the point on land that is named after a Captain John Sands (1649-1712) and his two brothers, James and Samuel, who were well-known at the time and settled in the area about 1691. John was the skipper of a packet which plied between New York and Virginia ports and is said to have introduced locust trees to Long Island.

Noah Mason, another sea captain who came to the area from New London, Connecticut, was awarded the contract to build the original lighthouse and was its keeper until his death in 1841. Mason, his wife Lucretia, and other members of the Mason family are interred in the nearby Sands' family burial ground on the old Conde Nast estate on Sands Point Road. A white marble headstone marks the grave of Noah and his wife. Mason, born in 1755 during the French and Indian War in Dighton, Massachusetts, enlisted in the Continental Army when he was 19 years old. He helped to build military fortifications at Dorchester Heights, Massachusetts and at Tarrytown, New York. Also, he took part in the Battle of Saratoga which resulted in the surrender of the British General Burgoyne.

Sands Point Light, Sands Point, NY

33

After the war, Mason moved to Connecticut, married, raised a family and engaged in the sea trade. In 1806, United States Senator Samuel Mitchell, owner of a home on Cow Neck (Port Washington today), sent a petition to Congress for the establishment of a lighthouse at Sands Point. The Point at the tip of Cow Neck peninsula had been known as Watch Point up to and during the American Revolution. Mitchell's bill was passed into law on January 26, 1806. Five acres of land on the Point were purchased from Benjamin and Jemima Hewlett who had come to Cow Neck in 1794 and had settled on the farm which had belonged to a Simon Sands. David Gelston, Collector for the Port of New York, issued proposals for the construction of the lighthouse. The contract was awarded to Noah Mason who carried out the project with such speed that the building was ready by the end of 1809 at the cost of $8,500.

Mason had a home and farm on the lower end of present day Hoffstot Lane, then called Mason's Island, The Island (also known at various times as Samuel Sands' Island, Mott Island, and Nostrand Island) was not strictly an island except at high tide when the water from East Creek crossed the salt marsh to mix with water from Long Island Sound. Part of Hoffstot Lane is constructed above the high tide level at the place where the salt marsh meets the beach, the former boundary of Mason's Island.

The lighthouse was originally white with a one-minute flash. Later it was changed to a fixed white light to avoid conflicting with the flashing white light of Execution Rocks Lighthouse, about a mile north. Eighty feet from the ground to the lantern room, the lighthouse is built of octagonal stone blocks, ten feet thick at base. The lantern room has been reconstructed and can be reached by a sturdy iron spiral staircase and is lighted by four large windows facing south. The original lantern burned whale oil.

Until 1868, the keeper of the light had to live at Barker's Point, but in that year the Government decided he deserved a house. The result was a simple, white-washed two-and-a-half story colonial brick house, attached to the lighthouse by an enclosed passageway. The date of the construction of the house is inscribed on tis exterior. It was enlarged in the 20th century to eight rooms, all big and well-lighted. The first occupant was probably John Seaman, keeper of the light in 1870, according to the Federal Census of that year.

Captain Cornelius Douglass, who entered government service when he was 15 years old, served as lighthouse keeper for 22 years at the turn of the century. The last keeper was Thomas J. Murray until December 1922 when the lighthouse was no longer used as a warning beacon. At that time, the Government removed the old lantern and lantern room and, as noted earlier, installed a flashing green light offshore in its place. This new light was later removed in 1968, and a maintenance-free, 38-ft. steel tower was then placed in the water at the end of the reef. This is still in operation today.

Mansions

Mrs. Oliver Hazard Perry Belmont, whose first husband was William K. Vanderbilt, became the first private owner of Sands Point Lighthouse in 1924. She paid $100,000 at a government auction (there were no other bidders) on Staten Island for five acres of land. This included the light tower and the lightkeeper's house to prevent visitors from passing over the government 12-ft. right-of-way through her land to the lighthouse. She had previously purchased the nearby property of the Sands Point Hotel in 1917. This was originally known as the Nostrand House, destroyed by fire in 1892. Mrs. Belmont built a luxurious French Gothic mansion (copied from a medieval chateau) called Beacon Towers.

While the lighthouse was in operation, Keeper Murray was almost deprived of his personal liberty. He was notified by the Superintendent of Lighthouses on June 22, 1922 (the light ceased operation in December) that he must discontinue receiving visitors at the lighthouse on Sundays and holidays during June, July and August, whether they were personal friends or otherwise. It was generally conceded that Mrs. Belmont had used her influence with the Superintendent to curtail Murray's social activities.

In the lush years following World War I, Mrs. Belmont, who had married the owners of two of America's largest fortunes, William K. Vanderbilt and Oliver P. Belmont, held sway at Beacon Towers. The showplace of the North Shore, with its 15 master bedrooms and 12 servants' rooms, ran up an annual tax bill of between 12 and 18 thousand dollars. It cost an additional 25 thousand dollars to keep the hordes of servants and the estate maintained. By 1927, Mrs. Belmont had had enough and fled the United States for her estates in France. Once again, Sands Point Lighthouse was put on the market.

This time, the buyer was William Randolph Hearst, just past his peak as a giant of the newspaper industry. He paid $400,000 for the Towers and the lighthouse. Mrs. Hearst was enchanted with the chateau and remodeled it, adding a banquet hall, a movie theater in the basement, and furnishing it with priceless works of art. She changed the name of the mansion to Chateau St. Joan after her favorite French heroine, Joan of Arc. In addition, the Hearsts built their own castle on the waterfront, 1,000 feet east of the old Sands Point Lighthouse. Although Hearst and his wife kept the mansion fully staffed with servants, they preferred to live in the simple lightkeeper's quarters. The mansion was left to guests. However, Mr. Hearst spent most of his time at San Simeon, his California home, while Mrs. Hearst remained in Sands Point.

Typical of the lavish hospitality at the Hearst mansion, which must have been an inspiration for Fitzgerald's *The Great Gatsby*, was a party in 1933 when 2,000 persons danced in the paved courtyard to the music of Paul Whiteman's orchestra. Four years later in 1937, Mrs. Hearst moved out of her mansion pleading that the estate was too expensive to keep up.

Although the chateau was offered for sale at a mere $150,000, there were no takers. Hearst transferred the title of his property to the Dime Savings Bank in 1940 to pay off a $93,000 mortgage. A year later in 1941, apparently unable to find a buyer for the million dollar mansion, the famous house was levelled by wreckers at a cost of over $11,000 to the bank owners.

The property was then sold to Edmund G. Burke, a real estate man, who at first wanted only the lighthouse and the land immediately surrounding it. The bank, however, which had just paid $11,500 to raze Mrs. Belmont's dream castle, would have nothing of such a deal. Burke had to purchase all 11 acres or none. With some misgivings, Burke and his wife bought the 11 acres and divided the property into one-acre lots for home sites. Less than 14 days later, he had sold all the subdivisions of the property and had netted a tidy profit. Ranch-type houses now dot the property where once two glorious chateaus had stood.

"Today, only the original wall towers and gate of the former Gold Coast mansions remain," calling to mind an ancient king whos visage lay scattered on the desert sand. "They mark the entrance to Sands Point Light Road where the lighthouse," now owned by a man who comes from a long line of ship builders and sea captains, "looks very picturesque as it towers above its ranch-house neighbors." The owner keeps the lighthouse structure in its original form and maintains it as a monument to the glory of its historic past. It is also a memorial to its builder, Noah Mason, and all the faithful keepers who kept the light burning through all kinds of weather and circumstances for the safety of mariners who passed up and down the Sound in ships.

Sands Point Light
Now a private residence

Photo By Carl G. Saporiti

CHAPTER 5

GREAT CAPTAIN ISLAND LIGHT, Greenwich, CT (1829)

Old Light List No.: 167 (Obsolete)
Location: Latitude 40° 58.0′ N
Longitude 73° 37.4′ W
Height: 51′ (HAW 73′)
Range: 17 miles, White, 100,000 candlepower
15 miles red, 25,000 candlepower
Alternate occulting White and Group Flashing
Red every 10 seconds, Horn
Lens: Fourth Order, Classical (Fresnel), electric
Rebuilt: 1868
Deactivated: January 30, 1970

Where Long Island Sound narrows and becomes New York's East River, there are three major lights. Inbound ships sail south of Great Captain Island and Execution Rocks and then keep the green light of Stepping Stones on their port side. Stepping Stones was automated in 1966, Execution Rocks in 1979. When Great Captain Island was automated in 1970, the light was moved to a nearby 65 ft. metal pipe structure. Great Captain Island lighthouse is now owned by the town of Greenwich, Connecticut and will, I hope, be preserved. The pipe structure (LLN 20445) is still maintained by the Coast Guard. It has an alternate flashing white and red light every 12 seconds, with a range of 14 miles. The lens is a DCB-10 with a 500 watt lamp. there is a horn. The light is ten nautical miles from Sheffield Island Light and eight miles from Execution Rocks Light.

Great Captain Island, about 35 miles from Times Square, New York City, has a history as elusive as the island itself and was little known to many Greenwich residents until town ferries began running there in the 1970s. Suspected to be a site of Captain Kidd's buried treasure, it had a casino which was destroyed by a mysterious fire. The island is 2,350 yards south of Greenwich, CT, and is shaped like a lamb chop. With 17.2 acres of beach, scrubby woods and a lagoon, the island remains relatively peaceful compared with its busy neighbor Little Captain Island. Because the town ferry schedule to Great Captain Island is subject to the tides, the island has long been a haven for boaters, now restricted to Greenwich residents only. It had been popular for boat clubs and Power Squadrons rendezvous. A picnic area had been set up then at the northwest end of the island.

The years have looked down on a succession of island owners and island uses. In the late 1920s, a plush, very private beach club sprang up, but the Depression ended that. Later, a syndicate attempted to profitably ferry throngs across the 1½ miles of water to a semi-private beach club/casino, but that did not pay either. Then, on the night of August 23, 1947, the casino was destroyed by a mysterious fire. While the casino blaze lit the sky, two army fliers lost their lives when their plane plunged into Long Island Sound. "Thousands of people jammed their way into Steamboat Road with cars and then on foot in an effort to get a good view of the fire, which filled the sky for miles around with an orange glow and clouds of smoke," according to a local newspaper account at the time. The casino, outbuildings, most of the boardwalk and some of the cabanas went up in flames while frustrated firemen watched helplessly from Greenwich Harbor. Overgrown foundations remain.

The Port-Green Corporation of Greenwich, the casino owners, argued it was a flare—dropped by a U.S. Coast Guard plane searching the area for the downed pilots—which ignited the blaze. The syndicate was awarded $19,500 by the Coast Guard in a 1951 court settlement for damages to their property. Five years later, the Aerotec Corporation of Greenwich purchased the island as a holiday spot for its 200 employees and their families and kept it until October 1, 1966, when they sold 13.7 acres of it to the town of Greenwich for $90,000. Aerotec had built cabanas on the beach at the narrow part of the island. In June 1973, the town of Greenwich purchased the remaining 3.5 acres of the island and the old stone lighthouse for $42,500 from the U.S. Government—except for a small area around the automatic signal light.

Early History of the Island: How it got its Name, etc.

In 1656, Captain Daniel Patrick was appointed military commandant to protect Greenwich and an island offshore from marauding Petuquapaen Indians. He was so successful, according to legend, that he named the island "Great Captain" in tribute to himself.

Important dates in the history of the light are:

March 1828: In a letter to Congressman David Plant of Stratford, Stephen Waring of Cos Cob requested that a lighthouse be built on Great Captain Island.

May 19, 1829: Samuel Lyons sold 3.5 acres of his holdings on Great Captain Island to the United States Government for $300.00 ". . . for a lighthouse to be built thereon."

October 21, 1829: The U.S. Government built the first lighthouse and keeper's dwelling on Great Captain Island on a rocky rise at the southeast end of the island.

February 18, 1868: a new lighthouse and keeper's home was built of stone to replace the original light on the island.

Until the light was automated in 1970, it was manned day and night by a four-man crew.

Caretakers

For four years after the lighthouse became automated, vandals caused heavy damage to it. For until 1974, there was no year-'round caretaker on the island. However, in 1974, Fred Parnell was appointed superintendent

U.S. Coast Guard Photo

Great Captain Island Light, Greenwich, CT

of the island by the town of Greenwich and lived with his wife in one of the cottages built by the Aerotec Corporation when it owned the island. Parnell was deputized as a special policeman with powers of arrest and served as caretaker until 1978.

From 1978 until the latter part of 1984, Robert Hendricks and his wife Helen were the caretakers of the island. They had to resign, because of Bob's declining health. The Hendricks' shared the light with Billy Joe, their black goat; Cappy, their German shepherd named after the island; three cats and a small dog. Otto Laversdorf and his family succeeded them.

The caretaker's life is not without its tribulations, in case anyone is interested in the job. He works for the Greenwich Department of Parks and Recreation for an annual salary of about $20,000. The perks of his job are free rent and utilities and lots of fresh, unpolluted air, free from the distractions of civilization on the mainland not too far away. This may sound good, but during the summer the caretaker works 24 hours a day, seven days a week. He is responsible for supervising beach staff, keeping bathrooms clean, and ensuring that the days run without a hitch. Also, the caretaker must have a knack with machinery, for he must maintain his own generator, since the island is self-sustaining. Loneliness usually sets in around February when, without visitors, life can be extremely desolate. Silence permeates the island. There are no telephones, movies, shops, restaurants or bars on the island. One caretaker's wife had to take a job in Greenwich to maintain her sanity. Clearly, the caretaker's job is not for everyone.

More Greenwich residents are getting to know their island sanctuary. From June 30, 1982 to July 1, 1983, Great Captain Island had 14,820 visitors. Hopefully, they will appreciate its natural attractions and preserve them for their descendents.

•

Parts of a Light and Early Fuels

From a ship, the twinkling light that guides the mariner safely along the coast, warning him of dangerous reefs, or giving him a guide by which he can determine course and position, looks like a very simple affair. Actually, it is a complex mechanism, consisting of three parts: the light, its lens, and the mechanism that supports and revolves the light.

Early lighthouse fires were sparked by wood and pitch; coal came into vogue for a time and then gave way to oil and kerosene with its incandescent vapor light, which gave keepers their time-honored title "wickies." Although most lighthouses today are equipped with electricity and Diesel generators in case of power failure, some lights still burn kerosene; the famous Eddystone Light (1698) near Plymouth, England, emitting a beam of 258,000 candlepower, is one of them.

CHAPTER 6

LEDGE OBSTRUCTION LIGHT, Stamford, CT (1882)
(Chatham Rock Light) (Stamford Light)

Light List No.: 23825
Location: Latitude 41° 0.8′ N
             Longitude 73° 32.6′ W
Height: 80′
Range: Appoximately 6 miles nominal range
          Flashing White every 4 seconds
Lens: 200 mm Clear Glass Lens, battery operated

No lighthouse in the First Coast Guard District has had so many owners as the Ledge Obstruction Light. "It has," an old salt wryly remarked, "passed through more hands than a bottle of beer on a hot day." Another wit commented that the light serves primarily as an 80-ft. high roost for passing cormorants and sea gulls.

Beset with shoals and reefs, the entrance to Stamford's twin channels was not always easy to find. As early as 1871, a large number of people petitioned for a light to mark Forked Rock, or "The Ledge," at the east side of the entrance. Officials at the time recommended that a day beacon be placed there, with a lighted beacon on the opposite side. The total cost, they estimated, would be $8,000. There was a lapse of nine years before anything further was done, a lapse which prompted the *Stamford Advocate* on November 25, 1881 to say that the delay was due to ". . . non-representation in the national legislature by a man who seldom got farther towards Washington than the Fifth Avenue Hotel."

Then, "For the first time in eight years," continued the *Advocate,* "the Fourth district was represented in Congress." On June 16, 1880, a preliminary appropriation of $7,000 was voted, and a further appropriation of $23,000 on March 3, 1881. The site chosen was Chatham Rock, opposite Forked Rock, and the State of Connecticut deeded the land for a lighthouse on March 16, 1881. A temporary pier was built to receive the cement, brick and iron necessary for construction, and the work began in earnest in mid-summer of 1881 with General Duane, a government engineer in charge. Captain John J. Ryle, a lobsterman, directed the placement of Byram Quarry rock on the shoal watersite. The first cement was used to form a vast artifical rock to receive the superstructure of the light. Immense masses of heavy stone (riprap) were dumped around it on all sides.

From the center of the mass of material, a cylindrical pier 28 feet high and 30 feet in diameter sprang up as a breakwater. It looked like "a huge hogshead standing on the chine," according to one observer, but the staves were of 1½ inch iron weighing a ton each. There were 120 of these staves forming the outside of the pier. A concentric iron structure, four feet less in diameter, was placed on the inside, which was lined with brick, and the space between filled with a solid mass of cement and stones. This pier formed a cellar for the structure and was used subsequently as a storage room for oil, coal and fresh water.

Above the completed pier, a tower soon rose, 22 feet in diameter at the base and slopiing gradually to 18 feet where the balcony deck comes out to a point in line with the base. The tower continued above the balcony to the parapet where its diameter is 15 feet. Still farther up was the lantern, nine feet high. Its apex was 49 feet from the base of the tower and 77 feet above the base of the substructure. The outside was painted with rust-resisting red lead and oil.

The heavy iron castings for the tower were fabricated in a Boston foundry and, during construction, a small "Mississippi Lamp" was displayed in the tower. The permanent lamp, visible 13 miles, was first exhibited on February 10, 1882. Other equipment included a fog bell operated by clock work. The lower of the five interior decks was made into living quarters for attendants.

Foreman James Fagan and a force of nine men lived in the wooden shanty on the temporary pier during construction and were visited occasionally by the lighthouse steamer "Mistletoe." When the Ledge Obstruction Light became inoperative on June 19, 1953, it had a crew of three men. The lantern in the white conical tower was a fixed green, fourth-order electric light, and the air diaphram horn blasted two seconds every 20 seconds during fog. The land on which the light stood reverted to the State of Connecticut and in turn to the City of Stamford.

Until June 19, 1953, the annual cost of operation of the light was approximately $14,500. On this date, when the light beacon became unattended, it changed its characteristic to a flashing white light every 2.5 seconds, flash 0.5 seconds, eclipse 2.0 seconds, and to 140 candlepower. The fog signal was discontinued, and Mr. Willard J. Ryle was appointed lamplighter.

Discontinuance of the light as an aid to navigation was the result of careful study and deliberation of a Coast Guard Board of Survey by direction of President Eisenhower. The Survey Board determined that funds for the provision and operation of aids to navigation in Stamford Harbor could be more economically utilized in the improvement of the Stamford Harbor West Breakwater Light and fog signal than for repair, protection and preservation of the old tower. Furthermore, the improvements offered more adequate service to mariners. The new West Breakwater Light has far greater candlepower and a vastly improved fog signal.

In 1953, when the Coast Guard discontinued the light, the General Services Administration, a division of the Federal Government, offered it for sale. Although unsold in 1955, 45 people wandered through the light that year and considered buying it for a summer home, but no one did. Eventually, 22 bids were received for the light, ranging from $1.00 to $57.50. The $1.00 bid won and was made by the former mayor of Stam-

Ledge Obstruction (Chatham Rock or Stamford) Light, Stamford, CT

Photo by Julius M. Wilensky

ford, Thomas F. Quigley, with the hope of giving the structure to the city. He wanted to have the lighthouse preserved as a historical shrine or landmark. In 1958, another former mayor of Stamford, Webster C. Givens, said he wanted to interest yacht clubs, boat owners, the Stamford Museum, and the Stamford Historical Society into making the lighthouse a combined marine museum and weather station. However, Stamford did nothing with the light, so in 1964, the General Services administration took the light back with the approval of yet another former mayor of Stamford, Thomas C. Mayers. No one seems to know when the Hartford Electric Light Company purchased the lighthouse from the General Services Administration, although it seems to have been in 1967. Helco wanted to build a power plant on their property in the west branch of Stamford Harbor, and to carry the cooling water out into the Sound via a huge pipe leading to the lighthouse property. During the early 1970s, they discussed this plan with still another Mayor of Stamford, Julius M. Wilensky, your editor. Their plan was scrapped because they were unable to satisfy the City that they could provide acceptable air quality. Helco apparently kept the light until 1982, when the company was taken over by the Connecticut Light and Power Company.

In 1982, Ledge Obstruction Light acquired its eighth owner, the Connecticut Light and Power Company, which became a division of the Northeast Utilities Company.The property was offered for sale on August 29, 1983. It was assessed by the City of Stamford for $55,000-$50,000 for the ten acres of underwater land and $5,000 for the lighthouse. The Coast Guard insisted that whoever bought the lighthouse must maintain a lighted, battery-powered navigational beacon on top of it. It had to be kept a working lighthouse.

The ninth and final owner (so far) of Ledge Obstruction Light turned out to be the Chairman of the Board of the First Women's Bank, New York City, who is also the owner of a textile company and a real estate investor. On Friday, December 14, 1984, Eryk Spektor purchased the light for $230,000 at an auction conducted by the Northeast Utilities Company. The latest owner's rationale for buying the light was quite simple: "I wanted a lighthouse," he said. "I would like to come by boat in the spring and see inside," he continued. "We'll paint it, fix it up, replace windows, do whatever needs to be done. It'll be a cheap place to park my boat." The new owner joins the owner of North Dumpling Light, Fishers Island Sound, New York (see Chapter 34), in having a unique place to escape to from the daily cares of business life.

Ledge Obstruction Light has seven levels and rises 80 feet in four, small, circular, fort-like stories. It is one of the 16 lighthouses of Connecticut's coast. The only time the light can be reached by boat is at high tide because of its 12-ft. high landing. It has no heat, no hot water and no electricity. The light is powered by a 12-volt battery. It is located 3,600 feet off shore and is less than three miles from Interstate 95. In its rooms, women gave birth, children played, heroic deeds were inspired, and a murder may have been committed. It has never been established if keeper Ray Bliven of Westerly, Rhode Island fell from the lighthouse or was pushed from it to drown in the waves below. There is no doubt, however, about the fate of another keeper's daughter who accepted a man in marriage only to discover that she preferred life on the lighthouse to life on the mainland. Her distraught husband persuaded her to go ashore one evening for a talk and shot her dead.

Martin Louther Sowle was the last keeper of the light from 1938 to 1953. When he assumed duties at the light in 1938, the family quarters had been transferred to the engine room. Residents of the Shippan Point and Old Greenwich waterfront areas said that Mr. Sowle was always on the lookout for small boats in trouble. For his quick action on October 2, 1939, he won a Congressional Silver Medal for life-saving. He set forth in heavy weather in a 16-ft. outboard motor skiff and rescued a man two miles off shore. When Ledge Obstruction Light was automated in 1953, Mr. Sowle was transferred to Greens Ledge Light off Norwalk, Connecticut, just eight miles east of his old light.

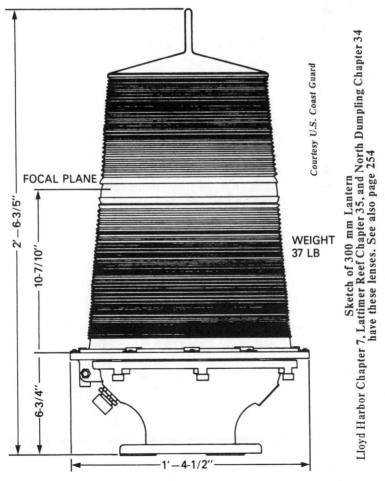

FOCAL PLANE

2' — 6-3/5"

10-7/10"

6-3/4"

1' — 4-1/2"

WEIGHT
37 LB

Courtesy U.S. Coast Guard

Sketch of 300 mm Lantern

Lloyd Harbor Chapter 7, Lattimer Reef Chapter 35, and North Dumpling Chapter 34 have these lenses. See also page 254

CHAPTER 7

LLOYD HARBOR LIGHT, Lloyd Harbor, NY (1857 and 1912)

Light List No.: 25260
Location: Latitude 40° 54.4′ N
Longitude 73° 25.5′ W
Height: 42′
Range: 9 miles, Horn
Lens: 300 mm, 3.05 amp lamp
Automated: 1949

The story of Lloyd Harbor Lighthouse is really the story of two light-houses, one built in 1857, the other in 1912. The original light was a wood-en, two-story keeper's house with a tower attached which was discontin-ued in 1925 and deeded to the State of New York in 1928. It was destroyed by fire on November 12, 1947. The second lighthouse, the one that exists today, was built in 1912 by Charles Mead Company in the water and not far from the original light. Its rectangular shape gives it the appearance of a castle. It was made of reinforced concrete, and therein likes its worth.

The First Light (on Lloyds Neck)

Northeast storms, churning the Sound from Mystic to Oyster Bay, can be wicked, as any mariner knows. At the widest reach, southwest from New Haven, a 45-knot easterly wind can create a real sea. At night, before 1857, ships had no choice but to run in the dark for shelter in land-locked Lloyd Harbor. Sometimes they came to grief along the spur that juts out southward from the tip of Lloyd's Neck. For this reason, the Government in 1847 bought five acres of sand on a peninsula from Jonah Denton (1812-1892), whose family had owned the property on the Neck for several generations, after having purchased it originally from Daniel Whitehead of Oyster Bay, and erected a lighthouse on it. In a low tower, a beacon was installed that was visible to any craft that cleared Eaton's Neck. It marked the entrance to Lloyd Harbor and, in moderate weather, served vessels making their way at night through "the Gut" into Huntington Harbor.

The keeper's dwelling was an 11-room, white frame wooden house, two stories high, with an attic and an offset light-tower, all resting on a deeply laid foundation of brick. In the many-sided light-chamber, a great lamp, fed with specially refined coal oil, cast its welcome beams across the wat-er from Asharoken and beyond to the Seawanhaka Yacht Club anchor-age in Oyster Bay and across a narrow stretch of Long Island Sound to the Connecticut shore. After the light was discontinued in 1925, the build-ing became increasingly damaged by vandals. On November 12, 1947, when the building was razed in a blazing inferno fanned by high winds, it took only a few hours to destroy the structure forever. It was believed that

Lloyd Harbor Light, Lloyd Harbor, NY

hunters had occupied the empty lighthouse and had carelessly lit a fire in one of the old fireplaces, thus setting off the blaze.

The last of the two official keepers of the light was Robert McGlone. The five acres of lighthouse property became known as the "eminent domain" of McGlone, his wife and five children. With infinite labor, McGlone brought topsoil from Lloyd's Neck to make a garden plot which had been cleared of native growth. Then, in 1900, tragedy darkened the happy home when Mrs. McGlone and her sixth child died in childbirth. The later celebrated Augusta "Gussie" Harrigan, a local, 31 year old spinster, came to the lighthouse to take care of the five motherless McGlone children. When the Government erected a new lighthouse at the Huntington Harbor entrance in 1912 and made Robert McGlone its first keeper, "Gussie" and his children remained at the old lighthouse. Ms. Harrigan eventually became the keeper of the light until she officially retired on October 1, 1925 at the age of 56 years. She lived long enough to witness the destruction of her beloved lighthouse in the fire of 1947.

The "New" Light (at Huntington Harbor entrance)

In the September 7, 1967 issue of the *"Notice to Mariners,"* the Coast Guard announced that it planned to close the Lloyd Harbor Lighthouse, which had been built in 1912, and replace it with a new buoyage system to mark the harbor entrance. The announcement triggered so many protests from boaters and various shipping and oil companies asking that the light be kept in operation as an aid to navigation that the Coast Guard cancelled its plan to discontinue it. For years the lighthouse had a keeper (Robert McGlone was the first). Later, a caretaker lived on it summers and serviced the light in the winter months until it was automated by the Coast Guard in 1949.

Located on the south side of the entrance to Lloyd Harbor and on the west side of the entrance to Huntington Harbor, the stately and picturesque light serves an important function. It can be seen from any point in the Huntington Bay area. Its fog signal is a necessary guide for commercial and industrial waterfront traffic during the winter months and on dark nights. The lighthouse has saved many barges from piling up on the rocks or on sandbars, thus preventing harbor congestion and loss of life. The light is particularly needed in winter by oil barges bringing fuel oil to schools, industry and homes. Their captains can pick up the light at a distance of ten miles and thus avoid potential disaster to their ships.

The "new" lighthouse consists of a tower and attached dwelling, both built of reinforced concrete. A reinforced concrete crib foundation supports the tower and dwelling. The site also includes a band of riprap (a wall of stones thrown together without order) which surrounds the foundation. The foundation was constructed on shore, about one-half mile from the lighthouse. It was towed to the site, then sunk (by filling it with water) to the hard-sand bottom that had been leveled and cleared of rocks. The interior spaces were then filled with concrete, resulting in an extremely heavy, stable footing for the lighthouse.

The two-story tower is surmounted by an octagonal lantern. Screwed to the floor of the gallery is a large fog-signal bell embossed with the date and city of origin: "Jersey City, New Jersey, 1911." From an historical perspective, Lloyd Harbor Lighthouse is essentially the same structure inside and out that was built in 1912. Rising through the center of the tower is an iron column from which hangs the circular, cast iron stairway. The original fourth order lens with an incondescent oil-vapor lamp has been replaced by a modern plastic beacon. The keeper's dwelling area has a lining of terra-cotta tiles, over which plaster on metal lath has been applied. Much of the interior woodwork remains, including beaded-board wainscoting and built-in cabinets. No significant exterior features have been removed or greatly altered. The only significant loss is its old illuminating equipment. Deterioration, however, has affected the structure and is evident everywhere.

The present lighthouse is significant as an example of one of the earliest reinforced concrete lighthouses in the nation and perhaps the earliest on the East Coast. By the mid-1870s, iron had assumed primacy as the structural material for lighthouses, particularly for water-bound lights on sand bottoms, such as Lloyd Harbor. Reinforced concrete gained acceptance in the second decade of the 20th century. The lighthouse is significant also, because it represents the maritime heritage of Long Island's north shore. Since colonization of the area, the many inlets and harbors along this coast served as home ports for vessels engaged in the salt water fishing and coastal trade. The light stands at the entrance to two small harbors, Lloyd and Huntington, which served such maritime interests. The importance of shipping in this locality is attested to the relatively early date of the first light (no longer extant) at this location— 1857, a time when many other such small harbors could claim only buoys or day markers for navigational aids.

Before the 1870s, shoal bottoms were marked by lights on substantial masonry footings. By 1877, however, the Lighthouse Board had developed the iron-caisson foundation, a hollow cylinder of cast-iron plates, bolted together at the site. Such foundations offered ease of installation and low cost relative to masonry, while still assuring the requisite stability for a lighthouse. The iron-caisson foundation was used into the 20th century for water-bound lighthouses.

Reinforced concrete was first used for a lighthouse in 1908, when the tower at Point Arena, California was rebuilt after its destruction in the 1906 earthquake. In the next several years, reinforced concrete lighthouses were built on the coasts of California, Oregon, Washington and Alaska. On the Atlantic Coast, the material had been used for minor structures, such as oil houses, but Lloyd Harbor Lighthouse was among the first major installations built of reinforced concrete. Its location was well-suited to such experimentation. The site was a water-covered shoal, but it was relatively protected, lying in the lee of Lloyd Neck. The installation of the light could thus be completed without the full exposure of an open-water site, and the risk to navigation, should the experiment fail, was also less than it would have been on the heavily traveled Long Island Sound.

The Lighthouse Board apparently found reason to encourage the use of reinforced concrete, because two major lights in the Delaware area were made of the material in ensuing years: Brandywine Shoal (1914) and Marcus Hook Range Rear (1920). Despite the evident acceptance of reinforced concrete in lighthouses, such structures are rare in the northeastern United States. The extensive construction programs of the 19th and early 20th centuries left few unmarked hazards, landfalls or ranges, so the need for new lighthouses was rather small. On the West Coast and in the Pacific, where construction continued into a later period, reinforced concrete lighthouses are quite common. It seems likely that Lloyd Harbor Light played a substantial role in establishing the fitness of such material. Its location made possible close observation of it by officials of the Lighthouse Board who, of course, were concentrated in the centers of government and commerce on the East Coast. Thus, "the Castle" stands today as a mute symbol of the historical development of lighthouses in the United States.

Lloyd Harbor is named after one of its early settlers, Henry Lloyd, who was born in Boston, Massachusetts on November 28, 1687. Henry inherited the property of what is now the town of Lloyd Harbor from his father, James, who bought the land in 1679 but never saw it. Henry settled on it when he was only 24 years old in May 1711. While he lived there, the area was called the Manor of Queens Village. During his life, Henry was a shipping merchant until his death on March 18, 1763. He is buried on Lloyd Neck. His house, still standing, is being restored by the Lloyd Harbor Historical Society.

•

A Dying Harbor Light

Unless funds are found to repair the extensive damage to Lloyd Harbor Light, the alternative, according to the Coast Guard, is to demolish it and erect an automated light on a steel tower in its place. Lt. j.g. Spence Byrum, the Coast Guard's former program manager, estimated it would cost about $500,000 to restore the 74-year-old fanciful Beaux Arts-style structure and make it habitable. Local residents have formed the Save Huntington's Lighthouse Committee in an effort to find ways to rescue the old beacon. The most effective way to save a lighthouse is for a community organization to "adopt" it; that is, to lease the structure from the Coast Guard in return for a pledge to restore and maintain it while the Coast Guard still operates the light. Another plan the Coast Guard would like to see carried out is to have the lighthouse become a museum with access by boat. Either way, the important thing is to maintain a high level of interest in the light in the community (and nation) or a dying lighthouse will be dead.

CHAPTER 8

GREENS LEDGE LIGHT, Norwalk, CT (1902)

Light List No.: 20390
Location: Latitude 41° 2.5′ N
                Longitude 73° 26.6′ W
Height: 52′ (HAW 62′)
Range: 12 miles, White
              14 miles Red
              Alternate Flashing WR every 20 seconds, Horn
Lens: FA 251, 150 watt lamp

Greens Ledge is a rock and sand ridge that extends 1.1 miles westward from Sheffield Island. Depths of 10 to 15 feet extend about 400 yards east from Greens Ledge Light. A rocky ledge, on which the least found depth is 21 feet, extends 0.8 mile west-southwestward from the light. Another rocky ledge, with a least depth of 20 feet, is about 0.4 mile south-southwestward from the light.

The light is shown from a conical tower on the north side of the west end of the ledge. It is 1800 yards from the Connecticut shore, or about one mile off the the mouth of Five Mile River. It marks the entry to Sheffield Harbor, the western (and main) entrance to the Norwalk River and also serves as an aid to navigation for Five Mile River. Viewed from afar, it looks like a king-sized spark plug. A severe hurricane (1938) cracked its base, so that from certain angles it leans slightly. In 1971, the Coast Guard wanted to tear the lighthouse down, but local outcry and effort against the plan saved it from destruction. Like most others, the light is automated. When Coast Guardsmen staffed it in the early 1970s, they spent two weeks at the lighthouse and had the third week off. In its day, the structure had two bedrooms, a kitchen (on the first floor), and a bathroom. The bathroom may be a very early example of indoor facilities in a cast-iron light tower.

Keepers of the Light

William M. De Luce - appointed February 15, 1902; took oath March 3, 1902. Paid $600,00 a year.

Robert Burke - appointed July 1, 1908

J. Th. Kiarskon - appointed October 12, 1909

William T. Locke - appointed April 3, 1910; resigned 1912

George Clark - served from 1939 to 1943

Edward Steiger - appointed in 1943

Assistant Keepers   Served from February 1902 to March 1904.
Paid $450.00 a year
Henry M. Bevedret

Granville F. Barlow
J. Ericson
Jason Sullivan

A Description of the the Light

Greens Ledge Lighthouse, established on February 15, 1902, is located on a wave-swept site at the southwestern end of the Norwalk Islands, an archipelago near the Connecticut shore in western Long Island Sound. It marks a rock ledge in the approach to Norwalk Harbor from the west, re-placing an earlier stone lighthouse which still stands more than a mile east on Sheffield Island. The structure consists of a cast-iron tower, rest-ing on a black cylindrical cast-iron foundation with a flared rim and sup-porting a circular watchroom and lantern. The tower presently is painted brown on the lower half and white on the upper half. Included on the site are a riprap protective breakwater and a boat landing.

Standing in ten feet of water, the foundation is made of curved cast-iron plates, fitted together with bolts through molded flanges on the in-side edges. The foundation cylinder flares out in a trumpet shape to accomodate a deck upon which the lighthouse rests. Concrete filling sta-bilizes and strengthens the foundation and surrounds a cavity left at the top for the brick-lined basement and cisterns. A brick lining strengthens and insulates the tower, providing an anchorage for the winding cast-iron stairs which rise on the periphery of each story.

The lantern, seven feet in diameter, contains glass panes, 25 inches across, framed with diagonal brass astragals. Cast-iron plates containing circular ventilators with adjustable covers make up the lower half of the lantern walls. Within the lantern stands the modern lighting equipment, four electric bulbs under a hinged dome of heavy glass. This equipment was manufactured by Automatic Power, Inc. The original equipment, in-stalled in February 1901, was a fifth order lens with a flashing red light. Three months later, a fourth order lens was installed, showing a fixed white light with red flashes every 15 seconds and visible for 13½ miles.

Significance of the Light

Greens Ledge Lighthouse is significant as a typical example of a pre-fabricated, cast-iron conical light tower on a cast-iron tubular founda-tion. Major George H. Elliott, Engineer-Secretary for the U.S. Lighthouse Board, developed this type of foundation in 1873 for underwater sites such as Greens Ledge. The materials, construction, architectural detail and interior finish at the light reflect the stabilized design for conical cast-iron light towers in the second phase of their development.

The light is significant also as a warning of a submerged rock ledge west of Sheffield Island. During the 1890s when Norwalk Harbor was be-ing developed by federal appropriations for increased commercial traffic, the approach to the harbor past the Norwalk Islands presented a hazard to deeper draft vessels. The Lighthouse Board decided to replace the old

Greens Ledge Light, Norwalk, CT

1868 Lighthouse on Sheffield Island, itself a replacement for a still earlier lighthouse built in 1826. Two new aids to navigation were to be located on wave-swept sites at either end of the Norwalk Islands to guide ships into the channel behind the islands from both east and west. Greens Ledge and Peck Ledge Lighthouses were proposed to Congress in 1896. On March 3, 1899 Congress granted an appropriation of $60,000 for the construction of Greens Ledge Light. In 1900, the Philadelphia Construction Company undertook the erection of the foundation and superstructure of the light.

During the last quarter of the 19th century, most of the remaining lighthouse sites posed engineering challenges. Wave-swept lighthouses off the southern coasts had been successfully secured at the sites by iron piles, either anchored in rock or screwed deep into sandy shoals. In the northern states, however, where floating ice made such construction unsafe, underwater sites such as reefs, shoals and ledges had been utilized only at vast expense in manpower and material. Massive masonry foundations were required, such as the one built for Race Rock in Long Island Sound.

With the development of cast-iron technology in mid-century, a tubular foundation constructed of that material and filled with concrete became a feasible alternative to stone. Made of identical, curved, cast-iron plates, with flanges extending toward the inside of the curve and knees molded in for reinforcement, these foundations were assembled with bolts into rings at the construction site. Then successive rings were bolted together, lowered onto the prepared site, and filled with concrete or stones. These foundations proved to be as strong and stable as masonry, and since they could be mass-produced, realized substantial savings in design time, production and transportation costs. Cast-iron became the preferred material for lighthouse foundations and was widely used between 1873 and about 1910. Greens Ledge Light is built upon such a foundation, here with a flared top and rim.

Little ornamentation was applied to the tubular cast-iron lighthouses. However, at least three different phases of architectural ornamentation may be discerned. The first phase is represented in the deeply molded, arched and pedimented windows and door hoods and segmentally arched window sashes at Stratford Point (1881, Chapter 17) and Saybrook Breakwater Light (1887, Chapter 22). The second phase is notable at Greens Ledge where cast-iron window and door surrounds and the brackets which support the watchroom gallery and covered deck have a simplified classical detailing and rectilinear window sashes are enclosed in shallower, plainer cast-iron surrounds. In 1901, a third phase of ornamentation was introduced at Harbor of Refuge, Lewes, Delaware. This phase was characterized by greater abstraction of door and window trim and a molded cornice in place of brackets.

Greens Ledge Lighthouse has been nominated to be included in the National Register of Historic Places.

CHAPTER 9

PECK LEDGE LIGHT, Norwalk, CT (1906)

Light List No.: 23560
Location: Latitude 41° 4.7' N
           Longitude: 73° 22.1' W
Height: 54' (HAW 61')
Range: 7 miles, Flashing White every 4 seconds
Lens: 250 mm, 1.15 watt lamp
Automated: 1933

Peck Ledge Lighthouse was the last manned light built on a wave-swept site in Long Island Sound. It is also the light manned the shortest length of time—27 years. A permit was obtained in 1901, it was built on a marine site in 1906, and it was automated in 1933. It may well stand as the most expensive structure holding up a 250 mm lens in the Coast Guard.

Keepers of the Light
George W. Bardwell - appointed July 15, 1906 at an annual salary of $600.00.
August Lorenze - appointed January 26, 1907 at a salary of $52 a month.

Assistant Keepers
Louis T. Tooker - appointed July 15, 1906 at an annual salary of $500.00
Ferdinand Heizman - appointed December 17, 1906 at an annual sala-
    ry of $500.00

Description of the Light
Peck Ledge Lighthouse stands on a shoal east of Cockoenoe Island and south of Norwalk, Connecticut. It marks the east end of the Norwalk Islands chain in Long Island sound. The light stands in seven feet of water, marking two hazards in the approach to Norwalk Harbor from the east, Peck Ledge to the west and a shoal extending north from Goose Island. The site includes only a protective ring of riprap around the foundation. No breakwater or dock provides a sheltered approach. The structure consists of a large conical, cast-iron tower which rests on a cast-iron cylindrical foundation. Presently, the foundation and lantern are painted black, while the tower is white with a wide brown band in the middle.

The foundation is constructed of curved, cast-iron plates, bolted together through flanges cast on the edge of the inner surface. Assembled on land near the proposed location of the lighthouse, the foundation was transported to the prepared site, sunk and leveled, then filled with 250 bags of concrete. Space was left at the top center for a basement containing cisterns for the storage of rainwater.

The tower is constructed of curved cast-iron plates in the form of a truncated cone, brick-lined for stability and insulation. Contained within

55

are three stories of living space, surmounted by a circular watchroom and circular lantern. A peripheral cast-iron winding stair connects the first, second and third floors. Storage space is created above and below the steps in the stairwell on each level in the form of a closet and a cupboard.

In the cylindrical lantern, diagonal brass channels divide the curved glass panes which fill the top half of the cast-iron walls. Each pane measures 36 inches on the diaagonal. The light originally had a fourth order lens when it first flashed its warning to mariners in 1906. Then it was a flashing white light every ten seconds and was visible for 12¾ miles.

This is one of the lighthouses I visited that was inhabited by a large number of birds. As I mention elsewhere in this book, when mindless vandals break the windows of lighthouses, birds frequently move in and use it as a nesting place. This situation presents a problem to Coast Guard personnel who have to perform routine maintenance on the light. If they try to evict their feathered trespassers, local environmentalists and bird lovers complain. They argue that the nesting pattern of the birds will be disrupted if they are disturbed, so they should be left alone.

The lighthouse is highly visible to the public and is one of the best preserved examples of circular cast-iron lighthouses in the First Coast Guard District.

Significance of the Light

Peck Ledge Lighthouse is significant as a typical example of a pre-fabricated, cast-iron, conical lighthouse and foundation developed by the United States Lighthouse Board to reduce the costs of design, production, and installation for difficult sites which remained unmarked by the end of the 19th century. These sites included wave-swept shoals, reefs, ledges and newly created breakwaters. The lighthouse is significant also as a component of late 19th century improvements to the approaches to Norwalk Harbor. Larger ships of deeper draft were in jeopardy from underwater hazards which previously had gone unmarked.

The archipelago of the Norwalk Islands forms both a protection and an obstacle for the harbor at Norwalk, Connecticut. When the desire for increased commercial traffic in the late 19th century brought dredging and improvement in aids to navigation to the Norwalk Harbor area, the old lighthouse on Sheffield Island (1826, 1868) in the Norwalk group was thought to be inadequate for guiding boat traffic around the east and west ends of the island chain into Norwalk Harbor.

Lobbying efforts were undertaken in 1896 for appropriations for two lighthouses, each to mark an underwater rock ledge at either end of the Norwalk Islands. Greens Ledge Lighthouse at the western end was approved in 1899 and completed in 1902.

Peck Ledge, at the eastern end of the archipelago, was the other site selected for a new lighthouse. Beginning in 1896, repeated requests for an appropriation were voiced until 1901, when an appropriation for $10,000 was made. A decision to include accomodations for two keepers in the de-

Peck Ledge Light, Norwalk, CT

sign led to requests for an additional $29,000 appropriation. By the beginning of 1905, contracts were let for the construction and fabrication of metal for the lighthouse. That summer the materials were delivered, and the foundation cylinder was assembled, leveled up and sunk.

Construction was halted in July 1905 due to a delay in delivery of the metal parts. By March 1906, assembly of the first and second story plates of the shell had begun. Both the foundation and superstructure were composed of curved cast-iron sections assembled on the site and bolted together with flanges molded around each section. The Lighthouse Board had developed this construction method in 1873 for the Hunting Island Lighthouse (discontinued) in South Carolina where the problem of erosion necessitated a lighthouse which could be disassembled and moved. By 1876, the Board employed such cast-iron plates to construct tubular lighthouse foundations for northern lighthouses where ice floes threatened the stability of screwpile lighthouses on wave-swept sites. The use of similar construction techniques for the superstructure led to the design of the round-plan, truncated cone cast-iron lighthouse which could be adapted to a variety of heights and dimensions to suit individual sites. It was widely used by the U.S. Lighthouse Board between 1880 and about 1910.

Peck Ledge Light exemplifies this lighthouse design. Window and door detail place it in the second period of cast-iron cone lighthouse design, as the deeply molded, peaked window hoods and arched-topped sash of the first iron cones (c. 1878-1906) were superceded by the flat-topped windows with simplified classical trim of later structures (c. 1885-1906). Peck Ledge Light is a late example of the second phase.

Peck Ledge Lighthouse has been nominated for inclusion in the National Register of Historic Places.

CHAPTER 10

SHEFFIELD (NORWALK) ISLAND LIGHT, Norwalk, CT (1826)

Old Lighthouse List No.: 176 (obsolete)
Location: Latitude 41° 02' 53" N
Latitude 73° 25' 11" W
Height: 46' (HAW 52')
Range: 12½ miles
Fixed White varied by Red flashes; 1" between flashes
Lens: Fourth Order Classical (Fresnel)
Rebuilt: 1868
Disontinued: c. 1900

Sheffield Island Light marks the west entrance to the Norwalk River on the north side of Long Island Sound. At one time it was called also Smith Island Light.

52.8-acre Sheffield Island has a very colorful history. The earliest documented reference to the island is a deed dated December 2, 1690, in which a Norwalk Indian chief named Winnipauk deeded the island property as an outright gift to the Reverend Thomas Hanford, Norwalk's first minister. It had been called many names prior to Sheffield: Winnipauk, Little Longe, Longe, White's, Smith's, Norwalk and Home. The names were changed, for the most part, according to the then current owner.

Uncertainty surrounds the history of Sheffield, from the time Thomas Harford obtained it until January 4, 1702, when town documents indicate that this island and all others around it became community property. For a while after Hanford's death in 1693, it remained in his family. Records show that in 1793, ten acres of the island were sold by Noah Smith to Joseph Franklin White of Danbury, Connecticut.

On January 24, 1804, Captain Robert Sheffield, a Revolutionary War veteran, purchased what became Sheffield and Tavern Islands. The captain gained fame in the maritime trade as the owner of the "Severn," the first ship to take a load of American cotton to Liverpool, England. He married Temperance Doty, a Mayflower descendant. Their daughter, also named Temperance, married Garsham Burr Smith, a widower who lived on Cockoenoe Island with his son, Nelson. Sheffield Island became their home where they maintained a large farm and raised a family of 12 children.

They brought cattle to the island in a most unusual manner. The cattle were led into the water of Long Island Sound at Wilson Point and then guided by men in small boats and forced to swim to the island. the cows on the Smith farm often wandered from island to island at low tide. When the tide came in, the cows frequently were marooned. At milking time, Mr. Smith took a boat and rowed to each island where his cows waited to be milked.

In 1826, Smith sold a small piece of land to the Government, which supervised the building of a tower 30 feet high that served as a lighthouse. Smith maintained it until his retirement in 1845. A succession of men continued to tend the light after that.

The Smith family enjoyed living on Sheffield Island for five generations. Most of their children were born on the island. School was taught on the island by teachers who lived with the family, and in 1859 the island became a school district. One member of the family, Theodore Smith, built a beautiful Victorian farm house which the press of the time declared to be the most spectacular in the area.

In 1868, the light tower was replaced by the picturesque lighthouse that still stands on the island, a continuing source of inspiration for painters and photographers. It is similar in construction to other lighthouses built about the same time and also discussed in this book: Great Captain Light, Greenwich, Connecticut, Chapter 5; Old Field Point Light, Port Jefferson, New York, Chapter 12; Plum Island Light, New York, Chapter 24; Block Island North Light, Chapter 29; and Cedar Island Light, New York, Chapter 26. The lighthouse is a fine example of mid-Victorian architecture. It had not been in use since about 1900, so the federal government sold the building and stone house behind it for less than $5,000 at a closed auction to Thurston C. Stabell and built Greens Ledge Light farther west. This was done because the reef at the western end was not well marked and pilots unacquainted with the harbor sailed too close to it. The reef is still just as dangerous and was the scene of an accident in 1977. For a long time, Mr. Stabell was the custodian of the Norwalk Yacht Club. His sons, Thurston and Anton, through the years, have maintained the lighthouse as a private summer retreat from the mainland where they both live and work.

Part of the island was auctioned off in 1923 and purchased by Robert Corby, a chemist for Fleischman Yeast Company, for a price rumored at the time to be $100,000. Corby, who had a reputation for being a playboy, developed his property into an elaborate resort which had a landing field for small aircraft, a golf course, tennis courts, polo ponies and race horses. Recognized as the "Island Club," it was a great attraction for European royalty and international celebrities. The club closed in 1937 because of a shortage of fresh water. Corby also died in 1937, and his dream of an island paradise died with him.

In 1942, Corby's large mansion suffered great damage, and mysterious happenings on the island were reported by people on the mainland and on boats sailing in Long Island Sound. Tales were told of mysterious lights on the island at night, ships navigating near it without lights, and weired flashing signals which no one could explain. Was it the ghost of Robert Corby which returned to haunt his beloved island? The extent and character of the property damage appeared to be more than the work of the usual mindless vandals. Strong suspicions were expressed that these strange happenings, if not caused by Corby's ghost, had something to do with the war effort. However, no one ever discovered, and no public report has ever

Sheffield (Norwalk) Island Light, Norwalk, CT

been made by the Government, of what went on around and on the island during this time.

In 1946, James Rand of the Remington Rand Corporation purchased the Corby property. He did nothing to improve the land, and during his ownership the bungalow burned to the ground. in 1959, the Sheffield Island Corporation of Hartford, Connecticut purchased the island and announced plans to build a country club on it. The project never materialized. A group of businessmen tried in vain during the 1960s to restore some of the buildings. New England storms, time, and mindless vandalism have taken a heavy toll on the island.

In 1978, "A plan for Long Island Sound" (prepared by the New England River Basin Commission), recommended that the City of Norwalk purchase and develop Sheffield Island into a general recreation area (similar to Great Captain Island, Greenwich) which would include a swimming beach, fishing piers and a ferry to operate from Norwalk to the island. However, this plan never materialized.

Sheffield Island always has been a prime feeding ground for the many herons and egrets which nest on nearby Chimon Island. Both of these islands are part of the new Connecticut Coastal National Wildlife Refuge. Chimon Island was purchased by The Nature Conservancy in the fall of 1984 and turned over to the United States Fish and Wildlife Service in the spring of 1985. Most of Sheffield Island, with the exception of 14 acres, was bought by The Nature Conservancy for an exorbitant price in June 1985, and was turned over to the U.S. Fish and Wildlife Service in the fall of 1985. A consortium consisting of the U.S. Fish and Wildlife Service, The Nature Conservancy, and the National Audubon Society, the Connecticut Audubon Society, and the Department of Environmental Protection will develop a management plan that will focus on establishing a nesting colony of herons and egrets on the island. Early in 1987, The Norwalk Seaport Association purchased the 118-year-old lighthouse for $700,000 and estimates that it will take another $250,000 for renovations and improvements. The Association would like to have the light added to the National Register of Historic Places.

●

The Case of the Missing Tugboat

Like other lighthouses in this book, Norwalk Island Light is not without its tales of marine disasters. One such tragedy occurred on Saturday night, November 17, 1984. The 85-ft. tugboat "Celtic," towing an 140-ft. unmanned barge "Cape Race" loaded with 1,400 tons of scrap steel, vanished mysteriously with her six crewmen on her way from Bridgeport Harbor, Connecticut to Port Newark, New Jersey. When she failed to arrive at Port Newark at 8 a.m. on Sunday, November 18th, Coast Guard and police boats and helicopters searched Long Island Sound and New York Harbor in vain for the missing vessels. Their disappearance puzzled authorities, because the "Celtic's" captain had 15 years experience with tugboats, and the working radios on board her had not been used to summon help. What had happened?

At eight o'clock on Monday morning, November 19th, a commercial fishing boat reported oil bubbling to the surface of Long Island Sound about two miles southeast of Sheffield Island and about one half-mile off the coast of Norwalk. Police scuba divers from Norwalk and Bridgeport descended into the water at about 10:30 a.m. and found the "Celtic" upright on her keel in about 70 feet of water. Her position was 41° 2′ N, 73° 25′ W. The barge "Cape Race" was found also somewhat later on the bottom of the Sound near the tug. The first team of divers brought up three bodies from the pilot house of the tug at about 11:40 a.m. At 9:41 p.m., divers found the body of a fourth crew member, the tug's cook. Since the police divers refused to enter the "Celtic's" interior, its owner, the Island Park Towing Corporation (a division of Eklof Marine Corporation, West Brighton, Staten Island, New York), hired commercial divers to continue the search for the missing skipper and deck hand. Their bodies were finally recovered on Tuesday, November 20th.

The cause of the sinking remained a mystery to everyone and gave rise to some interesting speculations and theories. Coast Guard officials, for example, thought the "Celtic" might have been dragged to the bottom of the Long Island Sound if the scrap steel cargo had shifted in the buffeting of wind and waves (winds were blowing up to 25 m.p.h. and waves were three feet high), and the barge had overturned and sank, taking the tug down with her. They noted that scrap steel could be an unstable cargo in heavy weather. The sinking happened "very quickly, perhaps in a matter of seconds," Lieutenant Commander (DPA) Marc Wolfson, the Coast Guard spokesman on Governor's Island, New York said. "No distress signals were received in the area, indicating that the crew did not have time to radio for help, and no floating debris was found, indicating that there had not been an explosion or fire."

On Wednesday morning, November 21, 1984 a formal Marine Board investigative hearing of the accident began at the Coast Guard's Marine Inspection Office in Battery Park, Manhattan. The hearing was jointly conducted by the National Transportation Safety Board and the Coast Guard and lasted until May 20, 1986 when they closed their investigation of the casualty. Some of their conclusions and recommendations follows.

Conclusions
1. The proximate cause of the casualty was not determined. The most probable cause was that the "Cape Race" suffered a hull failure below the waterline due to an unknown cause and sank. The sinking was rapid due to the lack of watertight integrity on the "Cape Race." The weight of the sinking "Cape Race" tripped the "Celtic" and pulled it below the surface before the crew of the "Celtic" could take action to release the towing

lines. The "Celtic" was towing the "Cape Race" alongside to starboard at the time of the casualty.

2. The watch in the pilot house of the "Celtic" was apparently unaware of a problem until the last moment before the vessels sank. The only indication of alarm or action on the part of the crew was the fact that the main engine control in the pilot house was found in the full astern position. It was not determined why this action would have been taken. All other crew members were apparently unaware of any impending disaster.

3. The weather did not contribute to the casualty. The "Cape Race" was not overloaded and probably had a freeboard of approximately five feet. The two to three foot seas probably did not break over the deck of the "Cape Race" to the extent it would have caused significant downflooding through the holes in the deck and coaming or the sounding tube stand pipes . . .

Recommendations

1. It was recommended that the Towing Advisory Council work toward encouraging the towing industry to further develop and use emergency release mechanisms for tow.

2. Towboat operators should be warned to make thorough examinations of barges which appear to be in questionable condition and to refuse to take any barge under tow than cannot be watertight. Additionally, operators should make frequent checks of these barges if they do decide to take them under tow.

3. It was also recommended that the Council consider means to persuade owners of uninspected scrap barges to increase their standards of repair and maintenance.

4. It was recommended that the report be given wide dissemination by means of the Marine Safety Council Proceedings . . .

CHAPTER 11

EATONS NECK LIGHT, Northport, NY (1799)

Old Light List No.: 20375
Location: Latitude 40° 57.2' N
           Longitude 70° 23.7' W
Height: 73' (HAW 144')
Range: 17 miles, Fixed White, Horn
Lens: Third Order, Classical. 1000 watt
150,000 candlepower. The Original French-con-
structed Fresnel lens is still in use.

Eatons Neck Lighthouse, situated on the northern extremity of Eatons Neck on a high bluff overlooking Long Island Sound, is the second oldest lighthouse (Montauk Light, 1797, is the oldest) on Long Island. It is located at the end of Lighthouse Road in the village of Asharoken (named after the chief of the Matinecocks Indians who occupied and claimed ownership of the north shore of Long Island from Hempstead to Smithtown), Huntington Township, Suffolk County. The sandstone structure in the past was called alternately "the Lighthouse of Stone" and the "Octagonal Pyramid." Its location marks an area where there have been more shipwrecks than any other spot on the north shore of Long Island. Over 100 major shipwrecks occurred there between December 1790 (when the brig "Sally" was lost with a crew of ten) to July 1935 (when the two-masted schooner "Lorelei" went down with six saved).

Mary Voyse, in her *History of Eaton's Neck* (1955), mentions the storm of December 23, 1811 "when sixty ships and their crews were lost in the snow, gale and zero weather. So severe was the weather that the sheep died and the chickens were frozen to death." And as early as 1795, Reverend Joshua Hartt, a Presbyterian minister and part-time surveyor for the Town of Huntington, noted in his field book that "a great reef of rocks dangerous to shipping existed off the north shore of Eatons Neck, and many vessels have been wrecked. Hereabouts, it is expected a lighthouse will be built for the advantage of seamen." Hartt had been seized by the British during the American Revolution and had shared a New York City jail cell with the celebrated Ethan Allen.

In 1969 the lighthouse was in danger of being destroyed. However, largely through the efforts of the Northport Historical Society, it was saved and subsequently listed in the National Register of Historical Places on April 3, 1973. Thus, the preservation and maintenance of the lighthouse should be insured on its ten acres by the United States Coast Guard. Eatons Neck lighthouse is rich in historical significance, as we shall see, for a variety of reasons. For instance, it is clearly associated with the early development of two branches of the Coast Guard: the Lighthouse Service and the United States Lifesaving Service. In addition, it has provided uninterrupted service as an aid to navigation since its founding and is essentially the same lighthouse that was erected in 1799, except that today it is automated.

The land at Eatons Neck currently occupied by the United States Coast Guard Station was located within the First Purchase boundaries of the Huntington settlers. Dispute over its ownership, however, arouse in 1646 when the peninsula was singled out for purchase from the Matinecocks Indians (one of the 13 Long Island tribes) by its namesake, Theophilus Eaton, a wealthy London merchant who was governor of New Haven, Connecticut. The property passed to Eaton's daughter, Hannah Eaton Jones, in 1659 and continued to be sold, first to Captain Robert Seeley in 1662 and to George Baldwin in 1663.

The legitimacy of these titles was contested by the Huntington settlers until the period of ownership by Alexander Bryan and his son, Richard, beginning in 1668 and lasting over 40 years. The property may have been used by tenant farmers after 1686 when the Bryans successfully petitioned to create the Lordship and Manor of Eaton. The manor house occupied by later owners was located near Cherry Lawn Lane and the bay. Its foundation remains on the Coast Guard property today.

The manor continued to change hands in the 18th century. Sold by the Bryans to John Sloss of Fairfield, Connecticut in 1710 it passed to Sloss's daughters and grandson, John Sloss Hobart, who was later instrumental as a senator in establishing the lighthouse. Hobart, who had occupied the property, sold it to James Watt of New York in 1788, who, in turn, sold it to John Gardiner and his wife in 1792. Gardiner ceded ten acres of land at the northern tip of the peninsula to the United States Government for the purpose of erecting a lighthouse.

The protection of coastal shipping by aids to navigation was the responsibility of local governments in colonial America. Boston Light, for example, the first lighthouse in America, was built by the provincial government of Massachusetts in 1716. With the establishment of a federal government after the Revolution, a more comprehensive system of providing maritime safety was made possible. An act of Congress created the Lighthouse Establishment on August 7, 1789 as an administrative unit to provide "necessary support, maintenance and repair" to aids to navigation. During the following decade, existing facilities were placed under federal jurisdiction and new facilities were developed. One of these new facilities was a lighthouse at Eatons Neck.

A hazardous reef off Eatons Neck demonstrated the need for a lighthouse there when, in December 1790, the brig "Sally" of Stamford, Connecticut was wrecked and the ten crew were lost. Five years later, a coastal survey of Huntington Township noted again the hazard of the reef. Legislation introduced in Congress by Senator Hobart and passed on March 14, 1798 authorized the erection of a light at Eatons Neck. President John Adams approved the Act, and the lighthouse was erected at the cost of $9,500. John J. McComb, Jr. (1763-1885), a Scot by birth and a bricklayer

Eatons Neck and Coast Guard Station, Northport, NY

U.S. Coast Guard Photo

by trade, was its architect. McComb had previously designed the first two federal lighthouse authorized by the 1789 Act at Cape Henry, Virginia (1798) and Montauk, New York (1797).

McComb also was responsible with Jospeh Mangin, a French architect, for the beautiful New York City Hall in 1812. He designed also Hamilton Grange, a Federal style building on Convent Avenue between 141st and 142nd Streets, New York City and, with Jonathan Williams, the Castle Clinton National Monument at Battery Park, New York City, between 1808-1811. Octagonal in plan like the Cape Henry Lighthouse, McComb's brick tower at Eatons Neck, completed and activated in 1799, was originally lighted by sperm oil stored in an adjacent subterranean cistern. A two-room frame dwelling house also was built with the tower. Gardiner's son, John H., is traditionally regarded as the light's first keeper, although some historians say it was a John Squire.

Lifesaving

The federal lighthouse system was designed to prevent shipwrecks under normal circumstances by identifying hazardous coastal conditions. With the advent of steam power, however, ships grew in capacity and so did the risk of extensive loss of life. The burning of the steamship "Lexington" off Eatons Neck on the way from New York City to Stonington, Connecticut on January 13, 1840, demonstrated this problem when an estimated 130 individuals died and only four or five were saved. Rending assistance to those shipwrecked was not then a federal responsibility. That duty fell exclusively to private citizens, volunteer benevolent associations and, at times, the lighthouse keepers. Ships in distress were first assisted in America by local individuals called "wreckers" who often collected salvage as payment for their services.

In 1785, the Massachusetts Humane Society was established, patterned after the British Royal Humane Society. This volunteer organization provided small houses of refuge stocked with food and clothing at intervals along the Massachusetts coast and is also credited with commissioning the first life boat built in the United States.

Similar New York area associations were formed in the first half of the 19th century to provide equipment for volunteer lifesavers and award prizes for individual efforts. But the maintenance of shelters and equipment by volunteers proved to problematic. Thus, an item added to the lighthouse appropriation bill for 1848 provided $5,000 for "furnishing the lighthouses on the Atlantic coast with means of rendering assistance to shipwrecked mariners."

On March 3, 1849, a small life saving station was built at Eatons Neck and remained standing until it was removed in 1954. However, it wasn't until 1876 that a lifeboat became part of the lifesaving equipment at Eatons Neck. Of historical note is that the Eatons Neck life saving stations, operated by the lighthouse crew, was the first one established by the federal government in the United States. By 1854, 137 similar stations had been built on the coasts.

The Civil War interrupted the further development and maintenance of these stations. A number of maritime disasters in the winter of 1870-71 necessitated a re-evaluation of existing life-saving systems. Congress appropriated $200,000 that year for new stations and repairs, and placed the system under the jurisdiction of the Revenue Cutter Division. In 1876, a new timber lifeboat station building and a lifeboat were built at Eatons Neck under the direction of Captain Darius Rutland who had been in charge of the lighthouse since January 18, 1862. The station crew lived on the second floor of the new building above the boat which was stored and kept in readiness on the first floor. The crew of this station was involved in saving lives and property from many shipwrecks.

Two years later, in 1878, the reorganization of the system culminated in the creation of the United States Lifesaving Service as a separate bureau of the Treasury Department. Then in 1938, it came under the jurisdiction of the United States Coast Guard. The life-saving fleet at Eatons Neck today includes: a 46-ft. steel buoy tender; two aluminum utility boats which are primary search and rescue vessels; a 21-ft. aluminum Monarch trailerable aids to navigation boat; a 14-ft. Boston Whaler; and a 21-ft. aluminum Monarch boat with a diesel engine—quite an addition from the single wooden rescue boat of a hundred years earler.

In the center of the glass-enclosed observation platform of the lighthouse at Eatons Neck is the large lens, imported from France, used to refract the beam cast by the four original whale oil lamps. Today, the lens performs the same service for a 1,000 watt quartz filament light bulb. The light is triggered automatically by a light-sensitive device. From the ceiling of the tower dangles the obsolete funnel-shaped "Smoak Ventilator." In the chamber below are four more copper ventilators built into the circular wall. The large, multi-tiered lens is anchored in this room also. At the base of the lens is a plate bearing the manufacturer's legend: "Henry Lepaute a Paris."

The lighthouse has been repaired and renovated several times. It was first renovated in 1868. A fog signal was recommended in 1867, and by 1871 a powerful steam fog signal was in operation. In 1904, a first class automatic siren was installed, sounding blasts for four seconds' duration separated by silent intervals of 40 seconds. In 1977, the lighthouse received a new coat of paint. As Mary Voyse noted in 1955 . . . "Eaton's Neck retains most of its early beauty. Although erosion has done great damage to the beaches and hurricanes have hurt the woods, its hills and shores are still unmatched for charm . . . Giant oaks, tulip and birch trees still stand . . . wild beach plum and shad bushes still line the beach road . . ." Today, in this beautiful area, with its status as a National Landmark, we hope that "the lighthouse of stone" will continue to be the beacon for sailors and their ships as it has been for almost two centuries.

CHAPTER 12

OLD FIELD POINT LIGHT, Port Jefferson, NY (1824)

Old Light List No.: 162 (obsolete)
Location: Latitude 40° 58.3' N
Longitude 73° 6.5' W
Height: 34' (HAW 67')
Range: 13 miles, Fixed White
Lens: Fourth Order, Classical
Discontinued: 1903

First Lighthouse

Since 1824, Old Field Point Lighthouse has been a mariner's land-mark. The rugged, wind-swept location for the light was purchased for $400 in 1823 from Samuel L. Thompson. The light was erected a year later when Congress appropriated $2,500 for it and added an additional $1,500 in 1825 to complete its construction. The first light consisted of nine lamps of whale oil in a large lantern. The light was magnified by parabolic reflectors. The lighthouse was made of rough-case stone and contained five rooms. Oil for the light was stored in the tower which was separate from the keeper's house. This little one and a half story lighthouse still stands serving as the Old Field Village Hall.

Second Lighthouse

A second lighthouse was built in 1868 when shipping on the Sound was at its peak. New ships were launched regularly from shipyards at Stony Brook, Setauket and Port Jefferson. Because the railroad had not yet reached this area, Long Island Sound was always dotted with freighters, passenger and mail ships of all sizes and shapes. The new lighthouse was constructed of granite blocks with walls two feet thick. Even so, former keepers of the light experienced the fury of storms on the Sound which drove rainwater into their house through closed windows and doors. The four-sided tower is 28 feet high and stands 67 feet above the sea. At the top of the tower is a circular, glassed-in room measuring six feet in diameter which is surrounded by an iron platform. When it was first built, kerosene was probably used to light the lamps instead of whale oil.

There has been little change in the living quarters of the lighthouse over the years, other than the installation of an oil burner. Its front door opens into a hall where there is a flight of stairs. The kitchen is to the right, a small office (used in former days by the keeper) is to the left, and straight ahead is the living room. Off both the kitchen and the living room is the dining room. Beyond that is a hobby room. There are three bedrooms and a bath on the second floor.

A door in the second floor leads to the tower, Halfway up the circular iron steps is a landing with a small window. From here you have a pre-

Old Field Point Light, Port Jefferson, NY

view of what can be seen from the top platform. At the top of the tower, an iron platform circles the circular, glassed-in room noted earlier. The view from here is unexcelled in this area.

All the windows of the lighthouse had white, louvered shutters which were a decorative touch and which were necessary as aids in keeping the rain and salt spray from penetrating the light. The shutters also kept out the rays of the former automatic red and green revolving signal. These shutters were imperative in the old days to keep the house lights from shining out to sea and confusing the mariners.

A diary, kept by the father-in-law of the first keeper of this second lighthouse, George D. Lee, records daily events there for a number of years. In the days before television and the telephone, life seemed to be, at least at the lighthouse, a continual round of visits. The diary notes that on one day in May 1870, over 500 sailboats passed the lighthouse.

Third Lighthouse

The third light (LLN 20305), the one currently in use, is a revolving beacon on a 50-ft. black skeleton tower erected in 1933. Height above water is 74 feet. It is automatically controlled, to the east and slightly in front of the second light. Because of erosion around the light, it was moved 30 yards 250° True from its original location by the Coast Guard in May 1963. Then in April-May 1981, the Coast Guard moved the light back to its original location. It has a DCB-10 lens and a 500 watt lamp. Its range is 20 miles.

The old keeper's house is now the home of the Chief Constable of Old Field and his family. It was acquired from the United States Government in 1935 with the understanding it could be reclaimed in time of national emergency. The Coast Guard did, in fact, reclaim the lighthouse during War War II, but at the close of hostilities returned it to the Village. A model of a corkwood carrier built in Conscience Bay by the Dickerson Shipyard is in the office of the lighthouse. Slightly to the west of the 1868 light is a small park and the turnaround point at the end of Oldfield Road. The park was donated to the Village in 1929 by Ecersley Childs.

Keepers of the Light

Edward Shoemaker 1824 - December 21, 1826
Mrs. Shoemaker (wife) December 21, 1826 - June 5, 1827
Walter Smith June 5, 1827 - April 22, 1830
Mrs. Elizabeth Smith (wife) and son Henry April 22, 1830 - June 21, 1856
Mary A. Foster June 21, 1956 - June 21, 1869
Bery Floyd June 21, 1869 - August 9, 1869 (removed)
George D. Lee August 9, 1869 - April 25, 1874 (resigned)
Charles F. Jayne April 25, 1874 - 1895 paid $520 year
Edgar Stanton Maclay 1895 - September 1, 1901
Richard Edwin Day September 1, 1901 - 1933

George D. Lee, seventh keeper of the light, was a Civil War veteran and a member of the G.A.R. He was the father of Holmes and Clarence Lee of Port Jefferson.

Edgar Stanton Maclay (1863-1919) was one of the more interesting keepers and apparently played a role in the development of Old Field. The son of a Methodist Episcopal missionary, he spent his childhood in China and Japan. In 1886, he graduated from Syracuse College where he obtained a B.A. and M.A. degree. He built a 100-room hotel, the Old Field Inn, which was destroyed by fire in 1899. Maclay married Katherin Koeber in 1893. They had four sons. In 1894, he finished a somewhat inaccurate two-volume history of the United States Navy which was published by D. Appleton & Company, New York. Maclay worked on the staff of several New York City newspapers. A statement criticizing Admiral Schley in the third volume of his history of the U.S. Navy led to his dismissal in 1901 from a minor post in the New York Navy Yard, after which he had great difficulty making a living. He wrote little except three biographies of naval officers, and these were scarcely noticed by the public. In 1904, he got a job on a Brooklyn newspaper, and shortly before his death obtained some research work in Washington, D.C. His home (circa 1900) still stands in Old Field.

Old Field Point Lighthouse is prominently located on a low bluff near the western entrance to Port Jefferson Harbor. Its photogenic tower is, of course, no longer in use. The light is about five miles south of Stratford Shoal (Middle Ground) Light. Sailors should check their charts carefully when approaching this light and steer clear of the boulders that extend a short distance off the Point. The lighthouse should be given a berth of at least 0.3 mile, even by small craft. A gong buoy is 0.6 mile north of the Point. Depths of 14 to 18 ft. are found about 0.4 mile north of the light.

CHAPTER 13

PENFIELD REEF LIGHT, Fairfield, CT (1874)

Light List No.: 20335
Location: Latitude 41° 7.0' N
Longitude 73° 13.2' W
Height: 51'
Range: 12 miles, Flashing Red every six seconds
Horn
Lens: DCB-24, 1000 watt lamp
Automated: September 4, 1971

Penfield Reef Light is one of Long Island Sound's more stylish light-houses. Its foundation was built by F. Hopkinson Smith who later built Race Rock Light in 1878. It is a two-story, white-capped granite house standing out in the Sound, with a red-topped white tower projecting from one side, like a chimney. It is a difficult light to pick up at a distance on an east or west course, because its colors blend too well with the sky. Built in 1874, the lighthouse is one mile south of the Fairfield, Connecticut shore line and marks the end of a long, curving reef exposed above water at low tide. Mystery and adventure, as we shall see, surround this famous snake-like promontory with a head of sawtooth rocks known as Penfield Reef. Until Saturday, September 4, 1971 when it was automated, the light was manned 24 hours a day by Coast Guardsmen.

Jutting out from Fairfield Beach like a great sea monster for more than a mile, Penfield Bar forms one of the most picturesque, interesting and dangerous landmarks along the shores of Long Island Sound. While it affords protection to the beach, it is a menace to shipping despite the warning light at the end of it. In all the length and breadth of Long Island Sound, there is no more notorious spot than Penfield bar and reef. Together they reach out from Fairfield Beach like a long arm ready to grasp its victims in its relentless grip. For years, as far back as the oldest residents of Fairfield can remember, Penfield bar and reef have lured many fine crafts to their doom. Despite the red eye that winks a ruddy warning night in and night out to mariners as if to say "KEEP OFF!," vessels of all kinds seem to be lured to the spot. Powerboats and sailboats sitting high and dry on the reef or bar at low tide are a familiar sight from the Fairfield shore.

Woe to the unwary sailor who fails to watch his chart in the vicinity of Penfield Reef and its sawtooth rocks. As noted previously, many ships have been battered and torn to pieces by the fury of the waves that engulf the reef. The bar claims its victims regularly too. Records tell of the fine yacht "Guinevere" that not so many years ago sailed into the clutches of Penfield Reef; of the schooner yacht "Flying Fish" that was battered to pieces within a few minutes of being stranded on the bar; of the freighter

Penfield Reef Light, Fairfield, CT

Photo by Julius M. Wilensky

75

"Industry" and her long enforced sojourn on Penfield rocks; and of dozens of other ships of all sizes and makes that have met their doom on this treacherous spot in Long Island Sound.

At low tide you can walk along the bar and reef almost to the lighthouse. However, you must be alert. Locals tell of a family of seven who were trapped by the oncoming tide on a high part of the reef and were never seen again. At high tide, only a portion of the reef's stony head rises stealthily above the tumbling waves, while the tortuous, reptile-like body lurks a few feet below the surface like a trap to catch mariners who venture too close to shore and ignore the red warning flashing from the tower of the lighthouse. To make matters worse, strong and conflicting currents sweep around the reef and drag unwary vessels to them onto the rocks that pierce the water even on the calmest days.

Barges by the hundred have met their fate on both bar and reef, battered and torn by the wind-whipped waters. After a storm, timbers are invariably strewn all over the bar or the reef and even on Fairfield Beach, mute evidence of the fury of the onslaught of the elements against man-made craft and the destructive power of Penfield Reef and its rocks. Perhaps the most famous wrecks were those of the Blue Line barges. During a storm in November 1916, nine barges of New York's Blue Line collided with a section of Penfield Reef, earning it the infamous title "the Blue Line graveyard." Every year four or five unsuspecting vessels are snatched from the sea by the reef.

Because of the long line of disasters on this location, the Coast Guard increased the candlepower of the lighthouse some years ago to its present 1,000. However, the reef still continues to claim its victims. A fragment of a vessel's deck house, a portion of a vessel's lifeboat, a broken spar, the shattered bows of a fishing boat scattered on the bar tell a tale of disaster and struggle with wind and wave.

Penfield was a peninsula at one time up to a few centuries ago. As years passed and the sea wore away the land, a group of islands were formed. Today it is a shoal. Old residents of Fairfield recall stories handed down from former generations of time when cattle and horses grazed on the land now periodically covered with water. Later, as the land sunk and weakened under the assaults of the ocean, islands were formed again. The "Cows and Calves" group of rocks located near the reef are names handed down from Colonial times. The resemblance of the rocks to grazing cattle is believed by some people to be the origin of their names. Nearly a century ago, cattle fed freely on the grass that grew in great abundance on a large island at the end of a grass-grown, tree-clad promontory. Where once green pastures basked in the summer sun and where cattle stood knee-deep in luscious grass, now are rocks and sand. Someday, Penfield bar and reef may be worn so deep that they will no longer lurk dangerously in the path of careless sailors.

Apparently the reef was named after an early resident of Fairfield. Shortly after the British burned Fairfield during the Revolution, a Reverend Andrew Eliot wrote to his brother, the Reverend John Eliot, in Boston and described how " . . . a servant of Mr. Penfield was brutally shot to death by the Hessian Hussars." No other record of Mr. Penfield survives other than this brief reference to him.

Before the Revolution rum runners and smugglers rounded Penfield Reef to dock in Black Rock Harbor with their cargoes of India rum and probably slaves. The King's excise collectors failed to catch the elusive Yankee smugglers. Rum-running was nothing new to these shores, since Black Rock was one of the largest rum-running ports of New England at that time. During the early colonization of Fairfield, a huge still was located off Westport and liquors were smuggled from there to the mainland to avoid British excise tax. A young boy was stationed there day and night apparently, "shooting ducks." He fired twice when the revenue officers appeared.

The Legend of Christmas Eve

On Christmas Eve 1916, the lighthouse keeper Fred Jordan set out in a rowboat for shore leave. A terrible storm was raging at the time, and his frail craft didn't have a chance in the heavy seas. Jordan capsized and drowned; Penfield Reef had claimed another victim. One of Jordan's successors told how he had seen the figure of a man, dressed in white, steal out of one of the rooms of the light, glide down the stairway of the tower and disappear into the darkness outside. Investigation showed that in the room downstairs the journal of records, kept in the lighthouse, was lying open on the table. It was a book that had not been taken from the shelf for some time. It was opened at the page on which the notation of Jordan's death was made. No one in the lighthouse could explain how the journal happened to be off the shelf opened and turned to the Jordan notation. Legend has it hat the lighthouse log is often found open to the page for Christmas Eve 1916.

Captain R. Iten, head keeper of the Penfield Reef Lighthouse, told the *Bridgeport Sunday Post* in the 1920's about an old saying that what the reef takes, the reef gives back. Poor Jordan's body was recovered not long after his drowning, and in the pocket of his coat was a note addressed to Iten which he probably forgot to leave behind before he started out on his fatal ride in that rough sea. The note instructed Iten to be sure to complete the entries of that morning—the day that Jordan died—as they had not been brought up to date.

On stormy nights a spector is said to poise on the rail of the gallery that surrounds the latern swaying, as if in agony, or to flit among the black jagged rocks that surround the base of the light. Not so long ago, a power yacht in trouble was said to have been piloted through the breakers to safety by a strange man who suddenly appeared amid the surf near the Spindle, in a rowboat. The man, so it was said, brought the yacht into calm waters with a skill that was almost incredible and then, getting back into his boat—disappeared.

Several years ago, two boys who had been fishing near the reef from a canoe were thrown into the water when their craft capsized. Death by drowning seemed imminent. At the moment when all seemed lost, a man suddenly appeared from out of the rocks and dragged the boys to safety onto the base of the light. They climbed the ladder and entered the living room of the lighthouse where they hoped to thank their rescuer, whom they thought was one of the keepers. But no one was to be found anywhere. Is it the ghost of Fred Jordan who is seen flitting among the rocks of Penfield Reef on on stormy nights? Many people believe it is.

●

Penfield Light has been also the scene of many daring rescues by its keepers. One such rescue is the story of a power boat that was cast onto the reef by wind and waves one stormy evening during the 1920s with 27 passengers aboard. The three men stationed at the light worked frantically and managed to save all 27 souls. When a member of the rescued party offered the crew a dollar for their heroic efforts, it was refused.

After 97 years of continuous manned service, Penfield Reef Lighthouse became fully automated at 1:30 p.m. on Saturday, September 4, 1971. In 1969, when the Coast Guard announced plans to demolish the light in the interest of economy and replace it with a pipe tower, local residents and politicians opposed the idea so strenuously that the Coast Guard decided on conversion of the lighthouse to automatic operaion without outward change to the structure. On the day of automation, local boaters joined in a sail-past salute in tribute to the three Coast Guardsmen who concluded their tour of duty at the light on that date.

Description of the Lighthouse

Penfield Reef Light consists of a square, two-story masonry dwelling with a mansard roof and wood-framed light tower above, mounted on a cylindrical granite pier. The pier is filled with concrete above the base level of riprap, except for a square cavity in the center of the upper portion which houses the cistern, cellar and water closet. There is a boat landing on the north side. The dwelling, measuring 28' 2" on a side, rises centrally from the pier. Several details contribute to a Second Empire style for the lighthouse, the square plan, mansard roof, quoins, and foot scrolled window surrounds. The first floor walls are lined with brick and faced with rough-faced, grey granite ashlar with slightly projecting quoins. The lighttower is 7' 6" square at the level of the second story and octagonal in plan at the level of the watchroom above. Surmounting the watchroom is an octagonal lantern with its surrounding gallery and conical roof. The first story has three rooms. The upper story has four. The center window on the first story of the south or tower elevation is false, recalling the Georgian sense of symmetry. The octagonal watchroom has three windows facing west, south and east. A ladder in the watchroom leads to a trap door in the floor of the octagonal lantern above. The lantern walls are composed of eight rectangular glass panes in their upper half and eight cast-iron sections in their lower half. The railing around the lantern gallery is supported diagonally, as illustrated in the 1874 *Annual Report* of the Lighthouse Board. The focal plane of the lighting apparatus is recorded as 51 ft. above water level. A fourth order bullseye lens, run by clockwork manufactured in the lamp shop at Tompkinsville, New York, was in operation in 1889. A fog signal operated by a fog detector sounds a blast every 15 seconds.

Significance of the Light

Highly visible from the sea and shore, Penfield Reef Light embodies one of the most popular masonry dwelling-with-tower designs used by the United States Lighthouse Board during the 1860s and 1870s. This Second Empire design, based on the domestic architecture of the period, reflected the national enthusiasm for picturesque revival styles. A picture of Penfield Reef Light was included in the Lighthouse Board's exhibit at the Centennial Exhibition in Philadelphia in 1876. The lighthouse is significant also in the history of aids to navigation in Long Island Sound as an important part of the federal program to accomodate increased commercial traffic in the Bridgeport Harbor area after the Civil War.

Penfield Reef Light was an essential part of the development of Bridgeport Harbor after the Civil War. Before the lighthouse was constructed, the site was marked with a can buoy. Beginning in 1866, lobbying efforts from Bridgeport maritime interests resulted in a proposal by the Lighthouse Board in 1868 for a lighthouse to be constructed in the five feet of water there. Marking the shoal with a light and fog signal would enable ships to travel directly between Bridgeport's burgeoning harbor and New York City at all hours and in all weather conditions. Compared with the depth of the site necessary for a masonry pier to be built at Race Rock in Fishers Island Sound, this was a modest challenge. However, the technology at that date required a costly circular pier of granite blocks, cut to fit together to form rings which could be filled with riprap. Cut stone foundations were the only solution available at the time for underwater sites in latitudes where floating ice made the slender legs of a tubular pipe foundation, such as a screwpile light, unusable. The foundation proposed for the Race Rock site by F. Hopkinson Smith was used as a model for Penfield Reef Light.

A model of Penfield Reef Light had been used previously in Hudson River lighthouses. Joseph Lederle, Acting Lighthouse Engineer for the old Third District of the Lighthouse Establishment, recommended in April 1868 that the Penfield Reef tower connected with the keeper's dwelling " . . . be built on the plan approved by the (Lighthouse) Board for the Hudson River stations." At Esophus Meadows, New York, Lighthouse, established in 1871, this exact design appears in frame construction instead of masonry. Bridgeport Harbor Lighthouse, CT; Hart Island in

Long Island Sound; Sabin's Point Light Station, R.I.; Long Beach Bar Light and Colchester Reef Lighthouse on Lake Champlain were listed in the Lighthouse board records as utilizing this design, as well.

Procuring the needed appropriations from Congress delayed the approval of plans for the foundation until after March 3, 1871, when a total of $55,000 was made available. From 1871 until 1873, the riprap foundation and granite pier were under construction. The dwelling, of cut granite blocks on the first story and wood framing on the second, was erected in 1873. The light was first exhibited on Friday, January 16, 1874.

A view of Penfield Reef Light appeared in the Annual Report of the Lighthouse Board for 1874, and, two years later, was included in the Centennial Exhibition. Ironically, the technology which Penfield Reef's foundation represented and the style of its dwelling-with-tower were already out of date as the federal government became interested in the prefabricated, cast-iron caisson type lighthouses, such as at Latimer Reef, Mystic, CT, for wave swept sites. Penfield Reef Light, based on the design work and engineering of the 1860s and early 1870s, thus represents one of the last examples of a masonry domestic model lighthouse on a masonry foundation. Its position near the Connecticut shoreline makes it one of the most visible lighthouses in the state.

A fog-bell, struck by machinery, was the first for apparatus at Penfield, The foghorn was audible 15-20 minutes away, according to early reports. This apparatus was replaced in 1892 by a Daboll trumpet operated by duplicate Rider hot-air engines. In 1898, the Rider engines were replaced by two Hornsby-Ekroyd oil engines.

Steeped in legend and history, Penfield Reef Light's fog detector blasts a rhythmic warning every 15 seconds to boaters when fog hovers about the light. Its sounds echoes over Long Island Sound warning mariners to beware of the dangers of Fairfield's voracious Penfield Reef.

The light has been recommended for inclusion in the National Register of Historic Places.

CHAPTER 14

BLACK ROCK HARBOR LIGHT, Bridgeport, CT (1809)
(Fayerweather Island Light)

Old Light List No.: 594 (Obsolete)
Location: Latitude 41° 8.3" N
Longitude: 73° 13.0" W
Height: 40'
Range: 11 miles, Fixed White
Lens: Fifth Order, 350 candlepower
Rebuilt: 1823
Discontinued: 1932

In 1789, the newly formed federal government passed a bill to assume responsibility for establishing buoys and lighthouses as aids and warnings to mariners and formed the Lighthouse Establishment as an administrative unit. The several states deeded their systems of lights to the federal government. The first land purchased by the new Establishment was at Eatons Neck, Northport, Long Island. In June 1798, the land was purchased from John Gardiner and his wife, Joanne. the lighthouse was built the following year.

The next site purchased in Western Long Island Sound for a light station was a portion of the 9½ acres of Fayerweather Island, purchased in 1807 from David Fayerweather for $200.00. The light was established in 1808 on the south end of the island. In 1923, it was rebuilt. A new keeper's dwelling was constructed in 1879 and was extensively repaired in 1887. The light was always a family station. The declining importance of Black Rock Harbor in the 20th century and improvements in aids to navigation caused the Lighthouse Service to close the light station in 1932. In 1934, Congress deeded the land to the City of Bridgeport as a park.

Despite its natural advantages, situated at the head of a deep harbor protected by Fayerweather Island, a high elevation along a low and marshy coast, Black Rock remained unoccupied until 1644. In that year, discord broke out among the Puritan congregation in Concord, Massachusetts, and the dissenters emigrated to Connecticut. Thomas Wheeler believed that the advantages of a good trading location outweighed the disadvantages of isolation, and became Black Rock's first English settler. He built a stone house with a flat roof upon which he mounted two cannons. One was aimed at the harbor in case of an attack from the Dutch at Niew Amsterdam (New York City), the other was aimed at the Indian fort located on a saltwater inlet near the present intersection of Fairfield Avenue and Ellsworth Street. Wheeler died in 1654, and for the next century, Black Rock was almost solely inhabited by his descendants. In 1676, the town granted John Wheeler, his son, the liberty to erect a "wharf in the harbor at blacke rocke," the first recorded use of the name.

Sometime before 1700, the Wheelers began Black Rock's profitable trade with the West Indies. Cornmeal, salt beef, and timber were exchanged for sugar, salt, rum, and molasses.

Black Rock's development changed abruptly about 1760. Within a decade, three major commercial wharves supplanted the old landing place at the Point, and shipbuilding had become a major occupation. The Revolution brought increased activity. As the base for several successful privateers, Black Rock was important enough to warrant the construction of a fort at the entrance to the harbor, and a large cannon was secured to guard the upper wharf. Captain Caleb Brewster used the port as the point of embarkation for his whaleboats on spy missions to Long Island, a key link in the famous "Culper Spy Ring."

A short depression followed the war, after which Black Rock began to boom. But after the trade embargoes of the early 1800s and the disastrous War of 1812, fortunes declined. Thereafter, Bridgeport usurped Black Rock's place as the new center of Fairfield County commerce, and the town became a self-contained backwater area. Building activity almost completely ceased for 20 years. Many of Black Rock's inhabitants moved. Most of the reasons for the decline of the port can be attributed to the emergence of neighboring Bridgeport and Southport.

The first lighthouse at Fayerweather Island was a frame and clapboard tower built in 1808. Disastrous hurricanes in 1811 and 1821 proved that the lack of adequate protection in Black Rock Harbor could bring calamity. William Wheeler, a schoolmaster who kept a journal of Black Rock happenings between Revolutionary times and the 1840s, recorded on 3 September 1821 that "Every vessel went ashore in this harbor . . . the Lighthouse laid flat." Bridgeport and Southport harbors, although shallower, were almost completely landlocked and offered far greater shelter in a storm.

West Indies produce, the mainstay of Black Rock's trade, fell sharply in price at this time. Many small shippers were wiped out. The final blow came with the opening of the Erie Canal, when cheap Western corn whiskey flooded eastern markets and replaced West Indian rum as a drink. Black Rock blossomed again but on a lesser scale in the 1830s. The ship chandlery and carriage industries attracted some new people to the village during this period, but no major expansion occurred at that time.

The present lighthouse was built in 1823, after the hurricane of 1821 destroyed the earlier light. It is a white, octagonal tower about 40 feet high with eight-ft. sides at its base. The walls are coursed ashlar of sandstone blocks lined with mortared rubble. An iron railing surmounts the corbeled brick cornice and surrounds the light cupola which was installed in the early 20th century when the light was electrified. Within 200 yards of the lighthouse are the foundations of the 1808 oil vault and the 1808 keeper's dwelling which was rebuilt in 1879.

John D. Davis was the last keeper of the light and served from 1907 - 1932. He was then transferred to Dutch Island Light in Narragansett Bay.

Black Rock Harbor Light, Bridgeport, CT

Rhode Island. A more modern, automatic "blinking light" was constructed about 1,800 feet farther to seaward than Black Rock Light at a cost of about $7,000.

Today Black Rock is an excellent Bridgeport neighborhood, possessing a sense of tradition rooted in a colorful past and a community spirit that sets it apart from other sections of the city. The historic houses in the old center, the pleasant tree-lined blocks of early 20th century developments, and the unsurpassed ocean front drive along Eames Boulevard make Black Rock most attractive.

The harbor has always been the focus of the community. In the 17th and 18th centuries, it was the only Connecticut port, except for New London, that could accomodate ships of 300 to 400 tons. Black Rock was one of the few places in the Connecticut colony settled exclusively as a trading center, and its population until the close of the 19th century consisted primarily of seafaring families.

At the beginning of the 20th century, commerce moved away from the once busy harbor front, but at the same time, urbanization spread to Black Rock. The wholesale destruction of the historic framework that occurred in the other old Bridgeport neighborhoods was prevented by the high quality of the new residential developments combined with a heightened appreciation of old architecture. What remains today is always something of a surprise to the uninitiated: 17th and 18th century homesteads surrounded by World War I era two-family houses; a largely intact wharf district with storehouses that predate the War of 1812; a carefully laid out section of Greek Revival houses from the 1820s and 1840s; and some especially fine examples of early Victorian Italian villas built in the 1850s. Unfortunately, Black Rock's historic old lighthouse was not one of the buildings preserved. After 51 years of neglect and vandalism, it was well on its way to becoming just a memory. Luckily, through the vision of some of the citizens of Bridgeport and Black Rock, the lighthouse was rescued from extinction. Other lighthouses should be so fortunate.

A Lighthouse Reclcaimed; a Paradise Regained
On Monday, January 21, 1980, the Bridgeport Environmental Protection Commission, headed by Kaye Williams, agreed informally to preserve the lighthouse on Fayerweather Island at the eastern tip of Seaside Park. The Commission noted that although the inside of the light had been ravaged by mindless vandals (a common occurrence at unattended lights), the basic structure was still sound. To prevent further damage, The Commission recommended that the entrances to the structure be bricked up. The Commission said that the lighthouse was part of the "visual environment" and should be preserved for its historic value.

In an effort to preserve the lighthouse, the Friends of Seaside Park began a "restoration of the landmark Fayerweather Island Lighthouse" drive in October 1983 with the Black Rock Community Council. Their aim was complete restoration of the famous old light as soon as possible.

In the summer of 1984, they hired Steven C. Engelhart, a graduate student in the Historic Preservation Program at the University of Vermont. It was largely through his efforts that the project was brought to a successful conclusion by September.

Steven and four local teenage assistants repainted deteriorated mortar joints, repaired the iron work of the lantern, and replaced the glass with vandal-resistant plexiglass at the top. For door and window openings, for years wide open to the weather and vagrants, Steve fabricated duplicates of the original fittings out of solid sheet steel. With material donated by Chapin & Bangs Steel Company and labor supplied by sculptor Robert M. Reilly, a 19th century batten door and three nine-light window sashes were recreated. Today, the lighthouse stands secure once more, a tribute to the community-wide effort that bought it about.

Besides complete restoration of the light, the Friends of Seaside Park also wished to rehabilitate Fayerweather Island and transform it into a nature preserve. The first thing they did in April 1984 was to clear the island of rubbish and debris which had been accumulating steadily for over 50 years. A second project was the construction of a trail network across the island. The trails vary in width between two and four feet, kept intentionally narrow to minimize potential erosion problems in this fragile ecosystem. The trails wind through the upland portions of the preserves, enabling hikers to reach virtually any point without endangering delicate plant materials.

The third and last phase in the recreation of a "primeval wilderness" on Fayerweather Island involved large-scale plantings of plant species suitable to shoreline habitats which probably would have been growing on the island in its undisturbed state. In a one-acre area around an old house foundation, the Friends planted various species of acorns, red maple, sweet gum, sassafras, tupelo trees, white and pitch pine and Eastern red cedar. Plantings of some locally endangered species, such as sweet bay magnolia and American persimmon, were also established. Shrubs installed include clethra, shadblow and witchhazel. On the gravelly neck at the north end of the island, the once common beach plum has been reintroduced along with red cedar, smoothstem sumach and chokeberry, all of which will eventually provide excellent cover and food for wildlife.

In all, some 2,000 individual plants have been set out by the Friends of Seaside Park. Although this may seem to be a large amount of plants, the reconstruction of a true wilderness habitat on Fayerweather Island's 9½ acres will require a continuing effort of equal magnitude for years to come. Readers wishing to support this most worthy endeavor may do so by sending their donations (Individual Annual Dues are only $3.00) to:

Friends of Seaside Park
38 Myrtle Avenue
Bridgeport, CT 06604
(203) 367-7056

CHAPTER 15

TONGUE POINT LIGHTHOUSE, Bridgeport, CT (1894)

Light List No.: 23070
Location: Latitude 41° 10.0′ N
Longitude 73° 10.7′ W
Height: 21′ (HAW 31′)
Range: 5 miles, Flashing Green every 4 seconds
Lens: 155 mm plastic, 1.15 amp lamp
Moved: 1921

Tongue Point Lighthouse, also known as the Bridgeport Breakwater Lighthouse, the Buglight, the Inner Harbor Light and The Bug, marks the eastern end of Tongue or Wells Point, a point of land which extends into Bridgeport Harbor from the western shore. This small, conical cast-iron lighthouse, painted black, rests on a ten-ft. high concrete foundation surrounded by riprap. The tower measures 12.3 ft. in diameter at its base. Unlike other cast-iron lighthouses of similar (but larger) construction, it has no brick lining within its cast-iron shell, since it was not designed to be habitable. The lighthouse originally stood 350 feet east of its present location (41° 09′ N, 73° 10′ W) on a breakwater constructed in 1891. At its old location, it had a fixed white light characteristic. In 1919, the breakwater was demolished as a hazard to shipping, and the lighthouse was moved to its present site in 1921.

Some rare survivors of aids to navigation apparatus remain at the light. The fog-bell stands outside the east wall of the tower. Inscribed "1881/U.S. Lighthouse Establishment," it predates the lighthouse and most likely was brought from another location in 1899. Before it is "salvaged" by a mindless collector, the Coast Guard should remove it and donate it to a maritime museum, such as the one at Kings Point, New York, or a local history museum. In addition, the clockwork striking mechanism and the weights within the center column, a rare assemblage of fog-signal apparatus, remain at the light. In the tower assembly, the numbering system for each of the pieces of the building, from the massive iron plates on the ground level, to the thin bronze closure strips for the window astragals, have been well preserved and provide a good example of late 19th century prefabricated buildings.

Tongue Point Lighthouse is significant for its association with the 19th century program of improvements for navigation in the Bridgeport Harbor area. The improvements were crucial to the development of the industrial base of the city. The light is significant also as a typical example of the smaller version of the Lighthouse Board's standard design of the later 19th century prefabricated, cast-iron tower which could be mass-produced into standard units, yet adapted to individual sites. The Lighthouse also played a role in the development of fog-signal devices, one of the major technical

Tongue Point Light, Bridgeport, CT

frontiers remaining in the lighthouse service in the late 19th century. In addition, as noted above, a rare assemblage of fog-signal apparatus remains on this site: the fog bell, the clockwork striking mechanism and its weights within the center column.

Until the 1840s, Bridgeport harbor development lagged behind that of neighboring cities with better natural harbors. With the advent of the railroad then, Bridgeport businessmen were awarded federal contracts to dredge a ship channel and to build breakwaters so that freight and passenger vessels could connect with rail lines at Bridgeport. As a transshipment location, development of the Bridgeport waterfront was assured. In the 1870s, the channel in the inner harbor was widened; in 1891, a harbor of refuge was created behind the breakwater. The breakwater, constructed by Brown and Fleming of New York, extended east 11,000 feet from Wells or Tongue Point to the site of the inner beacon. Local lobbying efforts succeeded in obtaining federal appropriations totalling, in 1893 and 1894, $4,500 to build a special foundation at the east end of the breakwater for the construction of a cast-iron lighthouse.

Lieutenant Colonel D.P. Heap of the Lighthouse Board supervised the installation of a 21 feet high conical lighthouse (on a 10 feet high concrete foundation) made up of flanged, curved sections bolted together to form rings, a standard design used by the Lighthouse Board between 1873 and about 1910 for different sites such as ledges, reefs, shoals and breakwaters. Of two stories surmounted by a lantern, the tower's lower story was used for storage and the second for a watchroom and record storage. Unlike many of the wave-swept lighthouses, this smaller version of the type had no living quarters within. Perhaps because of its short profile, it acquired the nickname of "The Bug" or "the Buglight." On March 1, 1885, a lantern light was removed and the sixth order classical lens was installed in the completed lighthouse. In 1896, a landing wharf for small boats was built on the breakwater, since the keeper was required to row to the light to perform his daily tasks.

In 1897, Congress appropriated $1,200 to establish an electrically operated gong fog signal at the light. The signal was developed in the General Lighthouse Depot on Staten Island, New York. However, the invention proved unreliable. Discontinued for repair on March 30, 1898, it was decommissioned seven months later and replaced in March 1899 with a 160 pound fog bell. During fog conditions, the bell was struck every eight seconds by a system operated by clockwork and 150 pound weights. This system still remains in place at the light. Although the mechanism was a 10,000 blow machine, it required attendance for starting and ending operations, as well as rewinding during extended periods of time.

In 1904, a reservation to contain a keeper's dwelling and garden was proposed in a sketch by the Third District Engineer. The reservation was to be located at the island end of a plank walk which had been installed in 1900. In 1906, the Annual Report of the Lighthouse Board reported that the keeper had, at his own expense, erected a small shanty in which he slept nightly "so as to start the fog signal at short notice." An appropriation of $5,000 was requested for construction of a dwelling, but within a decade plans were underway to move "The Bug" (or "The Buglight") to a new location on shore.

Ship captains had complained about the sharp turn they had to make around Tongue Point, or the Inner Breakwater, on their way into Bridgeport's Inner Harbor. In 1919, 350 feet of the inner breakwater was removed and added to the outer breakwater and, in 1921, a Lighthouse Department derrick moved the Tongue Point Lighthouse to a new, reinforced concrete foundation located 275 ft. closer to shore. As an additional accomodation to large vessels, the 18 ft. deep channel was dredged to a depth of 22 feet and a width of 300 feet.

The significance of and affection for "The Buglight" at Tongue Point in the local maritime community was demonstrated in 1967, when the possible discontinuance of the light and fog signal was vigorously protested. The lighthouse has been nominated to be included in the National Register of Historic Places. "the Bug" is a relic of a bygone era, but still welcomes mariners to Bridgport Harbor.

●

Women Light Keepers

Between 1825 and 1955, women lighthouse keepers were far more numerous than is usually believed today. Wives of keepers always assisted their husbands with the chores of the lighthouse, and their duties were varied and often difficult. However, there were women who kept the light just as ably as the men did. Actually there have been more than 250 women keepers who were either officially appointed as assistants to their husbands or who worked alone as keepers. For example, in 1857 Amy Buddington was keeper at Stratford Point Light, Connecticut, while Mary A. Foster ran the light at Old Field Point during the same year. Additional women keepers have been noted in this book in connection with various lights.

There is no more famous heroine in the annals of lighthouse lore than Ida Lewis (1842-1911) who kept the Lime Rock Light, Newport, Rhode Island for 50 years. During her lifetime, she saved 23 people from drowning. Her deeds of heroism were so well-known nationally that President Ulysses S. Grant and Vice-President Schuyler Colfax visited her at the light in 1869. Her lighthouse is now the Ida Lewis Yacht Club, and her impressive tombstone in the Newport cemetary is mute testimony of the love and respect people felt for her. Her story makes up the last chapter of Edward Rowe Snow's *The Lighthouses of New England* (New York: Dodd, Mead & Company, Inc. 1984) and is well worth reading.

CHAPTER 16

STRATFORD SHOAL (MIDDLEGROUND) LIGHT (1878)

Light List No.: 20290
Location: Latitude 41° 3.6′ N
            Longitude 73° 3.6′ N
Height: 60′
Range: 9 miles, Flashing White every 6 seconds, Horn
Lens: 300 mm, lamp size 3.05A
Automated: August 10, 1970

Middle Ground Light is located where it is to warn against disaster from the rocky shoal which lies in the "middle ground" of Long Island Sound. It is a dangerous shoal three quarters of a mile long, lying between Stratford, Connecticut and Port Jefferson, New York. Stratford Point bears north, a distance of five and a half miles. Old Field Point bears south by west, a distance of five miles. The lighthouse is a primary navigational aid which marks this hazard in the center of the main shipping channel through Long Island Sound. The lighthouse is difficult to spot during good visibility, because the gray granite octagonal tower does not offer enough contrast to the sea and sky. Light and fog sensors keep the light showing from just before sunset to just before sunrise, and also in poor visibility.

In order to point out the exact position of this shoal, a light-boat, (lightship or floating light as it was called, was first placed off its southern extremity in January 1838. The light-boat was a vessel of about 100 tons with a captain, mate and a crew of four men. The boat was well-provisioned for the crew, had enough wood and water for four months and enough oil for a year. The lights were shown from two masts, one 40 feet high, the other 50 feet high. Each lantern contained a compass lamp which was fitted to burn ten wicks. When the light-boat was first placed at Middle Ground, it was made to ride on a single anchor weighing 1,200 pounds. It didn't prove sufficient for anchorage in mid-sound. Several times, she was driven from her proper position. The light-boat was discontinued in 1877.

The lighthouse was begun in 1876, when a foundation was laid for a 60-foot tower on part of the shoal. In 1887, the lighthouse was rebuilt to serve increased shipping on the Sound, and on August 10, 1970, it was fully automated. The light was manned by members of the Lighthouse Service from 1910 until 1939, when the Service was absorbed by the United States Coast Guard. Until it was automated, the light was manned by uniformed Coast Guard personnel with four or five men assigned to it during differ-

Stratford Shoal (Middleground) Light

ent shifts. Today, the lighthouse doors and windows are sealed with sheets of steel as protection against mindless vandalism.

Wrecks

Long Island Sound has not been kind to those who venture into its waters in bad weather. The bottom near Middle Ground and elsewhere, as I have noted in these pages, is littered with the remains of passenger ships which sank in violent storms or were destroyed by fires or accidents. For instance, Bridgeport legends tell the story of the "Trustful," a fast, well-built cargo sloop similar to the reconstructed Hudson River sloop "Clearwater," which was scheduled to sail from Bridgeport to Port Jefferson with a cargo of church bells for a Setauket, Long Island, church.

The trip was to be made on a dark day with an overcast sky and a northeast wind whipping up the waves. Another sloop which sailed a few hours before the "Trustful" was seen flying distress signals by other vessels coming into Bridgeport. In spite of the bad weather, the captain assured his passengers and crew that it would be safe to cross the Sound. When some of his passengers argued with him, the skipper noted the church bells in the ship's hold and said, "The "Trustful" will be all right. The devil looks after his own. Anyway, if we go down, these bells here will never ring in Setauket, but they may peel a dirge for some of you white-livered folk at the bottom of the sea."

The "Trustful" set sail from Bridgeport a short time later while the weather got worse and the wind and the waves reached near hurricane proportions. A few hours later, people on the shore in Port Jefferson saw that the "Trustful" was in difficulty south of the Middle Ground shoals, but the seas were so high that it was impossible to go to her assistance. The "Trustful" disappeared a short time later, and no trace of her was ever found.

Sailors and fishermen on the Long Island and Connecticut shores believed that the "Trustful" was lost through the boastfulness of its skipper. Those who sailed the Sound often told stories of how they heard the sunken church bells ringing in muffled tones during storms. Others said they had seen the lost ship in full sail during rough weather and heard its bells ringing to warn of the coming of a storm. Bells do ring near the spot where it is believed the "Trustful" went down, because a bell buoy was installed in the area near the edge of Port Jefferson channel.

Many years after the loss of the "Trustful," the steamship "Mountaineer" steamed by the Middle Ground Light during bad weather when the lookout reported that he heard the muffled sound of bells. The captain ordered the engine stopped and, during a flash of lightning, he saw that his ship was only a few yards away from being wrecked on the Port Jefferson shore with a possible heavy loss of life. The story does not say whether this sound came from the ghostly bells of the "Trustful" or from the buoy installed by government near the harbor entrance.

Dedicated Keepers

The Middle Ground Lighthouse emits a white, flashing light to distinguish it from other nearby lighthouses. It is also a reporting point for planes approaching the Bridgeport Sikorsky Memorial Airport in Stratford. In the days of the old Lighthouse Service and up to 1970 when Middle Ground became fully automated, manning this lighthouse was a tough job. A *Bridgeport Sunday Post* story on September 4, 1927, describes the windswept water which confronted the keepers of the light:

"Rising straight out of the sea, this exposed tower combats the onslaught of wind and wave for 12 months of the year while its isolated keepers during the winter months look out on a great expanse of tumbling waters more often than not devoid of shipping. And yet the light must burn, for on its warning ray depend probably many hundreds of lives and much valuable property. And when the Sound is lashed to fury by the gale and the waves leap and curl against the sturdy masonry, the shock of the impact causes the building to shudder and tremble as if an earthquake had shaken the earth.

"Through the turmoil and windswept spume, people on shore see the light gleaming in intermittent flashes from Middle Ground scarcely realizing that out there in all that fury of element and tumbling water, a handful of men are keeping watch and ward over that dreary waste and insuring a safe passage for the country's shipping."

The men who manned Middle Ground and other U.S. Government lighthouses in those days were on duty for six hours and off for six hours all through the day and night. Each lighthouse keeper (at one time called "Wickies") also had eight days leave every month. Their duties consisted of cleaning, polishing lenses and brass, repairing and maintaining other machinery in the lighthouse, writing logs, bringing in supplies, cooking meals, and cleaning up their living quarters.

Lighthouse keepers in World Wars I and II helped save the lives of sailors from ships sunk by German U-boats off the Atlantic coast, and many other deeds of heroism and compassion are credited to them. Keeping the lighthouse was also a lonely, monotonous job, and many stories, including those involving superstition were told by men in this service, such as the story of Fred Jordan which I have told in connection with Penfield Reef Light, Chapter 13.

Despite ghosts, bad weather, monotony, sickness and other hazards, the lights at Middle Ground, Penfield Reef, and many other locations on Long Island Sound continue to flash their comforting warning beams, today not tended by dedicated keepers, but by an automated system that is monitored and maintained by the United States Coast Guard.

Description of the Light

Stratford Shoal Lighthouse marks a gravel shoal in the middle of Long Island Sound, five and one-half miles south of Stratford Point, Connecticut. Surrounded by a horseshoe-shaped breakwater of riprap, it consists of a grey granite, gable-roofed dwelling resting on a circular foundation of granite ashlar with a lantern tower projecting from its central south facade. Except for a two-stage concrete landing, there are no other structures at the site. This lighthouse replaced a lightship which formerly warned mariners of shallow waters in the middle of the shipping lane. Along with Race Rock Light and North Dumpling Light, I have always thought of this lighthouse as one of the "castles on the Sound," rising majestically from the water. And like a castle, it can appear mysterious, too, especially when fog hovers about it in bad weather.

Immense blocks of rough-faced granite form the outer rings of the light's foundation. The foundation measures 55' in diameter at the base, 46' at the top, and rises 18' 6" above the high water line. Within the concrete filled interior is a brick-lined cellar and below it, two cisterns.

In plan, the dwelling is a square 28' on a side. Skilled workmanship is evident in the dressing and laying of the smooth-faced ashlar blocks of which it is composed. The walls measure 18" in depth at the water table and 14" in depth at the top of the tower. The tower, three stories high, projects outwardly five feet from the south facade and measures 10'4" across at the base. Above the second story level, the tower assumes an octagonal plan, 7 feet in diameter.

Bricks form a lining wall for the tower. A cast-iron spiral stair rises in the center of the tower from the first story to the lantern. This stair furnishes the only access to upper stories of the lighthouse from landings on the second and third story level. Above the door on the first story is a curved stone plaque carved to read: "Stratford Shoals/Lighthouse/AD 1877/Lat. 41° 3' North/Long. 73° 6' West."

The octagonal cast-iron lantern contains eight large glass panes in the upper half of its walls and cast-iron plates in the lower half. A cast-iron frieze above the glass panes is ornamented with alternating panels of an embossed motif of foliage and a motif of repeated circles and double lines. Presently, the lantern is empty, and the spherical ventilator and platinum-tipped lightning rod designated in the original drawings are missing from the roof.

Significance of the Lighthouse

Stratford Shoal Light is significant as a carefully crafted example of the masonry lighthouse design employed by the United States Lighthouse Board for waterbound or wave-swept sites before the adoption of cast-iron tubular foundations and superstructures. Reflecting the domestic model which had been utilized earlier for some Hudson River Lighthouses, Stratford Shoal Light embodies the enormous cost and heroic effort required to put these designs in place in the tideswept and sometimes treacherous waters of Long Island Sound. Stratford Shoal Lighthouse is significant also for its important place in the aids to navigation system in Long Island Sound, standing in the middle of the Sound as its other name, "Middleground," implies. The middle ground had long been a hazard to shipping.

Stratford Shoal Light replaced earlier efforts to mark the hazard. In 1831, Congress appropriated $1,000 to erect a beacon on "the middle ground between Stratford and Crane Neck in Long Island Sound." A lightship was commissioned from a New York shipbuilder in 1837 for $8,500 to be positioned over the shoal; it had to be removed in 1866 and was replaced in 1868 with a new lightship. Ice floes were a formidable problem during the winter months. The uncertainty of the lightship's moving and its wavering beam during heavy weather finally made an investment of the magnitude of a masonry wave-swept tower justifiable to Congress in 1873.

During March 1873, a major development in lighthouse design and construction was introduced to the Lighthouse Board: "the tubular foundation for reefs and shoals in bays and rivers subject to the flow of ice" (*Journal*, Volume 5, page 220). One of the sites considered for this innovation was Stratford Shoal. However, the original plan for a granite, riprap and concrete foundation for the Stratford Shoal site, which had been presented by the Third District Engineer in 1872, was adopted. As such, Stratford Shoal Light represents a late example of the masonry foundation which was under construction contemporaneously with the earliest tubular cast-iron foundations being prefabricated and installed at Southwest Ledge near New Haven, Connecticut and Ship John Shoal in Delaware Bay.

At Stratford Shoal, a riprap ring was built up from the shoal to protect the construction site. Within the center of the ring, the gravel shoal surface was removed and concrete laid to provide a bed for the circular cutstone foundation, 55′ in diameter at the base, diminishing to 46′ at the top. Construction of the foundation, composed of huge blocks of granite backed with concrete, was completed with great difficulty by D.V. Howell between 1874 and 1876. The cut stone for the lighthouse was supplied by M.K. Chase and the metal work by Atlantic Steam Engine Works. A temporary wharf for materials was constructed, and the cut stone for the lighthouse was shipped from the quarries and stock-piled nearby. During 1877 and 1878, the building was erected. Work continued despite a major setback, the sinking of the construction schooner "Mignonette," which broke from her mooring in a storm. The men and supplies were saved, the men housed in the nearby completed building, and worked resumed. On December 15, 1878, the light was exhibited for the first time.

The design of Stratford Shoal Lighthouse represents the house-with-attached lighthouse classification, which had been used in North American lighthouses since the 1830s. For wave-swept sites, this design provided a more comfortable alternative to the tall, conical tower, and emphasized the domestic side of its function, combining lighttower and separate keeper's dwelling of on-shore sites. Both masonry and frame construction were used for the house-with-tower design, incorporating architectural details of the popular revival styles of North American architecture.

In the 1870's, the masonry model of the keeper's-house-with-tower as developed for Hudson River sites in the 1860s had been adopted in Long Island Sound and elsewhere. The same design was often used repeatedly: Race Rock Lighthouse, New York, closely resemble Stratford Shoal and was under construction at the same time. While Race Rock and Stratford Shoal share a basic similarity, differences between the two include: 1) variation in stone finishing; 2) different window arches; and 3) different roof shape.

Stratford Shoal Light exhibits some Gothic Revival details, such as pointed windows on the third story of the tower. These details point to the cultural lag of Federal design. The Gothic detail and tall tower lend an institutional air to the lighthouse.

Improvements in technology were reflected in the lighting and fog-signal apparatus at Stratford Shoal, which played a vital role in guiding ships away from its hazardous base and supplying information about location for major shipping lanes in the Sound. The second-class Daboll fog-trumpet and caloric engine of 1880 was followed by an 1897 installation of two Hornsby Akroyd 3½ horsepower engines and a Clayton air compressor for the improved trumpet. In 1915, a first class air siren was installed. New fog signal engines were added in 1923. Automation came in 1970.

The lighting apparatus originally installed at Stratford Shoal, a fourth-order Fresnel lens, exhibited a light that flashed every 30 seconds; this was improved in 1879 to exhibit 15 seconf flashes, and the following year, changed again to 10 second intervals. A new lens was installed in 1894, to be replaced in 1905 by a new fourth order flashing light The 60,000 candlepower lighthouse in place at Stratford Shoal in 1970 was visible for thirteen miles. It was automated in the same year and converted to battery power in 1978.

Stratford Shoal (Middleground) Light has been rightfully nominated to be included in the National Register of Historic Places.

CHAPTER 17

STRATFORD POINT LIGHT, Stratford, CT (1822)

Light List No.: 20265
Location: Latitude 41° 09.1' N
Longitude 73° 06.2' W
Height: 35' (HAW 52')
Range: 26 miles, Flashing (2) White every 20 secs.
Horn
Lens: DCB-224 1000 Watt Lamp
Present Light Built 1881
Radio Beacon: 316 kHz, SP (. . . . __ __ .) III, VI
20 miles

Stratford Point is a peninsula that juts sharply into the waters of Long Island Sound. On one side is the Housatonic River. On the other side, cliffs rise to a height of 40 feet. To the north of the Point, the shore forms a graceful curve, forming the line of a bay long known as "Half Moon Cove." The mouth of the Housatonic was always treacherous and dangerous because of its shifting sand bars and swift currents, ever a menace to navigation. This situation early made some sort of signal necessary to guide vessels entering the harbor, especially at night. There is no written evidence of the methods used, but tradition has it that a man was stationed at the Point where the present lighthouse stands to keep a bonfire burning during the flood tides when a vessel was expected and on particular foggy nights. Later, a pole was erected to which was attached an iron basket in which wood was kept burning.

In 1821, the first lighthouse was built at Stratford Point. It was the third lighthouse to be erected on Long Island Sound by the United States Government and occupied a four-acre tract of land purchased from Betsey Walker. There were two buildings, the light tower and dwelling house, which were erected by Judson Curtis, a local builder. In the fall (1822) when the light tower was built, occurred the memorable "September gale," which was the worst southeast gale that had ever passed over Stratford. Hundreds of trees were uprooted, houses blown over, and the salt spray was blown so far that the windows and trees in the town of Nichols three and a half miles away to the northwest were covered with salt. Although only the frame of the light tower was erected, it stood unharmed throughout the storm.

Later, to the east and close to the light, a bell tower was built. The bell ran by clockwork, striking every half minute. It took 20 minutes to wind and ran half an hour. Whale oil was first used to keep the light burning. Later, lard oil was substituted. On extremely cold nights the light needed almost constant attention, since the oil congealed, causing the light to go out. In the 1850s, a Fresnel lens imported from France was installed in the lantern. It was a fifth order light and considered the best of its class in the district.

On a cold, snowy night, the life of an old-time light keeper (known as "Wickies") was not to be envied, for the light had to be tended several times, and the bell had to be wound every half hour once or twice. If the wind was strong, the glass around the lantern had to be washed with alcohol to remove the sleet and salt spray. Once, on a foggy June day, the keeper at Stratford Point Light rang the bell for 32 consecutive hours. But even this record was broken when, in a blinding February snow storm, the keeper kept the bell ringing for 104 hours—not quite five full days and nights. The storm stopped and then continued with such unabated fury that the bell had to be operated for another 103 hours non-stop, thus ringing practically a total of 207 hours with but one brief stop. This certainly must be some sort of a record.

In 1881, the old dwelling was removed and a more modern one built in its place. A new light tower was erected also, but the old third order lens was kept. The structure was built under the direction of General Duane, a famous engineer. It is built mainly of cast-iron which, unfortunately, attracts lightning frequently. The light has been struck a number of times but without damage to the structure, the lightning each time having buried itself in the foundations. The old kerosene lamp that formerly made the light in the tower was a burner with a separate reservoir and a tiny flame scarcely larger than a pencil. About the lamp rotated two huge glass prisms that magnified the light beam from its tiny flame to a flash of 2400 candlepower, capable of being seen for many miles at sea.

In 1911, a modern siren fog horn was installed at the lighthouse, replacing the old bell which had served as a guide to sailors for many years during stormy or foggy weather. Two separate engines were installed in a building constructed for the purpose to operate a small air compressor. The air generated by the compressor was used to blow the powerful siren. Duplicate engines were installed for emergencies, so that if one broke down, the other could be started without interruption to the supply of compressed air for the siren, thus avoiding any possibility of having it stop blowing.

Stratford Point Lighthouse is the most powerful light in any of the waters discussed in this book. Its fourth order Fresnel lens has been removed and replaced with a DCB-224 rotating optic. The light tower is the second earliest example of the cone-shaped, cast-iron, prefabricated lighthouse discussed in this book, developed by the Lighthouse Board in the 1870s to cut costs in design, production and transportation, and intended to be used on a variety of sites. Here, as at Tongue Point in Bridgeport, the type is used on a land site. Separate from the keeper's quarters which were restored in 1983 and converted to government quarters, the tower today is used to house weather equipment. In form and materials, it is virtually identical to Bridgeport's Tongue Point Lighthouse, except it is larger.

The DCB-24 and DCB-224 are the Coast Guard's standard landfall

Stratford Point Light, Stratford, CT

lights. These optics are used for lights that must have a nominal range greater than 18 nautical miles. The DCB-24 and DCB-224 emit one and two pencil beams, repectively, which sweep the horizon.

Description of the Light

Stratford Point Lighthouse does the double duty of showing the way into the estuary of the Housatanic River and providing seamen with one of the most exact and perfect bearings that are to be found anywhere on the Sound. It stands 20 feet above the high water level on the shore of Long Island Sound to the west of the river's mouth. Established in 1881, this cast-iron lighthouse in the shape of a truncated cone presently is painted white with a horizontal brown band marking the middle third of its shaft. In addition to the lighthouse, the site includes a wood framed keeper's dwelling, also constructed in 1881, and a brick power house, built in 1911 for the fog signal apparatus.

A concrete foundation laid on grade to a height of three feet serves as a footing for the light tower. The tower measures 21 feet in outside diameter at the base, 18 feet at the top, and rises 35 feet to the focal plane of the light. Five courses of curved cast-iron plates form the walls of the tower. Bolts connect the plates through flanges cast at the inner edges. Although the Fresnel fourth order lens has been removed, the original cast-iron lantern deck remains, with modern lighting apparatus occupying the traditional central position on that level.

Since no living quarters were required, the interior is open up to the watchroom floor. A winding cast-iron stair curves gracefully around the periphery of the space. Storage space is provided by niches built into the brick lining wall on either side of the entrance. Additional storage space is provided in the watchroom. The watchroom, presently airconditioned, contains apparatus for measuring air pollution. A curved metal wall supports the ship's ladder which leads to the lantern.

The present lighting apparatus, manufactured by Carlisle and Finch of Cincinnati, Ohio, consists of two sealed beacon lights with double reflectors. It is mounted on a stand in the center of the lantern deck. Weather instruments and a small Fresnel-type modern lens are mounted elsewhere on this deck. About 1850, the light had a fifth order classical lens. In 1881 the lighting apparatus was a third order Fresnel lens with a constant level lamp manufactured by L. Sauter & Co., and rotated by a Henry Lepaute (Paris, France) clockwork mechanism. It emitted a flashing white light. In 1906, the apparatus was a fourth order lens, rotating in a mercury trough, according to the *Light List* for that year.

The keeper's dwelling, currently occupied by a Coast Guard family and located 45 feet north of the tower, is a wood frame building with cross gabled roof. In plan it measures 30 feet by 31 feet. The house was described in an 1887 inspection report as having brick nogging between the studs. When built, the dwelling contained eight rooms, including three bedrooms, one dining room, one kitchen, one sitting room and one pantry.

All that remains of that original detailing are the labels on the northwest corner porch and the porch posts.

The brick powerhouse, measuring 20 feet wide and 30 feet long, was built froma design used at Montauk Point, New York and elsewhere. Its well-considered symmetrical elevations, transomed windows and wide doors, imposing cupola (now removed), carved roof brackets, and brick dentil trim distinguish a building intended to house important machinery, and indeed it does. The building presently is used to house an important collection of aids to navigation equipment.

Significance of the Lighthouse

Almost from the beginning of the history of the white man in the eastern United States, there has always been a light of some description on what is called Stratford Point today, from an old wood and coal brazier to the present modern apparatus. Many legends are told how the first light was established on the point by some miraculous power. The lighthouse is considered as one of the most important leading lights among the aids to navigation along the Sound.

Stratford Point Light is significant as the earliest example in Connecticut of the cone-shaped, pre-fabricated cast-iron lighthouse, one of the earliest such lighthouses in the nation. Its construction and architectural details include characteristics which represent the earliest phase of development. Later, the type became more standardized and was utilized on land and watersites in many varied locations. The site represents the fourth oldest lighthouse station in Connecticut still under Coast Guard jurisdiction. Established by the federal government to mark the mouth of the Housatonic River, the light station at Stratford Point has made a significant contribution to the history of aids to navigation in Long Island Sound. In addition, Stratford Point is significant as one of the few light stations with three principal components remaining intact: the light tower, the keeper's dwelling, and the fog signal house.

Stratford Point has been the site of a lighthouse and keeper's dwelling since 1821. At that time, Ezekiel Gilbert of Derby and Robert Fairchild of Stratford contracted to build a wood frame lighthouse on a stone foundation to match the one at New Haven. It was to be painted red or white, as was the small 1½ story wood framed keeper's house nearby. In 1881, this shingled wood framed lighthouse was replaced with the present cast-iron structure, formed of curved cast-iron plates, flanged for bolting into courses. The Lighthouse Board approved this design for Stratford Point in 1880, a week after it approved a shorter version of the same design for Cold Spring Harbor, New York, front light. Present documentation suggests that Stratford Point is the earliest extant lighthouse of this design. Deeply molded cast-iron window surrounds, projecting pedimented hoods and recessed panels, and simple projections at the top and sides of the doorway all identify Stratford Point Lighthouse as an example of the first phase in cast-iron construction. This phase dated from 1880 to the mid-1890s.

A fog signal was established at Stratford Point in 1858. At the time the cast-iron light tower was built in 1881, a new fog-bell tower also was constructed, located about 20 feet southwest of the light tower. The new machinery was housed in a shed below the bell. In 1910, a compressed-air siren was ordered to replace the fog-bell, and a brick powerhouse for the first class sirens was erected to the west of the light tower, using a design also employed by the First District at Montauk Point Light. This powerhouse remains standing. In 1931, fog signal engines by General Electric and Ingersoll Rand were in use, operating a typhon whistle.

The complex history of lighting apparatus at Stratford Point began in 1821 with the introduction of eight lamps used in a fixed light. Within a year, Winslow Lewis, an inventor who had sold the United States Government the rights to his improved Argon type lamps and silvered parabolic reflectors, visited Stratford Point and installed a new mechanism. This device consisted of a revolving frame holding ten new lamps, ten new 16 inch reflectors, and two new spare lamps. A clock mechanism for lighthouse, patented by the renowned clockmaker Simon Willard, was fitted in the lantern as well.

The Lewis lamps were replaced with a fifth order Fresnel light in the decade before the Civil War. In 1867, the two range lenses with iron frames were described as providing flashes which were too brief and too infrequent. Thus, an 1881 inspection report identifies a third order flashing light as the apparatus in place at the lighthouse on that date. It consisted of a constant "level" lamp and two revolving range lenses, made by L. Sauter & Co. and were secured back to back. The Henry Lepaute clockwork required winding every four hours. In 1932, the inspector reported a fourth order electric incandescent light in place at Stratford Point, revolving in a trough of mercury and giving a light of 290,000 candlepower. Today, of course, the lighthouse has a DCB-224 rotating optic.

Stratford Point Lighthouse has been nominated to be included in the National Register of Historic Places.

CHAPTER 18

NEW HAVEN HARBOR LIGHT, New Haven, CT (1805)

Old Light List No.: 162 (Obsolete)
Location: Latitude 41° 14' 54" N
              Longitude 72° 53' 55" W
Height: 70' (HAW 93')
Range: 15 miles, Fixed White, Horn
Lens: Fourth Order, Classical (removed)
Rebuilt: C. 1840
Discontinued: 1877

Located on Lighthouse Point (formerly called Five-Mile Point or "Little Necke" as early as 1671) on the east side of the harbor entrance, New Haven Harbor Light is similar in structure to New London Harbor Light some 45 miles northeast of it. Its purpose was to guide vessels into the port of New Haven. The large deposits of oyster shells found on the Point many years ago led local inhabitants to suspect that it was once a meeting place for resident Indians. The property was part of an original grant made by the Colony of New Haven to the Morris family in 1660. A copy of the original deed may be found in the Towne Records of East Haven. The light was discontinued in 1877, when the Southwest Ledge Light was built a few hundred yards southwest of it.

The attention of the United States Government was first drawn to the importance of placing a beacon at Five Mile Point through a petition by citizens of New York and Connecticut who wanted a lighthouse erected on the eastern shore of the entrance to New Haven harbor. Since the harbor possessed considerable commercial importance at the time, the petition, presented early in 1804, was granted on May 5th. Records of East Haven show that the United States purchased from an Amos Morris for the sum of $100, a tract of land upon which to erect a lighthouse.

The deed recording the sale reads thus:

> Know ye, that I, Amos Morris, of East Haven, in the County of New Haven, and State of Connecticut, for the consideration of $100 received, to my full satisfaction, of the United States of America, do sell, etc., unto said United States, a certain piece of land, situated in said East Haven, at a place called Five Mile Point, for the accomodation of a lighthouse, being butted and bounded as follows, viz.: Beginning at the northwest corner thereof, to a rock three rods below high water mark; thence east three rods to high water mark to a stake and stone; thence west to a stake and stone to high water mark, eight rods; thence north by the shore, twenty rods to the first mentioned corner, being about one acre, together with the privilege of passing back and forth through my land for the

accomodation of said Lighthouse and keeper of it, in procuring and conveying the necessary supplies.

Amos Morris

Wit.: Nathan Beers
　　　Josiah Bradley

This was the beginning of the lighthouse which would stand guard over New Haven harbor for 72 years. The lighthouse would see hostile fleets approach New Haven, only to be driven off by the bravery of its defenders. It would see also the commerce of the town grow and then wane to become just a fraction of what it was. Finally, the light would become the main attraction in a town park (Lighthouse Park) where it has been preserved and admired as part of New Haven's maritime heritage.

Immediately after recording the sale of Morris's property, the Government began to erect the lighthouse and the keeper's dwelling. This first light was octagonal in shape and had shingled sides and roof. The lantern was provided with eight powerful reflectors, was 35 feet above high water mark and was visible in all directions for about six miles. However, the light was not efficient for vessels approaching the harbor from the east, because of a row of trees along the northeast and southeast shores which obscured the lantern's rays. This first structure lasted until about 1840, when it was replaced by a larger and better building made of sandstone and brick.

Keepers of the Light

During its active period, the light had frequent changes of keepers. The first keeper was Amos Morris who kept the post for three weeks and was followed by a Mr. Wedmore. He was succeeded by Jonathan Finch of East Haven who held the position until his death in 1821, at which time his son, William Finch, received the appointment. William Finch died three years later, and the care of the light was passed on to Elihu Ives of New Haven in 1824. He remained in charge of the lighthouse until 1846.

While Elihu Ives was keeper of the light, the first beacon was replaced by a new and more efficient structure at a cost of $10,000. The exterior of the new structure was constructed of East Haven sandstone and the interior of New Haven brick. The steps leading to the lantern were (and are) granite. The light was painted white and stretched towards the heavens for a distance of 97 feet above sea level. It could be seen at a distance of ten nautical miles when the weather was clear. The keeper's dwelling was painted red and attached to the tower. It was lighted in 1845 and discontinued as a lighthouse on January 1, 1877, the day that Southwest Ledge Light was lighted for the first time.

In 1846, Elihu Ives was succeeded as keeper by George W. Hicks of New Haven, and three years later Stephen Willard, also of New Haven, received the appointment. He remained keeper of the light until 1853, when Merritt Thompson took his place. In 1860, Elizur Thompson took charge of the light but relinquished the position in 1867 to try his luck in the gold fields of Alaska. Charles W. Bradley of East Haven watched the

New Haven Harbor Light, New Haven, CT

light during his absence. Returning two years later, broke and wiser, Thompson again became keeper of the light until his death on February 7, 1897.

Captain Thompson was one of the best known men in East Haven. During his 35 years as lighthouse keeper, he entertained many prominent men from all over the United States. Since his experience was wide and varied, he had a fund of stories for his visitors. When the new light was placed on the breakwater at the entrance to the harbor in 1877, Captain Thompson became the keeper there. When he died, his widow took charge of the light. After her death, her sister, Mrs. Adelaide Foster, received the appointment.

After the old light was discontinued in 1877, it was used for a number of years by the United States Weather Bureau to display storm signals during rough weather. For a small fee, visitors were allowed to climb to the lantern gallery to enjoy the view of Long Island Sound, New Haven and the surrounding country.

About 1900, Captain Hervey Townshend described Lighthouse Point thus: "In this vicinity the black sands and the rocky formations possess a magnetic power strong enough to affect the mariner's compass. The sea grasses are rare and beautiful, and superior fertilizing properties. White Irish moss grows here in abundance, and is used to some extent by the residents of the vicinity, and when properly cured and prepared, is a very acceptable acquisition to a shore dinner."

The British Are Coming!

British troops attempted to land on Five Mile Point on July 5, 1779, to to invade New Haven. However, American riflemen and field pieces were deployed on the Point to resist such an attempt. As the British approached the Point, Ensign and Assistant Adjutant Watkins in one of the lead boats shouted to the Americans on shore, "Disperse ye rebels!" Immediately, the Americans, under the command of Lieutenant Evelyn Pierpont, opened fire on the British troops in the boats, and Watkins fell back into the boat, dead, with a bullet through his heart. Watkins was subsequently buried just south of where the lighthouse now stands.

Amos Morris outwitted the British who one night approached his property on Five Mile Point for foraging. As he saw the enemy drawing near the shore, Morris mounted his horse and, as legend tells us, he pranced up and down the beach and called out in stentorian tones to the rocks and trees as though they were his troops. In the darkness, the ruse worked, for Morris was known to be a military man, and the British assumed that he had the shore lined with troops awaiting their landing. When they heard his loud and continuous commands, they immediately returned to their vessels.

Eventually the British landed at Five Mile Point, despite the initial repulse by Lieutenant Pierpont and his men. However, once ashore, they did not fare too well. The Americans made every effort to secure and hide all loose or movable property. Some of it was hidden in ditches and woods. The farm stock, with the exception of the pigs, were driven into the woods. The pigs, however, stampeded at the firing of Lieutenant Pierpont's muskets, broke from their pens and took refuge in the neighboring rye field. Just before Amos Morris left his house, and with the hope of appeasing the invaders and saving his property, he left his table in the dining room set with all the food and luxuries he possessed. Despite this gesture of hospitality, the British burned to the ground his house, barns and other buildings belonging to his estate.

The walls remained, however, and the interior was rebuilt. Before the fire, there were 16 large rooms in the house. The Morris House, as it is known today, still stands in the Morris Cove section of New Haven, near Lighthouse Park, a short distance north of the lighthouse. About a mile south of Fort Hale, it is one of the most interesting buildings within New Haven city limits. The mortar was made using oyster shells found on the beach, and the timber was cut on the Morris property. At least eight successive generations of the Morris family lived in the house. A well was dug on the property when the house was built and was a source of drinking water for many years.

During the War of 1812, the first alarm of danger to New Haven was sounded on a dark Monday night, September 13, 1813, when a British frigate and sloop of war stood close to the lighthouse. The following July, sailors allegedly belonging to a British man-of-war sighted off the coast at Guilford, landed at the lighthouse and made inquiries about the marine guard and defenses of New Haven.

The Lighthouse Today

With its white sides gleaming in the sun, New Haven Harbor Light stands on a rocky point projecting into Long Island Sound, flanked by two pretty, sandy coves. Conspicuous either from land or sea, this historic landmark is the object of more than passing interest to the landlubber and sailor alike. And it is even closer to the hearts of the residents of New Haven. In May 1949, it was given its first coat of white paint in 20 years to commemorate the opening of Lighthouse Park. In March 1986, renovation work began on the sturdy sandstone and brick structure when workers wearing special suits and masks began removing decades of pigeon droppings from its interior. Then workers steam-cleaned the exterior and interior of the lighthouse and repaired the cracked and chipped mortar that holds the sandstone bricks together. The lighthouse received the facelift partly because of its status as a historic landmark and partly as part of a broader plan to refurbish Lighthouse Park, which includes the only public beach in New Haven where swimming is permitted.

CHAPTER 19

SOUTHWEST LEDGE LIGHT, New Haven, CT (1877)

Light List No.: 20245, 20725
Location: Latitude 41° 14.1' N
           Longitude: 72° 54.7' W
Height: 57'
Range: 9 miles, Flashing Red every 5 seconds, Horn
Lens: FA-251, 150 watt lamp
Automated: 1953

Description of the Light

Southwest Ledge Lighthouse, established on Monday evening, January 1, 1877, marks a hazardous underwater rock formation , about one mile from land, on the east side of the main channel into New Haven Harbor. Presently painted white, the eight-sided lighthouse is a one-story, cast-iron dwelling richly detailed in the Second Empire style with a lantern capping its two-story mansard roof. The foundation, a cast-iron cylinder, is surrounded by a riprap which extends as a breakwater toward the northeast. The breakwater was constructed after the lighthouse was established. The only other structure on the site is the concrete footing for the crane, once used as a landing aid.

In plan, the superstructure is a square with beveled corners. It contains three stories, one at main deck level and two beneath the mansard roof. On the roof rests the octagonal lantern surrounded by a gallery with a railing and capped with an ogee octagonal roof. By 1911, points in the foundation had opened, and bands and straps were applied to mitigate the problem. The brick walls of the basement support the iron sills of the superstructure which are marked "Phoenix Iron Co., Philadelphia."

The sides of the octagonal lantern are divided in half horizontally. Each of the upper sections contains a pane of glass measuring 39" by 34," while each of the lower sections contains a cast-iron panel. At the bottom of each glass pane on the interior is a metal strip containing the original condensation channels. Four of the lantern panels contain round ventilators. Over each glass pane is a pair of attachments, most likely intended for shutters or curtain rods, since it was a standard practice in the 19th century to use shades to protect the lens against discoloration by the sun's rays. At present, the light equipment within the lantern is automated and electric, housed in a circular-plan lens with diagonal astrals mounted on a pedestal. The fog signal, manufactured by Pennwalt Corporation, occupies the southwest corner of the first story gallery.

The surface of the ledge is made to approximate a level by a layer of concrete at least four feet thick. Two courses of masonry, each 18 inches thick, are laid on the concrete. The upper surface of the masonry is four

Southwest Ledge Light, New Haven, CT

feet below mean low water, ten feet below mean high water, and 11 feet, three inches below extreme high water. The foundation cylinder rests directly on the masonry. It is composed of cast-iron plates, six feet high, four feet wide, and two inches thick, with a curve of 15 degrees. They are bolted together. This cylinder is 24 feet in diameter and about 30 feet high. The top of its gallery is a fraction over 18 feet above extreme high tide.

The cylinder is filled in solid with cement to the top. An encroachment of about 3,000 tons of large granite blocks surrounds the pier. The tubular foundation is surrounded by an irregular octagonal house and tower, 57 feet above the level of the sea. Originally it showed a fourth-order fixed white light that was visible for 13 miles.

The peculiarity of this structure is that, being round, it offers slight obstruction to floating ice during the winter months, and that it is a monolith of artificial stone, surrounded by a veneering of iron sufficient to retain it in place until the concrete filling gained the requisite hardness by age. This lighthouse was the first in a number of its kind. Its stability was thoroughly tested in a hurricane in September 1889, from which it emerged unscathed.

The Coast Guard says that a need for a light at this location will continue for the next 20 years. It is highly visible to the public and is an example of a lighthouse design that is rare in the United States.

Excerpts from the "Annual Reports" of the Lighthouse Board

1872 "Southwest Ledge lies in the middle of the main ship-channel into New Haven Harbor, and forms a great danger to navigation. there are but 7 feet 6 inches of water on the rock at mean low water, and the question is between the removal of the rock by the Engineer Department of the Army, and the erection by the Board of a light and fog-signal to keep vessels from running upon it and other dangerous rocks in the vicinity. The main light, on the east side of the harbor, and distant one mile from and inside of Southwest Ledge. It was established in 1805, & last refitted in 1855.

"There is no doubt but that a light in the channel on this ledge would serve the interests of navigation better than the present light, and that it and a fog-signal also placed on the rock would be of more benefit to commerce that the removal of the ledge, since vessels could always run for the light, and keep clear of all the many dangers to navigation, which it will be observed exist at the entrance to New Haven Harbor. A light-house at Southwest Ledge would involve a very large expense on account of its submarine foundation, and the strength which would be required to resist the large floes of ice by which it would be assailed. The expense is estimated at $117,800.

1877 "The work at this station was continued until July 18, 1876, when operations were suspended until an additional section of the foundation tube could be made. Upon its arrival work was resumed, and by the end of September it was completed to the dormer windows. The carpentry work was in the meantime done at the light-house depot, from whence it was taken to the station in October, and during November the principal part of the work was completed. The light was exhibited for the first time on the night of January 1, 1877. To complete the protection of this light-house from the dangers of floating ice, about three thousand tons of riprap were deemed necessary, and this was placed during the month of June.

1879 "This station is much complained of by the keepers as taking in every rain, and being very damp and uninhabitable. The water which is caught from the roof into the tanks is also complained of as not being fit for drinking purposes. The landing spaces left in the riprap breakwater surrounding the light-house are again filled up with stones, which have been forced into them during the winter's storms. Efforts will be made to remedy both these evils during the year.

1889 "A Daboll hot-air fog-signal was established at this station, and put in operation on August 20, 1888. a red panel was fitted in the lantern, covering Branford Reef and Gangway Rock, and exhibited on May 15, 1889, and various repairs were made.

1892 "A boat hoisting winch was fitted and set up. An oil house with a capacity of 50 boxes was built outside the landing gallery. Various repairs were made.

"This station was built in 1877 on a caisson in deep water. Two years ago it became necessary to place a hot-air fog signal in it. The space was not enough to give the engine proper draft and without it has proved inefficient as a fog signal. It is now proposed to replace this inefficient machine with one recently invented, which has been used elsewhere under circumstances so nearly duplicating those at Southwest Ledge that it is believed that it would succeed at that place. It will, however, be necessary to erect on a separate foundation outside the tower. It is estimated that this can be done for not exceeding $12,500, and it is hoped that the forthcoming general appropriation for expenses of fog signals will be sufficient to enable the Board to do this and defray the cost therefrom.

1893 "On January 7, 1893, the caloric engines and Daboll trumpet fog signal were discontinued. the machinery was removed on March 23, 1893. A new clock cord was fitted for the bell. the clock, stove-pipes, pump, doors, windows, etc., were overhauled and repaired. The establishment of a steam fog signal at Southwest Ledge light-station, at a cost not to exceed $12,500, was authorized by the act approved February 15, 1893, but no appropriation therefor has yet been made. The Board recommends that the amount named be appropriated.

1894 "...The Board has revised its plans, and now proposes to install a Daboll Trumpet here to be worked by petroleum engines in duplicate, which can be done at a cost not to exceed $3,000. Recommendation is made that the appropriation of this amount be made therefor.

"The gallery was extended, and platforms, one on the northeast and one on the southeast angles, built to receive the boat winches. Various repairs were made.

1898 "Some 200 tons of riprap were furnished and placed for protection of the site. the sounding of the Daboll trumpet was discontinued on May 20, 1898, until further orders. The cistern is occupied by an electric battery for use with the torpedo system. . ."

Significance of the Light

Southwest Ledge Lighthouse is highly significant from both an engineering and historical point of view among Connecticut lighthouses. The superstructure constructed for this site was installed on the grounds of the Centennial Exposition in Philadelphia in 1876. A lighthouse keeper lived within and tended the lamp which was exhibited nightly from July 4, 1876 until the close of the Exhibition. The pre-fabricated, cast-iron tube foundation "for an iron lighthouse for a marine site on the tubular plan," installed at Southwest Ledge in 1876, appears to be the earliest example of this type of construction remaining in the First District, if not in the nation. Designed by Major George H. Elliott, Engineer-Secretary for the Lighthouse Board in the early 1870s, the tube foundation was meant for northern underwater sites, where screw-pile lighthouses were menaced by floating ice during the winter months. This design is considered of great importance in the development of lighthouse engineering.

The superstructure of the lighthouse represent a transition. Its Second Empire detailing carries on the feeling of the combined dwelling and lighthouse of the 1860s and 1870s, which emphasized the domestic aspect of the structure and reflected the national preference for revival styles. Yet, in the utilization of cast-iron as a building material, pre-fabricated and bolted together on the site, the Southwest Ledge Lighthouse ushered in the succeeding period in which conical cast-iron towers gave little outward indication of their use as dwellings. The prototype for the pre-fabricated conical towers seems to have been the Hunting Island, South Carolina lighthouse. This was a much taller structure, established in 1873, designed for easy disassembly and reconstruction in a new location when erosion threatened the original site. Southwest Ledge Lighthouse is significant as well as a component of the post-Civil War program of improvements in New Haven Harbor.

The harbor improvements undertaken at New Haven after the Civil War included a recommendation from V.C. Houston in 1868 that Southwest Ledge, which impinged on the shipping channel, be blasted rather than marked with a lighthouse. However, after the funding was appropriated, he suggested that a new type of foundation and tubular pier be built to support a lighthouse on Southwest Ledge. At the Southwest Ledge site, as at Stratford Shoal, this new procedure involved forming a ring of riprap, within which cement was poured to level the rock of the ledge. But at Southwest Ledge, the Lighthouse Board planned to use a tubular pier made of curved plates of cast-iron, flanged toward the interior of the

112

curve for connection with iron bolts and connected into courses or rings which could be bolted together, one atop the other, to form a cylinder. A diving bell could be used to guide the setting of the lowest horizontal ring of cast-iron tube foundation into position. Filled with rocks and cement, the pier would form a stable base for the superstructure. The superstructure also was to be built of cast-iron plates, bolted together in the form of a Second Empire style house with a steeply pitched mansard roof. Atop the roof would be the lantern.

Ramsey and Carter of Baltimore were granted the contract for the metal work in June 1875. In 1876, they arranged to ship the lighthouse intended for Southwest Ledge to the grounds of the Philadelphia Centennial Exhibition for display. In June of that year, the Lighthouse Board decided that the identical lighthouse superstructure being manufactured for Ship John Shoal Light, Delaware, would be shipped to New Haven when completed, so that work could proceed at Southwest Ledge. The lighthouse on display in Philadelphia would be shipped to Delaware at the close of the Exhibition.

After completion of the Southwest Ledge Light, the program of harbor improvements continued with both the dredging of channels and the construction of riprap breakwaters. Southwest Ledge Lighthouse became the southwest terminus of one such breakwater. In 1911, the tubular foundation was reinforced with straps and buckles. During the Depression, more than $13,000 was appropriated by Congress for work on Southwest Ledge Lighthouse. Riprap was added surrounding the light, and two boat cranes on concrete pads were installed. Evidence of the cranes remains to the north and south of the lighthouse, on top of the riprap.

Southwest Ledge Lighthouse has been rightfully nominated to be included in the National Register of Historic Places.

DCB-24 and DCB-224 Lenses, the Coast Guards' standard landfall lights. Used at Race Rock Chapter 33, Stratford Point Chapter 17, Montauk Point Chapter 27, and Penfield Reef Chapter 13. See also page 255

Courtesy U.S. Coast Guard

113

CHAPTER 20

FALKNER ISLAND LIGHT, Guilford, CT (1802)

Light List No.: 20205
Location: Latitude 41° 12.7′ N
Longitude: 72° 39.2′ W
Height: 46′ (HAW 94′)
Range: 13 miles, Flashing White every 10 seconds
Lens: 190 mm, 0.77 amp lamp
Automated: March 17, 1978

Falkner Island and Goose Island, with Stony Island to the south, are about three miles south of Guilford Harbor. They are respectively 4½ and one quarter acres in area. Each is surrounded by reefs and rocks that are bare at low tide. A depth of about 16 feet can be carried between Goose Island and Falkner Island by staying in the middle of the passage and avoiding the 8t-ft. and 11-ft. spots, about 0.35 mile 224° and 0.4 mile 300° from the light on Falkner Island, respectively, and the shoals and reefs extending from the islands.

Falkner Island Light, 94 feet above the water, is shown from a 46-ft., white octagonal tower with a house at its base near the center of Falkner Island. The maker of the lens of the light and the year it was made are unknown. The light is a primary navigational aid in this part of the Sound. A lighted gong buoy marks the shoal at the northern end of the island, and a lighted bell buoy is off the southern end of Stony Island.

Falkner Island first appears in an agreement between Uncas (c. 1588-c. 1683), Chief of the Mohegan Indians, and the settlers on December 17, 1641, when the Chief sold the settlers "the island which lyeth in the sea before the said lands called by the English Falcon Island and by the Indians Messananunch." The name came from the falcons which frequented the island during colonial times; today, the island is a sanctuary for terns, more of which later. On October 18, 1677, Andrew Leete purchased the island, after he was given permission to do so by the General Court at Hartford, and Goose Island, a smaller island about a mile to the west.

Mr. Leete transferred the islands to an unknown person, since the deed was lost and not recorded. Somehow, Isaac Parmelee acquired half of the islands and sold his share on April 7, 1715 to Timothy Baldwin who already owned the other half, which he obtained in an equally mysterious manner. The same day, Thomas Islop bought the two islands and, on May 1, 1715, Thomas Stone, father of Ebenezer and Caleb, executed a deed in their favor for Falkner and Goose Islands, to which he must have had some claim. Ebenezer transferred his share to his sons Caleb and Reuben. In his will of October 18, 1780, Seth Stone bequeathed his part of "Fortune Island," as he called it, to Noah Stone. Noah probably bought

Falkner Island Light, Guilford, CT

out the other owners, for on May 19, 1800, he paid Medad Stone $158.34 for his share. then on May 12, 1801, he sold the entire Falkner Island to the United States Government for $325.00.

The Keepers

As soon as the United States bought the island, it began building a lighthouse on it which it completed in 1802. The first keeper (or "wickie" as they were called in the early days) was Joseph Griffing who remained at the light until 1808, when he was succeeded by Solomon Stone. During the first part of the 19th century, a ship was wrecked on Goose Island, and its crew of seven men perished from the cold. During the War of 1812, boats from British men-of-war visited Falkner Island several times but left Stone, his family and lighthouse unharmed when the keeper assured the British that the light would remain lit. Apparently the light was needed by both sides, and the British could not spare any of their own men to maintain it. A British ship's doctor even provided medical attention to Stone after he injured his leg in a fall.

In 1818, Eli Kimberly became the third keeper of the light and continued in his post for 33 years. He had the longest tour of service at the light. With his wife and 12 children, his family was the largest group to inhabit the residential quarters at the light. A nearby reef is named Kimberly Reef.

Captain Oliver N. Brooks, appointed on November 6, 1851, at a salary of $350.00 a year, succeeded Kimberly. Brooks's title referred to his nautical experience as a ship's master. He was given his first command at the age of 19. He was probably the most famous keeper of the light on Falkner Island. A native of Westbrook, he was a resident of neighboring Clinton for many years. The lighthouse was rebuilt in1871, during Brooks's tenure.

Brook's bravery in saving four lives from the wreck of the schooner "Noah F. Webb" on November 23, 1858, attracted nationwide attention and earned him a gold medal from the Society for the Preservation of Life of New York and the Life Saving Benevolent Association. The "Webb" ran aground at night in a howling storm on Goose island rocks, a mile southwest of Falkner's Island. Brooks bade farewell to his wife and children and set out in an open boat in the bitter cold November weather and succeeded in reaching the two-masted vessel after several failures. He found four persons on board lashed to the rigging. An infant, who also had been lashed to the rigging, was swept overboard by the heavy seas breaking over the ship. Brooks succeeded in returning to Falkner's Island with the victims, and his wife nursed them back to health after their harrowing ordeal. A grateful group of New Haven businessmen sent Brook's wife an elaborate sterling silver tea set and a purse of $126.00 for her part in the rescue.

During his 31 years at the light, Brooks assisted 71 vessels in distress, 18 of which were nearly total wrecks. For example, on Sunday, February 7,

1875, the steamer "E.A. Woodward" of Norwalk, Connecticut, on her way from Providence to New York, ran aground on the reef north of Falkner Island. Captain Brooks and his family saved the crew despite freezing weather and heavy seas. Because of this disaster, the fog bell in use then was considered totally inadequate. A steam signal of the "most approved pattern" was recommended to replace it. The estimated cost of protecting the site and establishing a steam fog signal was $7,500. A new fog horn was finally installed at the light in 1879. William Jones succeeded Brooks when he retired to the mainland in 1882, and became the fifth keeper of the light on Falkner Island. He was succeeded in 1890 by Earnest Herrman.

During the 18th century, it was the "custom of the farmers owning the island to go there in the spring, plow the land, plant the crops, and come home at night." The oxen were usually transported in a scow. A fine, large elm tree stood on the island for many years and was a conspicuous landmark until it was uprooted during the gales of the summer of 1893.

The ownership of Falkner Island was disputed between New York and Connecticut for many years. Finally, about 1800, Falkner was determined to be within the limits of Connecticut. Today, the island is owned by the Fish and Wildlife Service of the Department of the Interior, except for the lighthouse (now automated) which is still maintained by the Coast Guard.

On March 15, 1976, an electrical fire was reported in the house near the light at about 4 p.m. The fire apparently started in the walls of the building and spread rapidly to all floors. The station was unable to start the fire pump, so the house became completely engulfed; the south wall collapsed onto the main fuel tanks. Since these were in danger of exploding, the island had to be evacuated. The light tower was gutted, and the light, radio beacon, and fog signal became inoperative. There were no injuries to station personnel who were evacuated to the Coast Guard Station in New Haven. The Coast Guard installed a temporary light and fog signal and worked three days getting the light back into some kind of shape.

Falkner's Birds

Although the falcons have long since gone, three species of colonial terns now nest on Falkner Island, Arctic, common, and roseate. These birds were abundant until 1800 when hunting them for the millinery trade drastically reduced its population. When various protective measures were introduced about 1900, the population slowly grew until the 1940s, when the population again began to decline. Human intrusion, combined with competition with gulls for nesting territory contributed to this decline.

Uninhabited Goose Island, located one half mile west of Falkner Island, was the focal point for tern "harvesting" by the millinery trade. Hundreds of roseates nested on Goose Island in the early 1880s, but the colony was almost eliminated by a "taxidermist" in 1884. Falkner Island is now the nesting site for most of the common and roseate terns along the Connecticut coast and is one of the most important roseate tern breeding colonies in the United States. Most other islands in Long Island Sound no longer provide suitable nesting places. Thus, Falkner Island must be given maximum protection. The island is a valuable tern nesting habitat primarily due to its proximity to feeding areas and to the lack of mammalian predators or competing gulls.

In 1978, a long term study began of the common and roseate terns nesting on Falkner Island. About 1800 pairs were reported in 1981. The first three years of the study were devoted to the establishment of baseline data. The refinement of field techniques minimized the disturbing effect of the study to the extent that the colony of terns has adjusted to the presence of field workers and accepts the research activities without apparent agitation. In 1981, Dr. Jeffrey A. Spendelow responded to the growing concern over the decline of the roseate tern population by organizing an intensive study of the factors affecting the species' breeding success. Currently the research suggests that the population can be increased through feasible habitat modification. This research will continue and expand to include chick growth and chick mortality.

The project has been supported in the past by the Audubon Society, the Little Harbor Laboratory, and the New Haven Bird Club. The research program operates with limited funding and logistic support and depends primarily on volunteers to help out. Cash contributions are needed any time to help defray the cost of assistance, materials and supplies. Contributions, which are fully deductible, may be sent to:

Falkner Island Tern Project
c/o Little Harbor Laboratory, Inc.
69 Andrews Road
Guilford, CT 06437
(203) 453-3361

Description of the Light

Falkner Island Lighthouse stands at the center of a long, narrow island five miles south of Guilford, Connecticut in Long Island Sound. It consists of an octagonal-plan masonry tower, presently painted white, surmounted by a 16-sided lantern. Other buildings remaining on the site include a masonry powerhouse, built for fog signal apparatus in 1903, a wood frame boat house, and an observation shelter used by naturalists to monitor the colonies of roseate and common terns which breed on the island. A riprap breakwater curves west and south from the shoreward side of the island to shelter the boat landing and dock area. Of other buildings, only ruins remain: an old fog-signal house north of the light tower; the 1871 keeper's dwelling adjacent to the tower on the south, which was destroyed by fire in 1976; and a nearby privy.

Laid in courses of regular height, the walls of the light taper from a diameter of 16' 9" at the base to a diameter of 9' 9" at the top. the tower measures 36' 8" in height. The bottom course of blocks measures 4' 6" in depth, while the top course measures 18" in depth.

The 16-sided cast iron lantern room, 7' 6" in diameter, contains 32 glass panes, arranged in two ranks within the top two-thirds of its side walls. Each pane measures 18" by 24" while similarly sized cast-iron panels form the lower third of each side and contain ventilator slots in every other panel. A conical, cast-iron roof of shallow pitch covers the lantern and supports a spherical vent which is unique among Connecticut lighthouses. Resting on a bead molding above a small pointed dome, the vent is shaped like a covered pot with vertical slits below the rim, holding the top and bottom halves together. Mounted in the center of the lantern is an automated electrical lighting apparatus with a six-sided plastic lens, manufactured in Elizabeth, New Jersey. This lens replaced the fourth order fixed classical lens of six panels, made by Sauter and Co., Paris, France, which was removed to New Haven for safekeeping following the fire and mindless vandalism in March 1976. Because of repeated vandalism, the Coast Guard removed the radio direction finding beacon, relocating it to a land base at Horton Point, Long Island.

Another unique feature of this lighthouse is an external cast-iron spiral stair which connects the lantern gallery with a north-facing door on the watchroom level below.

The brick powerhouse measures 28' by 20'. Supports for the typhon horns, installed in 1932, stand outside the south wall. When built in 1903, the powerhouse housed two steam-powered fog signals. Presently, the structure serves as living quarters for the staff of naturalists conduction research on the nesting colony of terns. A wood framed boathouse with a gabled roof stands at the inshore end of the wharf in the boat landing area, probably a replacement for an earlier boathouse of similar construction. The frame bird blind at the north end of the island is of recent construction. Ruins of the older fog signal house lie north of the light tower. The site of an earlier boathouse, an early fog belltower, a workshop/barn, and oil shed, a coal bin and privy, all shown on an 1890 survey, are not readily visible.

Significance of the Lighthouse

Falkner Island Lighthouse is the second oldest lighthouse in Connecticut still under Coast Guard jurisdiction. It is significant as a later typical example of the masonry lighthouse design codified by the Treasury Department during the first half of the 19th century. It was the site of early fog-horn experiments carried out by Joseph Henry, head of the Smithsonian Institution and Chairman of the Lighthouse Board. Falkner Island was also significant for its role as a part of the on-going federal coastal aids to navigation program, dating from a time when federal financing first made possible the marking of hazards between the population centers. The external spiral stair connecting the watchroom and the lantern deck at the lighthouse appears to be a unique feature in the First Coast Guard District.

Falkner Island Light was built during the second decade of national control over lighthouse design, financed with a Congressional appropriation of $6,000 allotted from duties collected on imported goods. Governor Trumbull of Connecticut ceded the land to the United States on July 23, 1801, after the island had been purchased from Noah Stone by the federal government on May 12th of the same year for $325.00.

The builder of the lighthouse was Abishai Woodward, the designer, Jedediah Huntington. Their design of the structure follows a pattern which was prescribed in many early 19th century advertisements for lighthouse construction proposals. These advertisements were placed in newspapers by the United States Treasury Department, the federal agency responsible for building and maintaining aids to navigation at that time. Falkner Island Lighthouse was built as a tapering octagonal tower faced with hammered or edged brownstone, laid in courses, and lined with "rough stone." Wood stairs were replaced with iron in 1871.

In 1837, Warren Gates of Waterford, Connecticut and John and David Bishop of New London, Connecticut contracted to repair the light tower and enlarge the keeper's dwelling. They pointed the mortar of the light tower walls, painted the exterior of the walls with Portland cement, and applied whitewash inside and out. Repairs were made to the wood stairs and scuttle, the glass panes were re-puttied, and the lantern and lantern deck were painted black with a white cornice.

The original lantern was replaced in 1840. Within the old lantern, the lighting apparatus had consisted of 12 lamps with reflectors and eight lenses, placed around two circular tables. Sperm whale oil was used as fuel. For a cost of $2,842.00 in 1840, J.W.P. Lewis agreed to fit the new lantern with nine lamps and 16-inch reflectors. Perhaps the present lantern was installed between 1870 and 1872. In 1870, Congress passed an appropriation for rebuilding the keeper's dwelling and for installing an iron stair in the light tower. The brick wall was probably installed in 1870 as well. An inspection of the light in 1873 records a fourth order Fresnel fixed lens made by Sauter and Co., Paris, France, installed in a lantern with dimensions matching those of the one in place on the lighthouse in 1985.

Falkner Island Lighthouse is significant as the site chosen in 1865 and in 1902 for tests of different kinds of fog-signal apparatus, one of the most important fields of technological experimentation for New England coastal navigation. In 1865, Joseph Henry spent some of the his vacation setting up bells, steam whistles, reflectors, hot-air engines, etc. on Falkner Island, and during four days of observation, he and fellow scientists cruised Long Island Sound, recording the distance at which various devices could be heard. In 1879, the fog bell on Falkner Island was replaced by a first-class steam fog whistle installed in a large, gable-roofed shed to the north of the light tower. In 1902, a first-class compressed air siren, in duplicate, was installed in a new masonry engine house, which still stands south of the light tower. The siren was powered by two 16.5 horsepower oil engines. In September of that year, trials were made of the comparative range of sound, penetration of whistles, the compressed air siren and diaphone. In 1934, a Leslie typhon in duplicate was installed in the engine house.

The 1½ story wood framekeeper's dwelling erected in 1801 contained six rooms. The structure was enlarged in 1837. A three-story wood frame dwelling with eight rooms replaced the original keeper's house in 1871, remaining in use on Falkner Island for over 100 years until it was destroyed by fire on March 1976. The Coast Guard personnel stationed at the light were removed from the island thereafter. That same year the tower was sandblasted, repointed and painted. The lower windows were bricked in, a steel door and iron jamb were installed, and the Fresnel lens and pedestal were removed to New Haven for safe keeping.

The 1902 fog signal engine house south of the light tower, and a wood frame boathouse at the boat landing area on the western shore, are the only other light station structures which remain standing on the island. In addition, a wood frame observation post stands some distance north of the tower, used by researchers who are studying two species of terns, common and roseate, which have established nesting colonies on the island.

In July 1985, the island was transferred to the United States Fish and Wildlife Service by the Coast Guard, as part of the Connecticut Coastal National Wildlife Refuge which was established by Congress in October 1984. The Coast Guard retains responsibility for maintaining the light tower, the dock, and the rest of the navigational facilities.

Ironically, the presence of ornithological researchers on Falkner Island provides a limited amount of security for this historic old lighthouse from trespassers and mindless vandals. The structure could be more closely monitored than other historic lighthouses mentioned in this book.

Falkner Island Lighthouse has been nominated to be included in the National Register of Historic Places.

●

Birds and Lighthouses

Since the story of Falkner Island Lighthouse revolves mostly around its resident population of terns these days,I thought this would be a good place to discuss the age-old problem of birds and lighthouses. Since the establishment of the first lighthouse at Alexandria, Egypt, I suppose, lovers of wildlife have been saddened by the toll taken by the lights from the legions of sea birds that inhabit the coasts. Ornithologists have been baffled by the behavior of birds in the presence of a brilliant light. There are times when they seem to ignore it and fly by unaffected and unattracted by the glare. On other occasions, however, they hurl themselves against it with the utmost abandon. Weather or visibility seem to make little difference. Lightkeepers have observed large flocks of birds wheel away from a lantern on a calm, clear night and have seen similar flocks of the same species crash into it when atmospheric conditions were identical.

Neither fog, snow, rain nor wind seem to make any difference to bird mortality. Some people claim the light bewilders the birds, but close observation does not bear this out. It frequently happens that birds, particularly the smaller species, will flutter around the lantern and throw themselves against the glass like a moth against an electric globe. Fast-flying birds, like ducks and pigeons, have been observed to fold their wings as they approached a light and crash into it as if in a horizontal dive. Also birds will congregate on certain lights and ignore others. Why? No one seems to know.

When mindless vandals enter uninhabited (automated) lighthouses and break their windows (among other things), birds frequently take advantage of the situation and turn the lights into nesting places to which they return year after year. This creates a problem for the Coast Guard personnel who must service the lights from time to time. Sometimes they are attacked by the birds or slip on their droppings as they try to fulfill their responsibilities. If they try to evict the feathered tenants, they are criticized by environmental groups for disturbing the birds. There seems to be no solution to this situation as long as mindless individuals continue to trespass and destroy property which does not belong to them.

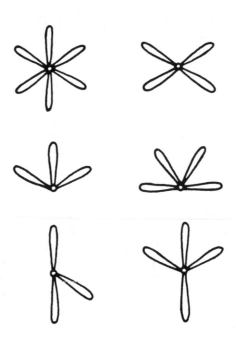

Possible beam patterns for 190 mm lantern. Orient Point Chapter 25 and Block Island North Light Chapter 29 , have this lens. See also page 253

Courtesy U.S. Coast Guard

CHAPTER 21

HORTON POINT LIGHT, Southold, NY (1857)

Old Light List No.: 154 (Obsolete)
Location: Latitude 41° 5.4′ N
Longitude 72° 26.3′ W
Height: 30′ (HAW 110′)
Range: 17 miles, Fixed White
Radio Beacon: 306 kHz, HP (. . . .   . _ _ .)
Lens: Third Order, Classical (Fresnel)
Discontinued: 1933

The entire northeastern shore of Long Island is nearly an unbroken stretch of beach from Plum Gut to Mount Sinai, a distance of 42 nautical miles. Goldsmith Inlet, Mattituck Harbor, and Wading River are only minor breaks in this long strand. Few aids to navigation are along this shore. Horton Point is the only lighthouse in this stretch of land, and it is one of the more powerful lights on Long Island Sound. It is perched on a cliff 103 feet above high tide. The light today (LLN 20185), unfortunately, is shone from a black skeleton tower with a green and white diamond-shaped day marker on a small white house on the northwest part of the Point. In has a DCB-10 lens and a 500 watt lamp and flashes green every 10 seconds. It is visible for 20 miles. A radio beacon is 72 yards south-southeast of the light (162° T): 306 kHz, HP (. . . .   . _ _ .) III, VI.

The former lighthouse tower and keeper's house (now a museum) are close by, southwest of the present light, a fact which moved President George Washington to recommend a lighthouse for the site, once known as Dead Man's Cove. The old lighthouse is no longer visible from the Sound, since trees and shrubs, left to grow wild and unattended, have grown up along the edge of the bluff and block it from view.

A rocky shoal with a least found depth of 26 feet is 1.6 miles north of Horton Point. The shoal is a ridge having a northeast-southeast direction, with abrupt shoaling on its northwest and southwest sides. From Horton Point for about 32 miles to Old Field Point, the shore is fringed with shoals that extend off a greatest distance of 1.5 miles and rise abruptly from the deep water of Long Island Sound. Boulders are found near the shore on the shoals which extend about 0.5 miles in places. A sand shoal about 0.5 mile in extent with a least depth of 26 feet is about 1.1 miles northwest of Duck Pond Point.

The bluffs begin about one mile west of Goldsmith Inlet and reach their greatest elevation just east of Duck Pond Point. A valley, formed by a break in the bluffs, is just west of the Point, and a bathing pavilion is on the beach. Boulders that bare at low water are on the shoals that fringe the shore between Duck Pond Point and Mattituck Inlet which is 6.7 miles southwest of Horton Point Light.

Barnabas Horton obviously was prepared for the worst when he landed in 1640 with an intrepid group of men on the Indian-inhabited shores of what is now the town of Southold. He even brought along his own tombstone. Horton was among the first settlers who arrived at Founder's Landing at the foot of Hobard Road in Southold Village. Later, in 1656, he was among the five freemen appointed to run the business in town. He owned the land where the lighthouse stands today. The Southold Historical Society has in its museum (located, as note earlier, in the old keeper's house adjacent to the light) collection a large oak cask which contained many of Horton's belongings when he arrived.

The leader of the founding group was the Reverend John Youngs of New Haven, Connecticut who had come to New England from his birthplace in Southwolds, England. The name of the new settlement stemmed from that name. It was known as Yennicat by the Corchaug Indians, the aboriginies from whom the land was purchased. Apparently the Indians and the settlers got along peaceably for a change, for no strife is recorded between them. The Reverend Youngs, a Puritan, and his flock came to Southold to found a town dedicated to religious freedom and established the Old First Church in 1640.

Southold and its neighbor on the south fork, Southampton, share the distinction of being the earliest English settlements on Long Island. Turpentine hunters came to Southold in 1636, making them the first English arrivals. They built a house on the site, but they did not found a settlement. New immigrants came in relatively large groups between 1730-1800, mainly of English, Welsh, Scotch, Dutch, and French Huguenot stock. The Irish arrived in the mid-1850s and, in the next 70 years, they were followed by numerous Poles and Lithuanians.

The land on which the lighthouse stands ran through from Long Island Sound to Peconic Bay. When its owner came upon hard times in 1850, the sheriff sold off eight acres of his property to Charles H. Paine and his wife Hannah for $100.00. Paine, in turn, sold it to the United States Government for $550.00 on July 24, 1855. Paine's scrimshaw walking stick is also in the permanent exhibit on display at the lighthouse museum.

Keepers of the Light
   William Sinclair June 4, 1857-April 13, 1861. Paid $400 a year
   A. J. Tillingast April 13, 1861-October 19, 1866
   Barnabas Pike October 19, 1866-April 15, 1869
   Huron W. Squires April 15, 1869-June 1, 1871
   Daniel Goldsmith June 1, 1871-February 24, 1877
   George S. Price February 24, 1877-September 10, 1896
   Robert Ebbitts September 10, 1896-May 1, 1919
   George Ehrhardt May 1, 1919-June 30, 1933

In 1877, a Civil War veteran, George S. Price, became keeper of the light and remained there until 1896. His daughter, Stella, was brought up at the light, so when her father died, she was appointed Assistant Keeper

U.S. Coast Guard Photo

Horton Point Light, Southold, NY

125

under Captain Robert Ebbitts who held the job until 1919. Eventually, Stella married and, as the saying goes, "went ashore."

On June 30, 1933, the lighthouse was decommissioned, an economy move dictated by the Depression. An automatic light with an electric eye was installed in its place, and the park district took possession of the 8.2 acre property for one dollar. The lighthouse had a brief revival during World War Two when the tower was used as a lookout for enemy aircraft. Military personnel were housed in the old building. After they departed, the vandals came as they always seem to do, removing bannisters and decorating the walls with graffiti. Doors were welded shut to keep them out, but that did not help. They pried open the doors and continued to mindlessly strip anything that could be moved. The director of the Southold Historical Society now lives on the second floor over the museum. Despite all precautions against intruders, he says attempts are still made occasionally to break in.

Restoration work on the light began in January 1976, as part of the Southold Park District's Bicentennial project. The museum and light were opened to the public for the first time early in July 1977. In the spring of 1978, the Coast Guard replaced the automatic light with an electric eye with an electronic light which is far more visible (the old light shone 14 miles, the new one, 20 miles) to ships at sea.

The ground floor of the museum has the original yellow pine flooring and the only one remaining of six fireplaces. The others were bricked up when central heating was installed in 1976. Exhibits of marine paintings are regularly featured, and the permanent display has such items of interest as a scrimshaw pie crimp, powder horn from colonial days, a whale tooth and a sawfish saw made from the bill. Also on view are lighthouse logs dating back to 1857, when the lighthouse was constructed. The museum also owns the first deed to the land on which the light was built.

Restoration of the tower of the historic lighthouse on Horton's Point continues. Broken windows are being replaced with shatter-proof glass and new iron railings have been installed on the circular staircase. Negotiations have been under way for six years for the return of the original lantern to its old place in the tower. The original light, made of French brass and glass prisms (a Fresnel lens), is in a Coast Guard storage area in Maryland whence it was taken in 1933 when the lighthouse was decommissioned. The museum attached to the light is open during July and August, Saturday and Sunday, 1-5 p.m., other times by appointment for scholars. Admission for adults is one dollar, for children, 50 cents. Funds are still needed to complete the restoration of this old lighthouse. Interested persons should contact:

The Director
Southold Historical Society
Main Road and Maple Lane
Southold, NY 11971
(516) 765-5500

CHAPTER 22

SAYBROOK BREAKWATER LIGHT, Old Saybrook, CT (1886)

Light List No.: 21435, 20155
Location: Latitude 41° 15.8′ N
Longitude 72° 20.6′ W
Height: 49′ (HAW 58′)
Range: 11 miles, Flashing Green every 6 seconds, Horn
Lens: 300 mm, 1000 watt lamp
Radio Beacon: 320 kHz, SB (. . . ___ . . .)
Automated: 1959

The first settlers of Old Saybrook noted that the sand bar at the mouth of the Connecticut River was a formidable obstacle to ships trying to enter or leave the river. This is one reason why Old Saybrook, in contrast to deep water ports like New York, New London or New Haven never became a major city. The size of vessels using the river was strictly limited to ships that, at high tide, could float over the bar. Even then, the constant shifts of sands made its crossing hazardous. In the *Light List* for 1906, mariners were warned that changes in the bar were frequent and that vessels should not attempt to cross it without a pilot.

The first official attempt to try to do something about the sandbar was in 1773. A public lottery was undertaken to finance the placing of buoys and other navigational aids, a rather paltry improvement. Finally, in 1875, the United States Governnment devised the plan of constructing two parallel breakwaters, or jetties, at the river's mouth and dredging a deep channel between them. It hoped the breakwaters would resist the shifting sands and thus keep the channel open. The west jetty was completed in 1875, but the east jetty was not finished until almost five years later. Since then, many additional tons of rock have been added. In the early days, no flat stones were placed on top of the breakwater to make walking easier. The rocks were simply placed at all angles and one needed the agility of a mountain goat to climb over them.

On August 7, 1882, Congress made a $20,000 appropriation for the erection of "a beacon light at the west jetty wall at Saybrook Bar on the mouth of the Connecticut River where it empties into Long Island Sound." The Lighthouse Board, governing body of lighthouse operations at that time, had requested almost twice that amount of money. Consequently, construction of the new lighthouse was delayed a few years until adequate funds were appropriated. Finally, on Tuesday, June 15, 1886, Saybrook Breakwater Light, popularly known as the "Outer Light," began operation.

In 1886, when the Outer Light went into service, it is possible that kerosene was used at the light. However, it soon began to be powered by wet batteries, 54 of them. It still used wet batteries when Laureat Le Clerc became keeper in 1954. In the old days, the lighthouse was equipped with a huge, 1000 pound bell that tolled out a thunderous warning to fog-bound sailors. The sound of this great bell was no doubt very comforting to mariners groping their way through dirty weather. However, the residents of the area complained about the noise it made, so the bell was replaced by a smaller 250 pounder, later also removed.

The Outer Light was once equipped with a diaphram horn run by an air compressor diesel engine. On foggy days and nights, the horn's deep bellow was quite thrilling and as comforting as an old friend to many residents within earshot. It was replaced in 1973 by an electronic whistle that tooted. Apparently, the whistle was easier to maintain and operate and was as efficient as the horn. However, the whistle was replaced eventually, and today the light again has a horn.

In April 1890, the schooner "Bella" of Wading River, Long Island, collided with a steamship off the Saybrook Breakwater Light. She wound up on the rocks off Greenport, Long Island. Although no lives were lost, the "Bella" and her cargo of farm produce were a total loss.

Description of the Light

Saybrook Breakwater Lighthouse marks a sandbar on the west side of the entrance to the Connecticut River, and a much shallower and more extensive bar east of the entrance. Presently painted white, the cast-iron tower stands at the south end of the Saybrook west jetty. The lighthouse is located southeast of the village of Old Saybrook near the older Lynde Point Lighthouse. Access by foot is not very difficult. The light is easy to pick up in any kind of weather, because it has a horn, a low-powered radio beacon for direction finders (320 kc) and a strong light.

The light's construction resembles that of Greens Ledge (Chapter 8) and Peck Ledge (Chapter 9) lighthouses consisting of a lantern, watchroom, four main floors and a basement. The structure is built on top of a cylindrical cast-iron caisson filled with concrete. Unlike other lighthouses, the main gallery has retained its roof and a fair amount of its original material has been preserved.

The foundation consists of a cylinder 30 feet in diameter and 32 feet high, composed of cast-iron plates bolted together through flanges cast on the inside edges. Assembled nearby, the cylinder was transported to the site and lowered through 17 feet of water onto a sand and ground surface. Riprap was deposited around it, while concrete was used to fill the bottom and perimeter, leaving a central cavity for the cistern and basement area. A corrugated profile was cast into the inner surface of the iron plates, presumably as a stabilizing factor for the concrete fill. Brick lining for the basement incorporates brick walls around the cistern in the northeast quadrant.

The 49' high light tower tapers from an interior diameter of 21' at the top of the first story to 10' 2" at the watchroom level. A brick lining, 12"

Saybrook Breakwater Light, Old Saybrook, CT

Photo by Julius M. Wilensky

thick at the bottom and 8 " thick at the top, insulates and stabilizes the bottom three stories of the tower.

A cylindrical cast-iron watchroom rests atop the fourth story, supporting the 12-sided cast-iron lantern above. The cast-iron plates of the tower are one story each in height and overlap the plate below in a semi-circular ridge. On the northeast facade is an elliptically arched entrance. Above the entrance is a plate with the inscription "G.W. and F. Smith Iron Co., Boston Mass." On the interior of the light, only structured elements remain from the period prior to automation in 1968.

The 12″ brick lining on the first story was utilized for round-arched niches for storage purposes. Additional storage was provided on upper floors in closets and cupboards fitted into the space between the brick lining and the interior metal staircase wall. All of the windows in the lighthouse have been boarded up as precaution against the encroachment of mindless vandals.

The lantern is decogonal in plan, the upper half of its walls containing rectangular panes of glass. The *Light List* for 1906 noted that the lighthouse had a fourth order white light visible for 13 miles, and a fixed red sector between E ⅝ N and ESE ⅜ E. The present lighting apparatus is electrified and automated. It replaced an earlier incandescent oil-vapor lamp which, in 1917, replaced the 17-light oil wick lamp noted above.

Keepers of the Light
Frank Parmelee (acting) - appointed June 2, 1886 at $540 year.
   His salary was increased to $560 year on November 1, 1888.
   Eventually he was transferred to another light.
John G. Shipworth - appointed March 29, 1890 at $560 year. He was born in England and eventually resigned from the service.
George W. Fife - appointed on August 26, 1896 at a salary of $560 year. He was born in Scotland and also resigned from the service. Fife served in the U.S. Navy.
Robert S. Bishop - appointed March 23, 1897 at $560 year. Eventually he was transfered elsewhere.
Nathaniel Dodge - appointed May 26, 1898 at $560 year. He was transferred.
Thomas Bunker - appointed on June 22, 1898 at $560 year. He was born in Ireland and served in the U.S. Navy. He was transferred too.
John Dahlman - appointed October 15, 1899 at $560 year. He was born in Germany.
Sidney Gross - keeper in 1938; appointed - ?

Notes from a Keeper's Log
Landlubbers who think that the waters of Long Island Sound are gentle and not to be feared, because the long arm of Long Island lies between it and the Atlantic Ocean, are sadly mistaken as anyone who has sailed the Sound knows. The coast of Connecticut is frequently lashed by

storms and hammered by destructive seas. The famous hurricane of 1938, which did unprecedented damage on Long Island and in New England, slammed onto the Connecticut shore and did severe damage along the Connecticut River all the way to Springfield, Mass. Bound to live forever among lighthouse logs are the entries of Keeper Sidney Gross who kept a running record of the storm. His notes are here reproduced in part:

"At 2 p.m. on the afternoon of September 21, a light southeast breeze sprung up from a perfect calm. At 2:15 p.m. it became so hazy that it was necessary to start sounding the fog signal. By 3 p.m. it was blowing a gale, and I was unable to step outside the engine room door, the only door through which we can enter of leave the building. I made several attempts to get outside to save some of the small articles on the platform, part of them not being lashed down, but I found it impossible, as the wind pushed me right back into the engine room. Assistant Keeper Bennett also made an attempt to get out and save some of the gasoline for the engines, but the velocity of the wind had been increasing every minute, and we were absolutely helpless as far as saving anything outside the tower was concerned.

"The tide was coming in, and the waters of Long Island Sound and the Connecticut River were becoming tougher every minute. The fog signal was being sounded continuously. At 3:30 p.m. the water level almost reached the platform, and at that time the gasoline drum and the bridge to the breakwater were carried away. The wind then shifted from the southeast to the southwest, and the water pounded still harder. At 4 p.m. the platform encircling the outside of the tower was torn from its fastenings and carried away with everything on it, including a 12′ rowboat.

"By this time the water was so high outside that it backed into the cistern through the overflow pipe, spoiling all our drinking water. Dozens of rocks, weighing several tons, were carried away from the breakwater and from around the tower. Some of them were moved as much as 60 feet from their original locations. The wind was so strong that it carried away the tops of the combers in the spray, so that we could hardly see more than 25 or 30′ from the station. At 4:30 p.m., the 1500 gallon oil tank, which was full of kerosene, was carried away. At almost the same time, the 600 gallon oil tank was lifted out of its cradle and carried away.

"At 5 p.m. the water level was about even with the deck, just a few inches below the engine room floor. As the wind shifted, the waves started to pound at the two fog horns and the south window of the engine room. Assistant Keeper Bennett and myself boarded up the window as best we could, but at 5 p.m. the waves were pounding so hard that all the boards were torn out and the glass was smashed in. Tons of sea water started to pour into the engine room. We made other attempts to board up the opening, but the water was too powerful. During these efforts, a great wave came through the window, carrying the sash and the board with it . . .

"I could not ring the bell, as it was impossible to get out on the bell deck; if I had gotten out, I would have been promptly swept overboard. At sunset I disconnected the electric light fixtures and installed the incandescent oil vapor lamp. The lens was shaking so badly that I expected it to fall of the pedestal and break to pieces. I started up the oil vapor lamp, but the mantle collapsed from the vibrations as soon as they were put in place. I then removed the oil vapor lamp and put in a fourth order oil wicklamp. The vibrations were so great and the draft from the wind so strong that I had to stay up there with the light the whole night to see that it did not smoke up or go out altogether.

"At 6 p.m. the water was pouring through the second story window in the hall. I boarded up the window with the doors of a small cabinet and what loose material I could find. At this time I could hear the battery house being broken up. Seven of the batteries and my outboard motor were carried away. Everything outside the building was now carried away, and I certainly did not expect to see another sunrise as the whole structure was shaking under the violent pounding. When daylight came at last, what we saw seemed more like a dream than reality. There was nothing around the tower. Everything was gone except the battery house and even that was badly out of shape . . ."

Significance of the Light

Saybrook Breakwater Lighthouse is significant as an early example of the cone-shaped, prefabricated cast-iron lighthouses which dominated the new construction of the Lighthouse Board in the old Third Coast Guard District from 1881 until the second decade of the 20th century. Minor variations in detailing distinguished succeeding models of conical cast-iron lighthouses. Saybrook Breakwater Lighthouse represents the first phase of development. The light is significant also as an integral part of the late 19th century campaign to improve aids to navigation on Long Island Sound, marking a hazardous bar at the mouth of the Connecticut River.

Saybrook Breakwater Lighthouse stands on a breakwater only 1½ miles from Lynde Point Lighthouse, a land-based masonry tower established in 1803 to mark the west side of the entrance to the Connecticut River. The challenge of marking waterbound hazards to navigation had been met in the first few decades of federal control through the deployment of buoys and lightships. For many years there was a lightship off Cornfield Point to the west , both to serve as a marker for the point, and for Long Sand Shoal. A buoy was approved by Congress on March 3, 1831 to mark Saybrook Bar at the mouth of the Connecticut River. However, this was inadequate for the increased maritime traffic in Long Island Sound after the Civil War.

The technology required to build an adequate lighthouse foundation from cast-iron for underwater sites where ice floes were a danger during the winter months was well developed by the late 1870s. At that time, Major George H. Elliott, Engineer-Secretary of the United States Lighthouse Board, designed a tubular cast-iron lighthouse foundation to be prefabri-

132

cated in curved sections and assembled near the site. This design was a major accomplishment in the history of North American lighthouse engineering. The earliest known use of this type of foundation was at Southwest Ledge Light, near New Haven, Connecticut in 1877 (Chapter 19). Saybrook Breakwater Light was one of the early structures which resulted from this development.

In 1883, an inadequate appropriation was made for a lighthouse for the Saybrook "Bar." An additional appropriation was requested and approved. The subfoundation on the sand and gravel bottom was finished in 1885, and an iron tubular foundation 32 feet high and 30 feet in diameter was bolted together and sunk into place in 17 feet of water. The foundation followed the design worked out by Major Elliott. Curved, cast-iron plates of identical dimensions were bolted together to make rings, or courses, by means of wrought iron bolts attached through flanges cast into the inner edges of the plates. The cast-iron rings were then bolted together vertically before being submerged onto the subfoundation. Concrete made with Portlant cement was used to fill the foundation, leaving a cavity at the top for the basement and cistern of the superstructure.

The lighthouse superstructure has a truncated cone configuration, made of five courses, or rings, of curved cast-iron plates, which, like the foundation, were flanged to facilitate a bolted assembly. It was fabricated by the G.W. and F. Smith Iron Co., Boston, Mass. A lining of brick was installed, which supports the outer edge of a peripheral cast-iron winding stair and five cast-iron landings. Saybrook Breakwater Light represents an early example of this stairway design, which was continued in later lighthouses of this configuration into the 20th century. Closets built into the brick lining on the first or living room story were fitted with shelves and drawers in a unique manner. On the kitchen, bedroom and radio room levels, the storage space is fitted above and below the stairs as closets and cupboards. Openings for the windows and the entrance door have the segmented arches and cast-iron trim typical of the first phase of cast-iron lighthouse development. By June 15, 1886, the pier, superstructure and lantern were completed, and the light was first exhibited on that date. Riprap was placed around the site for protection up to the level of the high water mark.

Fog-signal equipment was supplied in 1889, at which time Saybrook Breakwater Light took over the fog-warning function from Lynde Point Light, 1½ miles north. In 1890, a fourth-order Fresnel lens was fitted, replacing the original fifth-order lens. Six years later, a Gamewell fog bell striking machine was approved for the lighthouse. In 1917, a 17 wick oil lamp was converted to an incandescent oil vapor lamp. Since 1958, the fog-signal has been operated by remote control. At that time, Coast Guard personnel from Saybrook Breakwater Light lived at Lynde Point and stood watch only during inclement weather.

Saybrook Breakwater Lighthouse has been nominated to be included in the National Register of Historic Places.

CHAPTER 23

LYNDE POINT LIGHT, Old Saybrook, CT (1803)

Light List No.: 21455
Location: Latitude 41° 16.3' N
Longitude 72° 20.6' W
Height: 71'
Range: 13 miles, Fixed White
Lens: Fifth Order Classical, 1000 watt lamp
Rebuilt: 1838
Automated: Summer 1975

On April 6, 1802, Congress authorized the construction of a "sufficient lighthouse to be erected at Lynde's Point, at the mouth of the Connecticut River," and on November 3rd, the United States Government purchased from William Lynde a small piece of land (116 rods) on Lynde Point. The price was $225, and the deed included a right of access across the Lynde farm. The purchase involved the passing of a resolution by the Connecticut State Legislature ceding to the federal government the state's jurisdiction over the land at the end of Lynde Point. This was done in May 1802 and signed into law on November 29th by Governor Jonathan Trumbull.

No time was wasted in beginning construction of a lighthouse. On Tuesday, November 30, 1802, Jedekiah Huntington, collector of the port of New London and supervisor of lighthouses in the state, executed a contract. Abishai Woodward, a master carpenter from New London, was hired to build a wooden lighthouse. The structure was to be 35 feet high, 20 feet in diameter at the base and eight feet in diameter at the top. It was to be surmounted by an iron, whale-oil lantern, six feet, ten inches in diameter and and seven feet, three inches high. The foundation was to be of stone and the building of pine covered with shingles. The contract called for a total payment of $2,200. There was a house already on the property which was to serve as the lightkeeper's dwelling. The lighthouse was first lighted on Wednesday evening, August 17, 1803.

On March 3, 1832, Congress appropriated $5,000 to remove the original wooden lighthouse and to build the present structure which local residents call the "Inner Light." As no bids were received within the appropriation, the matter was deferred until July 1838, when Congress made an additional appropriation of $2,500. Evidently there was some confusion about specifications, and the contract was let, jointly, to the three lowest bidders on August 18, 1838: Jonathan Scranton, Volney Pierce and John Wilcox, all from Madison, Connecticut. The contract was signed by I.W. Crawford, Superintendent of Lighthouses for the New London District.

The structure was to be completed by December 1, 1838. It was to be built of granite, 25 feet in diameter at the base, graduated to 12 feet in diameter at the top. The walls were to be five feet thick at the base and grad-

Lynde Point Light, Old Saybrook, CT

uated to two feet at the top. The old wood structure was to be moved 50 feet to the south until the new structure was completed so that there would be no interruption in the light. A new house was also constructed as a home for the lighthouse keeper and his family.

The fuel originally used to illuminate the Inner Light was whale oil. On August 25, 1879, kerosene was substituted. No one has recorded exactly when electricity first began to be used by the Inner Light, even though electricity was introduced into the borough of Fenwick where the lighthouse is located in 1915. However, apparently it had been substituted for kerosene by the time George Sheffield was the keeper. In 1958, the Connecticut Light and Power Company began providing electrical service to the light for certain. In the old days, the light was equipped with a bell used as a warning to fog-bound mariners. At one time it also had a fog horn.

In passing, it should be noted that the borough of Fenwick, in which the lighthouse is located, is an exclusive summer community which is a local historic district itself. Twenty or so years ago, land (if you could get it) went for $50,000 an acre, and the houses (if you could get one) began at $100,000. Katherine Hepburn, the well-known actress, has had a summer home there for years.

A Description of the Light

Lynde Point Lighthouse, erected in 1838, is located on the west side of the entrance to the Connecticut River on the northern shore of Long Island Sound. It replaced an earlier octagonal wood-framed light built on the same site in 1803. The present octagonal light tower, painted white, supports a cylindrical, grey cast-iron lantern, fitted with 12 glass panels and capped by an ogee iron roof presently painted red. To the west of the light tower are the ruins of the old keeper's dwelling, demolished in 1966. A modern building is located immediately to the north.

The three builders in 1838 were given a choice of using split granite or freestone in their construction of the light. Their choice of brownstone resulted in carefully dressed blocks laid in pseudisodomic patterns, described in the contract as "regular courses of stretches and headers" by laying up walls of alternative courses of two different heights of carefully dressed and fitted ashlar blocks. According to the contract, walls were laid in lime mortar, the points, "thoroughly painted with Roman or hydraulic cement" and the exterior and interior given two coats of whitewash. The most striking feature of the interior is the wood spiral stair, supported by a central mast 11 inches in diameter and faceted into 16 sides.

The concrete base for a fog-signal bell stands opposite the southeast face of the light tower near the perimeter of the property, while a seawall of large, coursed stone blocks protects the site. Built 36 years after the two other early masonry towers in Connecticut, New London Harbor (1801) and Falkner's Island (1802), Lynde Point Light possesses the finest masonry work of the three. Inscribed at midpoint on the southeast face of the tower is the date: "A.D. 1838" (or 1839; the last numeral has been partly obscured by repainting). This inscription, crude and uncentered, seems to have been a later addition.

Centered on the lantern deck and bolted to it, is the cylindrical cast-iron lantern room, seven feet, three inches in diameter. The upper half of the existing lantern contains 12 panes of glass set in iron mullions, each pane measuring two feet by three feet, two and one-half inches. The lower half of the lantern consists of six curved cast-iron sections, unlined and bolted together on the inside.

A fixed fifth order Fresnel lens, one of the only two such lenses in Connecticut is mounted in the lantern atop a cast-iron pedestal. The other one was located in Black Rock Harbor Light, Bridgeport [Chapter 14], before it was discontinued and removed in 1932. Built in 1881 by Barbier and Fenestre of Paris, France, it replaced the original fourth order lens in 1890. In 1988, the classical lens may be removed and an optic of greater intensity installed.

The earlier keeper's dwelling, demolished in 1966, was replaced by a tasteless masonry duplex dwelling of contemporary vernacular design. Hopefully, this building will be torn down in the near future, since its presence strongly detracts from this historic site. A barn, an oil house, and a privy reported to have stood on the site in 1936 no longer remain.

Keepers of the Light

From 1803 to 1973, many keepers lived in the two Saybrook lighthouses. Sad to say, no official records seem to have been kept memorializing these men and their often equally heroic wives who did so much to guard the lives of the mariners of their day. The Inner Light always included a family residence, so wives and children are necessarily part of the lore of that beacon. On the other hand, it was generally the custom to have a strong, young bachelor at the Outer Light. All we know about these keepers is fragmentary:

Daniel Whittlesey - an early keeper of the Inner Light. For several years after his death, his widow, the mother of several young children, tended the light singlehanded.

Henry Clark - another early keeper.

James Rankin - a former silk weaver from Glasgow, Scotland, came with his bride to seek his fortune in this country. He was a careful oberver of of his surroundings and kept minute records of weather conditions and bird migrations. Rankin was appointed keeper on July 21, 1852 at an annual salary of $350; the sum was increased to $400 on July 31, 1853. Keepers were paid monthly which meant that Rankin received $29.17 and then $33.33 a month for his services.

Richard Ingham - probably a local man, since his name is very prominent in the area.

Elmer Gildersleeve - Came from Portland, Connecticut. Probably was in charge of both the Inner and Outer Lights between 1880 and 1915. His wife was a very kind woman, the mother of ten children. She often used to clean cottages in nearby Fenwick before and after the summer season to earn extra money for her family. One evening, Captain Gildersleeve became very ill. Dr. Thomas Hepburn rushed him to the Hartford Hispital, but the Captain died before help could be given to him. Mrs. Gildersleeve retired to Old Saybrook with her children.

George E. Sheffield - a fairly recent keeper. He was in charge of both the Inner and Outer Light.

Captain Wolf - his name is remembered, but there are no records about his tenure at the light.

William Chapel - a recent keeper.

Norman Boyd - born in 1915 in Broken Bow, Nebraska. Joined the Coast Guard in 1936; retired in 1957. Boyd served as keeper for only two years, 1952-1954. Thereafter. he was stationed on a lightship. Hale and hearty at 71 years, he still lives with his wife in Old Saybrook, one of the few living keepers I know.

Laureat Le Clerc - served from 1954 to 1970. The last civil service keeper, he lived in the little old house at the Inner Light with his wife. Although the Coast Guard assumed management of all United States lighthouses in 1939, it waited for the old civil service keepers to retire before it moved in its own men. Captain Le Clerc began his career when he was 12 years old by working for his uncle who ran the lighthouse in the St. Lawrence River, Quebec, Canada. He ended his career by working 15 years at Lynde Point and Saybrook Breakwater Lighthouses. When he retired at 69 years, he was the oldest lighthouse keeper in the United States. His hobby was repairing clocks.

Significance of the Light

Lynde Point Lighthouse is significant as a carefully crafted, typical example of the masonry lighthouse tower built in the first half of the 19th century to specifications of the U.S. Treasury Department. Containing a well-preserved wood spiral stair of early date, which is unique for Connecticut lighthouses, Lynde Point exhibits superior stone work in its tapering brownstone walls. Although there are three other early masonry lighthouses in Connecticut, New Haven Harbor Light (1801), Falkner Island Light (1802) and New London Harbor (rebuilt 1801), Lynde Point Light's construction is the best documented. Two advertisements for construction proposals survive, containing the government's specifications and a construction contract. Lynde Point Light also is significant as part of the federal government's early efforts to improve aids to navigation in Long Island Sound when the mouths of important harbors and rivers were among the first sites chosen for lighthouse appropriations. Lynde Point Light marked the mouth of the Connecticut River.

In April 1837, the federal government published in the Connecticut newspapers advertisements for proposals from contractors to build a granite or freestone light tower, 45 feet high with the stipulation that the old lighthouse was not to be dismantled, but was to be moved a short distance away and was to continue in operation while the replacement tower was under construction at the old site. In addition, alternate proposals for a 65-ft. high tower were requested, the builder to receive the old lighthouse, its lantern, lamps and reflectors as partial payment.

Pierce, Scranton and Wilcox, the builders who won the contract, eventually built an octagonal masonry tower 65 feet high. On top of the tower, six stories high, the octagonal wrought iron lantern rested with 28 panes of best quality Boston glass, 10 inches by 12 inches, set in iron racks on each side. Cooper panels with sliding ventilators filled the lower part of each lantern wall. A cooper sheathed dome, formed of 16 iron rafters, roofed the lantern.

At the end of the Civil War, a Congressional appropriation was used to repair and renovate the Lynde Point Lighthouse. In 1867 and 1868, the *Annual Report* of the Lighthouse Board records the intention to remove the wood shutters and stairs in the lighthouse, which were rotten, and to replace them with iron ones. A brick lining wall was to be built at the same time. However, the present stairs are of wood, in good condition and constructed with cut nails. The brick lining wall was never installed. It seems likely that the present wood stairs date from the 1868 period of renovation. No record of a later stair construction appears in the annual reports of the Lighthouse Board during the period when cut nails were still in use. The lantern was to be repaired, and an iron deck plate for the lantern was to be installed at this time. The sea wall, built in 1856, was repaired and suitable buildings constructed, including both a coal and a wood house.

Lighting apparatus for the 1839 lighthouse at Lynde Point consisted of ten patent lamps and ten reflectors. Each reflector was 14 inches in diameter and contained six ounces of pure silver in its coating. The United States Treasury Department advertised for someone to supply this equipment at Lynde Point. The fitting out formerly had been a monopoly of Winslow Lewis, inventor of the patent lamp system. Although the Lewis lamp system had been outdated for more than a decade, since the vastly superior Fresnel lamp (first order) had been first placed in the famous lighthouse at Cordouan at the mouth of the Gironde River, France in 1822. The 1839 Lynde Point tower was constructed three years before the first Fresnel lens was installed in the United States lighthouses at Navesink, New Jersey. At Lynde Point, the ten lamps were still in place in 1850. It was not until 1852 that the Lighthouse Board began to reject Mr. Lewis's intensive lobbying efforts and began to replace all reflectors with the more efficient (and expensive) imported French Fresnel lenses. Lynde Point received a fourth order lens.

Lynde Point's importance as an aid to navigation is reflected in the activity and funds involved in trying to upgrade the fog-signal apparatus there during the second half of the 19th century. The record of fog-signal apparatus at Lynde Point begins with an $800 appropriation in 1850. In 1854, a fog-bell was established for $1,000. The machine for striking the fog-bell was completed in 1856. During the renovation program of 1867, part of the appropriation was for a more efficient fog signal to take the place of the old fog bell. In 1874, the bell was rehung and its striking apparatus was installed. Again in 1883, a new fog-bell striking apparatus was introduced.

The original keeper's dwelling with a frame kitchen addition dating from 1833, was joined to the lighthouse. In 1858, a gambrel-roofed, 1½ story wood-frame keeper's house was ornamented with Gothic Revival elements, including a cross gable with pointed arch windows (later made rectangular) and a central chimney with recessed panels. Physical evidence of a gable-roofed wing connecting the dwelling and the lighthouse remains on the west side of the tower. Photographic evidence suggests that the wing was part of the earlier dwelling. This historic and charming old 1858 dwelling was demolished, and replaced in 1966 by an incongruous contemporary high veneer and siding duplex residence to the north of the light tower. Currently it houses Coast Guard families. The duplex was built despite outcries from the Old Saybrook Historical Society. It does not in any way contribute to the historical significance of the site; conversely, its presence greatly detracts from it. The foundation of the old keeper's dwelling remains, while evidence of the oil house and privy is minimal.

Fortunately, Lynde Point Lighthouse has been recommended for inclusion in the National Register of Historic Places. Some consider Lynde Point the most beautiful lighthouse in Long Island Sound.

Entrance to Connecticut River. Saybrook Breakwater Light in foreground.
Lynde Point Light on shore

140

Photo by Julius M. Wilensky

CHAPTER 24

PLUM ISLAND LIGHT, Plum Island NY (1827)

Old Light List No.: 146 (Obsolete)
Location: Latitude 41° 10.1' N
Longitude 72° 12.2' W
Height: 34' (HAW 63')
Range: 14 miles
Lens: Fourth Order, Revolving
Rebuilt: 1869
Discontinued: June 1, 1978

When Plum Island Light was discontinued, Plum Gut Light (LLN 937.50) was established to replace it. Orient Point Light (LLN 940), operated from New London, was upgraded at the same time to compensate for the loss of this historic 158 year-old lighthouse which marked the treacherous Plum Gut waters for so many years. However, with its 350,000 candlepower and range of 14 miles, the old light in its heyday was more powerful than Plum Gut Light and Orient Point Light combined. Now it stands like a gaunt specter oblivious to its glorious past.

In its day, Plum Island Light was a leading beacon to vessels passing up and down Long Island Sound and was useful to mariners sailing into Gardiner's Bay, either from the east or through the narrow passage between Plum Island and Oysterman's Point on Long Island. Discontinuing Plum Island Light is part of a nationwide Coast Guard move to eliminate manned lighthouses for economic reasons. Citizens sent in few letters of protest to the Coast Guard when it announced the closing of the light. Apparently the sailing public was content with the two substitute lights.

Plum Island is located 110 miles east of New York City, about 10 miles from Connecticut, and about 1.5 nautical miles from the northeastern end of Long Island. The island is slightly more than 840 acres (1.3 square miles); it is 2.9 miles long and is 1.7 miles wide at its western end. About two miles west of Great Gull Island, Plum Island is hilly and bare of trees, except near the southwest end, and has several large buildings (more of which later), a prominent tank and flagpole. The island is a federal government (Agriculture Department) reservation and is closed to the public.

Plum Gut Harbor, on the southwest side of Plum Island, has an entrance between jetties with private seasonal lights on dolphins off the outer ends. The lights are shown daily from sundown to 0130. A private fog signal at the west jetty light is sounded occasionally when Department of Agriculture vessels are navigating in the area. A depth of about 14 feet is in the entrance. Small yachts seeking shelter in an emergency may lie along the wharves. The harbor is under the supervision of the Department of Agriculture and the Coast Guard and may be used only with permission.

Plum Island was anciently known as the "Isle of Patmos." Later, explorers observed many beach plums growing along its shores and a new name, "Plum Island," was subsequently accepted. The island was occupied by the Circhug tribe of Indians who owed allegiance to the Montauk tribe and who recognized Wyandanck, Sachem or the Montauk tribe, as the Grand Sachem of Paumanake, or Long Island. The first written deed read:

> Know all men by these presents that I, Wyandanck, the Montauk Sachem, for me and my heirs forever, for and in consideration of a coat, a barrel of biskitt, 100 muxes (iron drills Indians used to make wampum beads from different shells) or fish hooks, at these subscribing by mee, received of Samuel Wyllys and his heirs forever; I, the said Sachem, hereby declare myself to bee the rightful owner of the sayd Island and I covenant with the said Samuel Wyllys, his heirs and assigns, that I will never molest him or his assigns in the possession of same and will prohibit my men from doing so, by killing any of his cattle that shall bee put upon it. And for the true performance hereof, I have set my hand at Gadiner's Island, April 27, 1659.
>
> (Signed) Wyandanck
> His X Mark

For two centuries, Plum Island was owned privately and used for farming and raising sheep. The original deed to the land on which the lighthouse now stands belonged to Richard Jerome and his wife. They sold three acres of their property for $90 to the United States Government on August 29, 1826, and the Government promptly began constructing a lighthouse on the site. One of the early keepers was William Boothe who was appointed on May 19, 1853 at an annual salary of $350.00. In his *Annual Reports,* the inspector of lighthouses had the following to say about Plum Isalnd Light:

1868. 121. Both the tower and keeper's dwelling are in bad condition and should be rebuilt. The tower, built in 1827, leaks badly; the masonry is soft and crumbling; the lantern is of the old pattern and with small lights and large astragals, and it leaks badly. It is thought that the old buildings are not worth the money which would be required to put them in good order, and it is therefore proposed to rebuild them. . . .

The light was subsequently rebuilt in 1869/70.

1878. 158. The slate roof of the dwelling house at this station, which leaked badly, has been replaced by a shingle roof, and no further leaks have been reported. The fog bell has been raised about ten feet higher on the bell frame where it is believed it will be better heard in fogs and storms.

Lt. George M. Bache, USN, was an early lighthouse inspector. He wrote many annual reports (but not this one) on the lights until at least 1838.

Plum Island Light, Plum Island, NY

Students of lighthouses will find his reports worth reading. Bache wrote practically all of the early reports.

Like other nearby islands, Plum Island was often the stopping place for the tall ships that sailed along the Atlantic coast and eventually became part of the observation system established to protect Long Island Sound and New York Harbor. The United States Government bought the entire island in the 1890s and established Fort Terry, a coast artillery post. The island was considered important to the defense of Long Island during the Spanish-American War. It was used also as a training camp for young recruits in World War I and World War II. During World War II, the Army built the Plum Island Rail Road (now defunct) to move submarine mines to and from boats. The island was assigned to the Army Chemical Corps after the second world war.

In 1950, your editor hiked across Plum Island from the northeast bight to the lighthouse to obtain aid from the Coast Guard to tow our disabled centerboard sloop through Plum Gut to Orient Point where we could get repairs. I found remnants of Fort Terry, and the three Coast Guardsmen had landscaped their lighthouse beautifully with flowers and nice lawn all around. I spent a couple of hours there with one of the men. The other two had taken their boat to Greenport for supplies. On their return, they towed us through Plum Gut, which was having one of its bad days. After the Agriculture Department took it over, they used some of the disarmed gun emplacements for cattle pens. While I appreciate the need for economy, the Coast Guard's Search and Rescue capabilities have certainly been hurt by lighthouse automation. Private and other public rescue operations have sprung up all over the Sound to take up the slack.

On July 1, 1954, Plum Island was formally transferred to the United States Department of Agriculture to establish a laboratory to study hoof-and-mouth disease and other exotic diseases of economically important domestic animals. A new, high-containment laboratory was opened in 1956. Since then, diagnostic, research, and training programs at Plum Island Animal Disease Center have been extended to cover many foreign animal diseases. No visitors are allowed on the island. About 350 people are employed at the Center, most of whom commute daily from Orient Point. From the Sound, substantial buildings are visible as you sail by the west shore or the northwest shore.

Persons wishing to send samples collected for diagnostic evaluation or other materials known to contain infectious micro-organisms should first contact:

Director, PIADC
P.O. Box 848
Greenport, NY 11944-1298

The preferred method of submitting samples to the Plum Island Animal Disease Center is to hand-carry them. If this is not possible, arrangements should be made to ship via nonstop (or at least the same plane) service to New York. But contact the director first!

CHAPTER 25

ORIENT POINT LIGHT, Orient Point, NY (1899)

Light List No.: 20135
Location: Latitude 41° 9.8' N
          Longitude 72° 13.4' W
Height: 64'
Range: 15 miles, Flashing White every 5 seconds, Horn
Lens: 190 mm, 2.03 amps
Automated: 1966

Orient Point Lighthouse (known affectionately as the "Coffee Pot" by locals) is cirular-plan, cast-iron tower on a concrete-filled, cast-iron foundation. A beacon on the tip of Long Island since 1899, the light is painted brown at the top of the tower and white at the bottom. Besides the lighthouse, the site includes two riprap (stones thrown together without order to prevent erosion) breakwaters which form a protected approach south of the tower, a concrete dock, and the riprap shoring which encircles the foundation.

The lighthouse marks the western end of Plum Gut, a channel which connects Long Island Sound with Gardiners Bay and points south, east and west, and overlooks Plum Island to the east. Orient Point, so named in 1836, because it was the most easterly tip of the North Fork peninsula of Long Island, lies to the southwest of the light. The meeting of waters converging from several directions produces violent and potentially dangerous currents to the unwary in Plum Gut. Currents can be five to six knots, and a mean chop develops when the wind is counter to the tidal current. The word **gut** refers to a narrow passage of water between two larger bodies of· water. Thus, Plum Gut is a narrow passage of water named after adjacent Plum Island..

Orient Point Lighthouse stands at one end of Oyster Pond Reef, a body of rocks submerged under only some 10 feet of water and which extends nearly one third the way across the Gut, while the channel in the Gut offers depths of more than 100 feet. Every summer, many yachts from Long Island Sound and New England sail past this aid to mariners to rendezvous at Shelter Island, Greenport, Montauk, Sag Harbor, and other excellent harbors in the area.

Description of the Lighthouse

The shell of the foundation of the light is a cast-iron caisson 25 feet in diameter and 32 feet tall. It rests directly upon the rocks of Oyster Pond Reef which was levelled to provide a stable footing for the light. The caisson is made of curved cast-iron plates which have flanges projecting into the shell's interior. Bolts through these flanges hold the plates together. The cast-iron sections were made in New York City and brought to the Orient Point Wharf Company dock (where the New London Ferry now docks) by sailing ship. A barge then floated the structure to the reef for assembly at low tide. The caisson was then filled with concrete; a space in the top of the shell was left unfilled to provide space for equipment and supplies.

The tower rests directly upon this foundation. It takes the form of a truncated cone, 24 feet tall, with diameters of 21' at the base and 18 feet at the top. The circular watch deck surmounts the tower and in turn supports the circular lantern. The three stories within the tower held living quarters for the crew in the days of manned operation. construction of the tower walls resembles very closely that of the foundation, curved cast-iron plates bolted together by internal flanges. The tower is lined with brick. The brick lining is three feet thick at the bottom and tapers to a smaller thickness in the upper stories. The windows and door openings of the first two stories are presently fitted with steel plates to deter vandals. Four round ports light the tower's third floor.

Galleries with railings are found at both the watch deck and lantern levels. The lantern walls are cast-iron at the bottom and glazed over their upper halves in a diagonal-lattice pattern with bronze muntins. the sheet metal-covered lantern roof is pitched with a ventilator ball at its apex. Inside the tower, a cast-iron stairway ascends around the periphery, separated from the living areas by a wall of sheet iron. The stairs are set into the brick lining of the tower. The watch deck features beaded-board walls. No early illuminating equipment remains in the lantern, since the original fourth order lens showed a fixed red light visible for 11¼ miles. It was replaced by an electric lamp and a modern plastic lens when the light was automated in 1966.

Orient Point Lighthouse retains its historical integrity virtually intact. Besides the main structural components, the beacon still has such features as the hoodmolds and gallery brackets which identify the light as a product of a distinctive period, the late 19th century. Cracks in the foundation which were repaired with patch plates and regrouting behind the patches may have given instability in the footing of the light. As a result, the structure, as every sailor knows, now lists about five degrees out of plumb.

Keepers

N.A. Anderson, who was born in Norway, was appointed first keeper of the light on October 20, 1899 at an annual salary of $600 a year. He served until 1919. His assistant, Daniel McDermott, born in Ireland, was appointed on December 10, 1899 at an annual salary of $450 a year. He later resigned. At the turn of the century, lighthouses were considered too dangerous for women. For example, Mrs. Anderson, wife of the first keeper, roomed at Orient Point. During her husband's 20 years of service as keeper, some very cold winters occasionally formed great ice sheets around the lighthouse, thus preventing boat passage and literally marooning him from the mainland and his wife.

Orient Point Light, Orient Point, NY

Reports of the Commissioner of Lighthouses

1896. The beacon off Oyster Pond or Orients Point, on the west side of Plum Gut, Long Island Sound, was carried away by ice. It is proposed to replace it with a lighted beacon and fog signal. It is estimated that this will cost $5,000.

1897. On June 4, an act of Congress approved $30,000 for a light and fog signal on the site of the beacon formerly standing at this point to guide (ships) through Plum Gut, entrance to Long Island Sound, New York.

1898. ...It now appears that it will be necessary to place some 600 tons of riprap stone around the base of this structure on account of its exposure.... On October 26, a second course of plates had been sunk in position when a gale swept them away, breaking 20 beyond repair and damaging 19 others ...

Preservation of the "Coffee Pot"

The Coast Guard manned the lighthouse between 1939 and 1966, at which time it was automated. However, by 1970, the old "Coffee Pot" was rusting away and listing a little to a point where the Coast Guard considered it a hazard for servicing personnel and uneconomical to repair. Accordingly, in one of its *Notice to Mariners* in 1970, the Coast Guard announced that the Orient Point Lighthouse would be extinguished forever by being demolished after the boating season and replaced with a pipe stem fixture. A United States Navy disposal team with its arsenal of high explosives was slated to do the dirty deed.

Upon reading this notice, the outcry from the east end Long Island residents was loud enough to be heard at the Coast Guard's headquarters in New York. Also protesting were many Long Island Sound sailors who had developed affection for the "Coffee Pot" as they sailed by. Local historical societies and other members of the community expressed their overwhelming sentiments about the beauty of the old-fashioned lighthouse and how it should be maintained as a historical landmark. As a result of this protest, the Coast Guard at first offered to defer demolition until some local group or organization could take over the lighthouse.

The Coast Guard then took another look at the "old girl" and sent a team of engineers from New London to survey the site. It announced a stay on the destruction of the cast-iron caisson, which listed even then, and had a few see-through holes in its base. Then the Coast Guard remained silent for three years. Orient Point Lighthouse continued to function as a signal light from the tip of Long Island. Her lamp was lit by remote control from Plum Island, because the underwater cable from Orient Point had long since been inoperable.

Nothing was known of the light's long term future until early October, 1973, when workmen were sighted climbing scaffolding on the structure. Rumor spread locally that the Coast Guard was probably getting around to finally demolishing the landmark as it had promised in 1970. However, a quick check with them showed the contrary was true. It had decided not to jilt the "old girl" but to keep her in service indefinitely.

Sandblasting was begun by Chesterfield Associates in preparation for applying a preservative coating and epoxy base finish coat. "This will protect the lighthouse for at least ten years," said Gregory Drubeck, project engineer for the Coast Guard at the time. Existing holes in the base of the cast-iron shell were filled in with concrete and the lighthouse "restored to its former condition," said Drubeck. "The lighthouse is going to be around for awhile." The light was upgraded in 1978 to compensate for the loss of Plum Island Light. It is now automated and operated remotely from New London, Connecticut.

Sometimes the Government transfers ownership of property like this to municipalities, museums and other non-profit organizations free of charge as long as they maintain the property. Inquiries should be addressed to: Commander, First Coast Guard District, 150 Causeway Street, Boston, Massachusetts 02114.

Significance of the Lighthouse

As I mentioned earlier, Orient Point Lighthouse is significant as a relatively unaltered representative example of late 19th century lighthouse construction. Its concrete-filled caisson foundation, its iron tower built according to a standardized format, architectural details such as hoodmolds and gallery brackets, and even such interior features as the cast-iron stairway are characteristic elements of the period.

In addition, the lighthouse is significant as an important part of local maritime heritage in eastern Long Island, an era of long-standing involvement, and even dependence, upon sea-going activities. Fisheries and coastal trade have comprised important portions of the local economy since colonial times. Today, the eastern Long Island Sound fisheries remain active. Ship-borne commerce now has as a prime element the ferries connecting Orient Point with New London, Connecticut. The place of the lighthouse in the region's historical awareness was evident when local residents protested its destruction in 1970.

In the 1870s, the United States Lighthouse Board developed the technique of placing concrete-filled, cast-iron caisson foundations on water-bound sites. Made of prefabricated plates bolted together on site before filling, the caisson offered relative ease and low cost in comparison to the best prior means of leasing wave-swept lighthouses (see Stratford Shoal, Middleground, Light, Chapter 16 for my comments on these lights) with stone masonry. The filled caissons had the requisite mass and hard shell to withstand the strong currents and ice floes encountered at water-covered shoals and reefs in the harbors and channels of the Northeast. The earliest caisson-based aids to navigation featured superstructures which followed the practice, in the 1860s and 1870s, of using current architectural styles, such as the Second Empire lighthouse at Ship John Shoal or Classical Revival at Fourteen Foot Bank, both in Delaware Bay.

In the early 1880s, however, apparently in an effort to conserve design costs and to speed development of new lights in places like Stamford, Connecticut (Ledge Obstruction Light, 1882) and Mystic, Connecticut (Latimer Reef Light, 1884), the Lighthouse Board established a standardized iron tower. Circular in plan with inwardly tapering sides, the standard tower had walls similar to the caisson shell, curved and flanged iron plates, prefabricated and bolted together on site. A thick brick lining ballasted the tower, creating a very solid structure. The standardized design format extended even so far as the few exterior details, such as gallery brackets and hoodmolds. The Lighthouse Board prepared pre-printed specifications for all the elements in the format, greatly speeding the process of requesting bids for metal work and construction.

Orient Point Lighthouse is an example of the long period of the standard design's use, having been erected in 1899, nearly 20 years after the first such lighthouses appeared. Similar lighthouses were constructed about the same time in Norwalk, Connecticut and are also discussed in this book, Greens Ledge Light (1902) and Peck Ledge Light (1906). The archtype remained virtually unchanged until after 1910, when several improvements were made. The tower cross-section was widened, and the living areas were given more windows. But the overall scheme still resembled very closely that of the 1880s. Orient Point is one of some three dozen such lighthouses erected in the Northeast. In its comparatively well-preserved condition in an exposed location subject to occasional severe wave-buffeting, it stands as a fine representative of late 19th century American lighthouse technology.

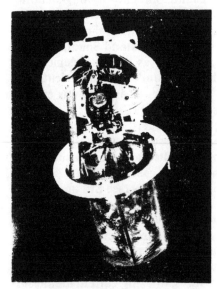

Motor and turntable drive
for 190 mm lantern

See also page 253

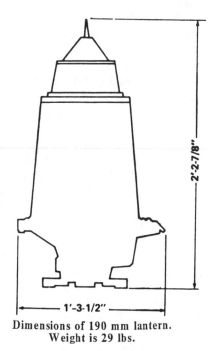

2'-2-7/8"

1'-3-1/2"

Dimensions of 190 mm lantern.
Weight is 29 lbs.

Courtesy U.S. Coast Guard

CHAPTER 26

CEDAR ISLAND LIGHT, Cedar Point, NY (1839)

Old Light List No.: 160 (Obsolete)
Location: Latitude 41° 02' 25" N
          Longitude 72° 15' 41" W
Height: 35' (HAW 45')
Range: 11 miles, Fixed White
Lens: Sixth Order, Classical (Fresnel)
Rebuilt: 1868
Discontinued: 1934

Cedar Island Lighthouse is one of the chief naval landmarks of eastern Long Island. It was the first and last beacon passed by Sag Harbor sailors on their famed whaling expeditions to the Brazil Banks and elsewhere. One story has it that the American flag was hoisted at the lighthouse whenever a ship returning home was sighted. The light is one of Long Island's best examples of the Boston granite style of architecture. It has survived despite a recent fire, in more or less unaltered condition from its construction in 1868. The lighthouse marks the tip of Cedar Point Park on the east end of Long Island. The park extends west, pointing like a finger toward Shelter Island and separating Gardiner's Bay from Sag Harbor, providing protection for Northwest Harbor.

The first federally administered lighthouse was built on the island in 1839, but the site had been used for years to guide ships into the whaling port of Sag Harbor. Navigation was not easy even under the best conditions around the outer islands of Long Island Sound, skirting first Gardiner's Island and then the southern tip of Shelter Island, around long spits of land and into the safety of Northwest Harbor. The location was extremely hazardous because of rip tides, fierce "nor'easters," and shifting sandbars. On October 28, 1809, for example, the Swedish brig "Fahlum," sailing from Newport to New York, struck a rock off Plum Island and went down off Cedar Island. The present lighthouse was originally constructed in 1868 to replace the older wooden building and tower which had been built on the site 30 years earlier.

When Sag Harbor was a great whaling port, agents and owners of whaleships and brigs maintained "stake lights" marking dangerous water areas in that vicinity prior to the building of the lighthouse in 1839. Captain Joshua Penny, who lived in Three Mile Harbor, tended these "stake lights." According to legend, Penny's wife saved Sag Harbor from destruction by the British in 1814. The officers of the British fleet at anchor in Gardiner's Bay went ashore one evening to dine with Lord Gardiner on his island and to plan their attack of the town. Mrs. Penny saw them go and sent word to Commodore Stephen Decatur, then staying in New London. Decatur formed a company of men, rowed over to the island

151

and captured the officers in ambush as they returned to their ships after supper. Lights on nearby Cedar Island and the beach were important during the time Long Island was in the hands of the British, particularly during the War of 1812 when so many able-bodied seamen from New England were forced to serve in the British navy.

East Hampton records tell us that a road was laid out at Cedar Beach as early as 1736 and that it was widened in 1795. The trustees of East Hampton Town appointed a committee to investigate the town's claim to Cedar Island and, on August 13, 1838, the trustees agreed to sell it to the United States Government for $200 and ordered the deed executed. At that time, the island was a three-acre tract known to seafaring men as a "sandspit." It had a grove of 40 or 50 cedar trees on it, hence its name. The town trustees enforced penalties for destruction of the cedar trees. Until 1938, the island was separated from the mainland by a strait and lay 200 yards off Cedar Beach.

By the turn of the century, the island had washed away from the original three acres to less than an acre, so keeper Captain (it seems all keepers liked to be called "captain") Charles J. Mulford of East Hampton, descendant of an old Sag Harbor sailing family, requested that the Lighthouse Service Board reinforce the shoreline. Keeper Mulford was a Civil War veteran with a wooden leg and kept spares in the large attic of the granite lighthouse. When a fire swept through the old light on June 6, 1974, several of Mulford's "legs," which had been gathering dust in the attic, were destroyed in the blaze. In 1904, following his suggestion about the shoreline, the Lighthouse Board had 4,000 tons of riprap deposited on the northern exposure, and in 1906 another 2.000 tons were deposited along the same location. The breakwater was constructed after 1908, when a high tide, which accompanied the blizzard of January 24, covered the island and swept much of it away. The concrete and rock foundations of the tower and house remained quite solid and unaffected by the pounding of the waves. However, that old nemesis of many lighthouses, erosion, gradually wore away the island so that by 1937 only 0.947 of an acre remained of the original three acres of 1838. Gone, too, was the beautiful grove of cedar trees which had lent the island its name.

In October 1923, the yacht "Florence B. Simmons" sank near Cedar Island. Although the four crew were saved, the yacht was a total loss.

In 1934, Cedar Island was turned over to the Treasury Department by the Lighthouse Division of the Commerce Department and declared "surplus property." The last keeper of the light was William H. Folllett. Because the light lacked modern conveniences, he used the kitchen range and individual room stoves in the winter to heat the building. He also pumped water from a cistern into which eaves of the lighthouse drained. In place of the old lighthouse, an automatic light was installed atop a 57-ft. skeleton tower (LLN 26710) on a breakwater several hundred feet in front of the island. The steel tower still diverts traffic with its flashing green light every four seconds, which can be seen for five nautical miles.

Cedar Island Light, Cedar Point, NY

In 1937, the lighthouse was sold at an auction by Secretary of the Treasury Henry Morgenthau, Jr. The high bidder was Phelan Beale of Bouvier and Beale, New York City attorneys. Mr. Beale acquired the entire island, now only 0.947 of an acre and devoid of cedar trees, including the nine-room lighthouse, a boat house, and an oil house for $2,002. He said he bought Cedar Island to protect the several miles of shorefront behind it, which he leased as a shooting preserve. Although his newly acquired lighthouse was stucturally sound with granite block walls two feet thick, it lacked modern improvements. Beale planned to install a heating plant and running water and to give his 20 office employees the run of the place for fishing and swimming during summer vacations.

When Beale bought the light at a public auction in Washington, D.C. on January 12, 1937, he lived at 40 East 62 Street, New York City. When interviewed and asked why he bought the property, Beale said that he was a lessee of a 452-acre private game preserve along the shore of Gardiner's Bay within 200 feet of the lighthouse and wanted to keep strangers away. Also, he said, "I want to preserve the lighthouse as a monument to the past." He believed the tiny 0.947-acre island was an integral part of the mainland. His 17-year lease on the game preserve was not due to expire until 1947, but he sold his property in 1943 to Isabel P. Bradley of Darien, Connecticut. Beale was a native of Montgomery, Alabama and was president of the New York Southern Society. His law firm was located at 165 Broadway, New York City. His hobby was game breeding and hunting on his fenced-in estate on Gardiner's Bay where two breeders raised 1,500 pheasants for him annually and smaller numbers of wild turkeys, Canadian Geese, wild ducks, quail and rabbits.

On September 21, 1938, a fierce hurricane hit the Northeast and filled in the 200-yard strait of water between the island and the mainland, thus connecting the island and Cedar Beach with a sand spit and changing the name of the island and its steel beacon forever. The storm created Cedar Point as we know it today. The island became a peninsula. In 1967, the property was acquired by Suffolk County for a public park, along with other parcels of land. The lighthouse, like many other unmanned lighthouses, has been thoroughly vandalized by mindless persons and was gutted by equally mindless arsonists on June 6, 1974. The damage was estimated at $50,000-$100,000. The fire destroyed the roof, oaken interior and cracked the heavy stone walls in some places. The Cedar Island Lighthouse was dedicated to the Suffolk County Historic Trust in 1984 and has been nominated for inclusion in the National Register of Historic Places.

Description of the Lighthouse

The lighthouse is encircled by a five-ft. wide granite walkway that was once enclosed with a white picket fence. It consists of a 2½-story, L-shaped main house approximately 33 feet square and a four story tower about eight feet square set in the "L" of the main building. The tower cul-

154

minates in a lookout walk around an octagonal beacon which is capped with a conical roof and ball ornament. Some of the downspouts are still in place at the various corners of the house. They originally carried rain water to a cistern in the cellar. The windows and doors were sealed with concrete blocks in 1974 following the fire mentioned earlier which gutted the interior of the building. A new roof was installed at the same time.

The light is a Victorian example of the Boston granite style of construction. Its architect is unknown, but the contractor was W. & J. Beattie Company, Fall River, Massachusetts, owners of a granite quarry from which the granite for the lighthouse probably came. Above the main doorway is a beaded ovolo moulding bearing the construction date "1868" in relief. On this same level, there is a wider doorway, about seven feet across, which probably provided an opening for a small row boat. The Cedar Island Light bears a close resemblance to several other Victorian masonry lighthouses discussed in this book. For example, the 1867 Execution Rocks Lighthouse is designed in the same formal Boston granite style as Cedar Island Light, although the light tower is a separate and different structure.

A generating plant still survives on the northern end of the property. This small brick structure was probably built at the turn of the century or soon thereafter. Like other unattended lighthouse property, it has been subjected also to mindless vandalism.

A shoal extends 0.3-0.4 mile north of the shore of Cedar Point. The shoal has boulders, and its edge is marked by buoys. A portion of Northwest Harbor, between Cedar Island Light and Barcelona Point, is strewn with boulders covered by only four to six feet of water. The mariner is thus urged to sail with caution when in these waters. Strong tidal currents are encountered between the south shore of Shelter Island and the north shore of Long Island's South Fork.

CHAPTER 27

MONTAUK POINT LIGHT, Montauk Point, NY (1797)

Light List No.: 650
Location: Latitude 41° 4.3′ N
          Longitude 71° 51.5′ W
Height: 108′ (HAW 168′)
Range: 19 miles, Flashing White every 5 seconds, Horn
Lens: DCB 224
Radio Beacon: 286 kHz, MP (__ __ · __ __ .) III,
    125 miles
Automated: December 1986

Montauk Point and its sturdy old tower are the sources of much history and the scene of many marine disasters. The Indian name for Turtle Hill, upon which the lighthouse stands, is "Womponamon," an Algonquan word meaning "to the east." The proud Montauk tribe gave their name to the region and ruled the surrounding tribes. Their sachems called councils by lighting fires on Womponamon, and many of the tribesmen came to them in dugout canoes large enough to hold 18 paddles.

During the American Revolution, eastern Long Island and Montauk Point were occupied by the British. The Royal Navy kept a huge fire burning on the bluff overlooking the sea to serve as a beacon for the ships of the squadron that blockaded Long Island Sound. During the winter of 1780-81, a good part of the British fleet lay in Gardiner's Bay, including the H.M.S. "Royal Oak," flagship of Vice Admiral Arbuthnot. The British were keeping an eye on the French fleet, sent to aid the American colonies, then at anchor in Newport Harbor, Rhode Island.

On January 22, 1781, the British received a report that three ships of the French fleet had left Newport and were within range of the British fleet. Vice Admiral Arbuthnot sent three frigates in pursuit of the Freench: the 1487 ton H.M.S. "Culloden," a 74-gun vessel, 161 feet long with a beam of 46 feet and a draft of 16 feet, sister ship of the "Royal Oak"; the H.M.S. "Beford"; and the H.M.S. "America." A heavy northeast snowstorm sprang up and made pursuit impossible. The "Bedford" was dismasted. The "America" was lost for several days in the storm. And the "Culloden," despite the efforts of her skipper, Captain George Balfour, was blown onto Skagwonggonac (Skagwong for short) Reef which ripped her hull open. Somehow, Captain Balfour managed to get his ship off the reef and sailed her, hole and all, into the smoother waters of Fort Pond Bay where she promptly sank off the eastern headland at the entrance. Apparently, the entire crew of 600 was rescued.

Built at Deptford, England in 1747, the "Culloden" had seen service in the battles of Minorca (1756), Gibraltar (1759), and elsewhere in 1762 and 1778. Her name came from the Battle of Culloden (1746) when the troops

Montauk Point Light, Montauk Point, NY

of Charles Edward Stuart ("Bonnie Prince Charlie") were defeated by the Duke of Cumberland's army. After she sank, her masts were salvaged and used by the "Bedford" which had been towed into Fort Pond Bay after the storm has subsided. The "Bedford" was once again made seaworthy on March 9, 1781. After everything of value had been salvaged from her, the "Culloden" was burned to the waterline. The headland has ever since been known as Culloden Point. At low tide, the ship's timbers are visible even today, making it an interesting spot for scuba divers to visit.

After the struggle for independence was over, the new American Government realized that if it was to exist, it would have to stimulate trade with other nations. In order to do this, it would have to eliminate some of the hazards along the coast and make the principal ports of New York, Philadelphia and Baltimore more easily accessible to world commerce. Montauk Point was certainly one of the most dangerous areas on the new trans-Atlantic trade route. Records show that the rock-studded point projecting out into an often fog-ridden Atlantic Ocean took a heavy toll of shipping during the early years of settlement in the New World. A vehement group of shipmasters and owners protested that along the more than 100 miles of Long Island's southern, treacherous, Atlantic-hammered shoreline there was no haven for vessels. A shipmaster who cleared Coney Island and headed east from New York Harbor had only six small, shallow inlets between him and Montauk Point. Wrecks of brigs, sloops, ketches, and schooners lay in the surf on Fire Island, on the long, exposed beaches at Quogue, Southampton, East Hampton, and on Montauk Point itself.

In 1792, to prevent this loss of ships and trade, Congress appropriated $255.12 to buy land upon which a lighthouse was to be built to warn passing mariners of the perilous rocks at Montauk Point. Three years later, President George Washington signed the authorization for the construction of the light. A contract was awarded to New York bricklayer, John McComb, Jr. McComb's bid of $22,300 was the lowest offer of the four bids that were received. Also in his favor was the fact that he had already built a successful lighthouse at Cape Henry, Virginia in 1791. McComb was later commissioned to build also Old Field Point Light, Port Jefferson, New York in 1799.

Work on the light began almost immediately. Heavy blocks of sandstone were hauled to Montauk in horse-drawn wagons. McComb ordered a 13-ft. deep foundation dug into the crest of Turtle Hill. At its base, the lighthouse was to have a 28-ft. diameter with walls nine feet thick. At the top of the 80-ft., octagonal tower, the walls were to be three feet thick. The contract also called for the construction of a two-story keeper's house and a vault for "nine strong Cedar Cisterns" which would store the necessary oil for the beacon. It should be noted that at this time in history, it was only possible to build lighthouses on land. It was not until 1878 with the construction of Race Rock Light near Fishers Island, New York and Minot's Ledge Light (1850-1860) near the southern entrance to Boston

Harbor Pass, that the construction of wave-swept lighthouses was possible. The construction of Race Rock Light presented a formidable challenge to engineers, and it represents a major break-through and accomplishment in lighthouse building. Its story is told in Chapter 33 of this volume.

When Montauk Point Light was first lit in 1797, it burned whale oil. Whaling was a growing industry at the time, and for more than half a century Montauk Point's lantern used fuel from the huge mammals. By the late 1850s, however, whales began to be scarce as ships ranged the globe in search of them. For a time, Montauk Point Light was forced to burn lard oil when whale oil was unavailable. With the discovery of petroleum came kerosene which was cheaper and easier to obtain than whale oil. In the 1860s, finally, the light was converted to a kerosene wick permanently.

Because of its location, Montauk Point Lighthouse stood, to some extent, as the symbol of the New World for almost a century. In 1886, it was upstaged by the Statue of Liberty in New York Harbor. Lieutenant George M. Bache, U.S.N., noted in his report of 1838: "(It) is passed by all vessels approaching Long Island Sound from seaward, and is a good point of departure for those leaving the Sound." Thus, Montauk Point Light has been the first welcoming beacon to the New World for travelers sailing from Europe to New York. With independence, the flow of immigrants from Europe to the United States increased, trans-Atlantic trade boomed, and New York became the preferred destination for ships carrying settlers or merchandise. Montauk Point Light, like the Statue of Liberty, symbolizes the United States's emergence from a colonial enclave to an independent trading nation which opened its arms to the millions of Europeans who saw it as the promised land. Most recently, the light was the first welcoming beacon for the returning American hostages from Iran in 1981. The lighthouse sported a giant yellow ribbon wrapped around the deck beneath the lantern and was created by the officer-in-charge, BM1 Paul Driscoll, his family and crew members. On the ribbon was printed in large letters the greeting: WELCOME HOME.

Since 1797, then, Montauk Point Light has safely guided mariners around treacherous reefs and shoals which surround her jagged coastline. Indian canoes, whaleboats, revenue cutters, and smuggler's ships (then as now) passed the lighthouse during the early days of operation. During the War of 1812, British men-of-war prowled beneath the reassuring beacon. Schooners, brigs, and all manner of sailing craft used the light as a guide. Today, fast, sleek nuclear ships glide under this historic light's winking eye high atop Turtle Hill.

Early Keepers of the Light

Jacob Hand - Appointed November 4, 1796. Hand was reprimanded by
  Thomas Jefferson for nepotism. He wanted his son to succeed him
  without taking a competitive examination.

Jared Hand - Appointed January 28, 1812. Jacob's son apparently passed the competitive examination to be appointed on his own merits.

Henry Baker - Appointed February 24, 1814. His annual salary was $333.33.

Patrick F. Gould - Appointed May 9, 1832

John Hobart - Appointed October 29, 1849

Silas P. Loper - Appointed August 17, 1850

Captain Jonathan A. Miller - Miller was injured in a naval engagement during the Civil War. He served as keeper from January 1, 1865 to May 13, 1869 and December 3, 1872 to October 15, 1875 (?)

Captain John E. Miller - The son of Jonathan, Miller was a member of an old East Hampton family and was a New York City policeman for 23 years before he was placed in charge of the light at Montauk Point. He served as keeper from May 16, 1912 to 1929.

For many years, Montauk Point Light was a desolate, often inaccessible place, and the early keepers of the light, their wives and families led solitary and very lonely lives. There was only one rock road leading from the Point to East Hampton, the nearest village 20 miles away, and during the winter months, snowdrifts usually made the journey to it impossible. Children were taught their school lessons at the light by their mothers. A few visitors during the summer made the job of the keeper a little less lonely. Although his work was often tedious, it had its advantages if he like bass fishing which was excellent at the Point. Life at the light continued this way until the early 1900s when the new motor cars brought droves of visitors to the light and created new problems.

Wives replaced keepers at tending light when they died or when they were called to other duties such as rescue work. Such was the case in December 1856, when the brig "Flying Cloud" ran aground on the rocks at Montauk Point and Patrick T. Gould, the keeper, climbed down the face of the bluff in a gale to save the crew from drowning in the surf. He was awarded a gold medal by the grateful Lifesaving Benevolent Association of New York. The inscription on it told of his "courage and humanity saving from inevitable death the crew of the brig "Flying Cloud," wrecked on Montauk Point December 14, 1856." However, apparently nothing was mentioned of his wife's role in maintaining the light during her husband's heroic rescue efforts.

Two Tales: the "John Milton" and the "Washington"

The construction of Ponquogue (Shinnecock) Light with a steady beam in January 1858, and the changing of the Montauk Point Light from a steady beam to·a flashing signal (which it has to this day) at the same time were blamed for one of the worst wrecks that ever took place off the south shore of eastern Long Island. It was a rare error made by the Lighthouse Board. To make matters worse, there was no way to notify ships at sea about these changes. As to be expected, tragedy struck soon thereafter. Since 1797, Montauk Point Light had been the only beacon, casting a steady beam, on that lonely wind-swept 76-mile stretch of coast between Fire Island Light and Montauk Point.

Captain Ephraim Harding had sailed from New York on the 1445 ton full-rigged ship "John Milton" on December 6, 1856, bound for San Francisco via Cape Horn. On the way home, he stopped at the Chincha Islands off Peru and loaded a cargo of guano. When he reached the south shore of Long Island again on February 18, 1858, he ran into "strong gales and a thick snowstorm," which he recorded in the ship's log. As he proceeded east along the south shore, the snowstorm continued unabated. There was, of course, no way for him to know that Montauk Point Light had changed its characteristic from a steady beam to a flashing one or even that a new light had been built at Ponquogue which now cast the steady beam.

When Harding reached Ponquogue Light and saw its steady beam, he mistook it for Montauk Point Light and, after sailing on his course a bit farther, he steered his vessel to port and headed north, believing he was in the open water of Block Island Sound. He was not. The "John Milton" crashed on the rocks before dawn on Saturday February 20, 1858, about five miles west of Montauk Point Light, all sails set. There were no survivors of the 33 persons aboard. Men, spars, sails and cargo were found subsequently in hideous confusion, encased in ice.

"She melted like a lump of sugar," an old man, first on the scene said of the "John Milton" years later. When dawn came, the ship's bell could be seen poised upon two beams projecting from the bow of the wreck, all that remained of the vessel. There, swaying with every swell of the waves, according to a contemporary newspaper account, "... it tolled out the requiem for the departed." Later, the bell was bought and given to the Session House in East Hampton where it rings to this day.

The bodies of Captain Harding, three mates and 18 sailors washed ashore on the beach, along with their pitiful belongings—their personal letters and daguerreotypes of their loved ones whom they expected to see again so soon. The dead were carried to East Hampton in wagons. Reverend Stephen L. Mershon preached the funeral sermon. Twenty-three of the men were buried in a common grave in the Old South End Burying Ground, and a stone was erected above them by public subscription.

Captain Henry Babcock, skipper of the whaling ship "Washington" out of Sag Harbor, returned from a long voyage to the Pacific about the same time the "John Milton" foundered on the rocks on February 20th. He, too, had received no word of the change of lights at Montauk Point or of the new light at Ponquogue. He sailed along the same southern coast of Long Island toward Montauk Point as Captain Harding did. There, he planned to turn to port and head west to Sag Harbor. When he raised Ponquogue Light, he refused to accept its steady beam as belonging to Montauk Point Light. He had taken a reading of the sun at noon and believed that the light which appeared to be Montauk Point Light had been made too soon. He was worried and called a conference with his officers and crew.

Everyone on board the "Washington" was eager to get to Sag Harbor. They favored nothing but the quickest possible passage home. They argued, "There is no other light but Montauk on this part of the coast." but Captain Babcock was, fortunately, a man of great wisdom and strong will. He sensed something was wrong and refused to give into the admonitions of his men. Instead, he gave the order: "Tack ship and stand ashore!" His judgement proved to be correct when a second lighthouse was raised and positively identified as Montauk Point Light. But for his decision, the "Washington" would have gone to the same watery grave as the "John Milton" had earlier.

Captain Babcock eventually was keeper of the light for many years at Montauk Point after he retired from whaling. It pleased him, we are told, to stand on the bluff at Turtle Hill on a fair summer day and look down at the rocks below which almost claimed him, as they did Captain Harding and his crew, when he sailed the "Washington" home years ago.

Recent Disasters

During World War II, three American ships were sunk by Nazi submarines near Montauk Point: the 5031 ton "Maiden Creek" went to the bottom on December 31, 1942; the 1371 ton "Wilmington" and the 5303 ton "Black Point" were lost on May 5, 1945. A British vessel, the "H.M.S. Mattawin," was sunk by two Nazi torpedoes just 20 miles southeast of the light. She went down in three minutes. Fifty-three seamen perished in this disaster, but 39 escaped to safety in two life boats.

●

As the needs of maritime shipping changed, the lighthouse at Montauk Point was further modified. Sometimes the weather forced changes. On one occasion during a freezing winter gale, the light's barn was blown into the sea. Another time, the front porch of the keeper's house was swept away. Thus, buildings were improved upon or added to as the years passed. In 1860, the lighthouse was rebuilt and the tower increased in height to 108 feet which it remains to this day. Eventually, the light was converted to electricity. Later, automatic fog signals, a watch tower and radio beacon were installed. In 1939, the Lighthouse Service was combined with the United States Coast Guard which then took charge of the operation of the light.

Although times have changed, the tower in use at Montauk Point today is basically the same one that McComb built in 1797. Every year it is whitewashed, and its distinguishing day signal, a red band, is renewed with metallic paint. Super highways have made a visit to the lighthouse a pleasant drive, a welcome change from horse-and-buggy days when a single, hole-ridden dirt road made travel difficult if not impossible. Thousands of sightseers annually picnic at beautiful Montauk State Park and visit its historic adjacent beacon. However wonderful this may seem, the flood of visitors to the top of Long Island unwittingly has contributed to the problem of erosion which threatens to destroy the very land they enjoy.

Montauk Point Lighthouse is one of the few remaining 18th century American Lighthouses still standing. Others included in this book are: New London Harbor Light, New London, Connecticut (1760); and Eatons Neck Light, Northport, New York (1799). Montauk Point Light is one of the best-known American lighthouses for some of the reasons I have given here. Standing a majestic 169 feet above the pounding Atlantic Ocean, it continues to serve seafarers as faithfully as it has for nearly two centuries.

The Montauk Historical Society took custody of the lighthouse on Friday, September 12, 1986, in a colorful ceremony which brought school children and their parents, military personnel in full dress, prominent citizens and the United States Coast Guard Band to the bluff at the tip of the Island. Petty Officer W. Gene Hughes, the 32nd and last keeper of the light, led the formalities that "disestablished" the U.S. Coast Guard Light Station at Montauk Point and put the future of the site in the hands of the Historical Society. The Society will lease the property from the federal government free of charge and assume responsiblity for all maintenance.

Plans for the lighthouse, according to Richard White, chairman of the lighthouse committee, include a museum in which, among other things, the Historical Society hopes to display the classical Fresnel lens which has been moved down stairs from the tower. A DCB-224 has replaced it in the lantern room. The Coast Guard has agreed to leave the Fresnel lens on site. Two apartments in the lighthouse building will be occupied by a patrolman from the Long Island State Parkway Police and the museum's curator. The Society will charge an admission fee of $1.50 for the museum, which will be open weekends in the spring and fall and six days a week at the height of the season during the summer months.

Thus, Montauk Point Light becomes the last lighthouse discussed in this book to be automated in 1986. Two earlier ones were New London Ledge Light and Watch Hill Light. That leaves Point Judith Light and Block Island Southeast Light as the only remaining manned lighthouses. They will go, too, in time, I suppose. An era has passed forever.

Montauk Light inspired Walt Whitman to write six lines subtitled "From Montauk Point" in 1888 as part of his most famous poem *Leaves of Grass:*

"I stand as on some mighty eagle's beak,
Eastward the sea absorbing, viewing (nothing but sea and sky),
The tossing waves, the foam, the ships in the distance,
The wild unrest, the snowy, curling caps—that inbound urge and urge
    of waves,
Seeking the shores forever . . . . "

How a Remarkable Woman Saved a Lighthouse: Erosion at Montauk Point
John McComb built his lighthouse 297 feet from the eastern edge of a

high bluff which overlooks the Atlantic Ocean. "Far enough back to last for centuries," he must have thought. He would have been shocked if he knew that in less than 200 years, erosion would have destroyed most of the land and brought his lighthouse to within 55 feet of toppling into the sea. As recent as 1983, the edge of the southeast bluff came as close as 50 feet to the light, but concrete rubble was dumped over the edge to fill the bluff's gaping hole. Such are the facts. Although the wind, rain, and waves have played their part in destroying the bluff over the years, it has been mindless man who has done the most damage and must be held responsible for it. In fact, most of the erosion on the Point has occurred since about 1900 with the invention of the automobile and new, improved roads which brought people there to fish, climb the bluffs and picnic.

Until 1970, the slope down the face of the bluff was not much more than muddy gullies, down which yards and yards of soil and some stones tumbled annually into the ocean. The Coast Guard, quite frankly, did not see any way to stop this wearing away of their property. The only option it saw at the time, since it would have been prohibitedly expensive to dismantle the old, historic light brick by brick and rebuild it farther inland, was to build a steel tower farther back on the cliff, place an automated flashing light on top of it, and move its operation to nearby Star Island, letting the lighthouse go it its destiny.

Such was the fate of another lighthouse, the historic Cape Henlopen Light (1767) on the south side of the entrance to Delaware Bay. Wind erosion blew the sand away from the light, exposing its foundation. The Lighthouse Board put in a brush cover to stop the erosion, but that strategy only slowed the movement of the sand. Then, on April 13, 1926, a severe storm undermined the tower, and it toppled into the sea. The lighthouse was lost forever. Such could have been the fate of Montauk Light also.

Fortunately, in the fall of 1969, a remarkable woman by the name of Giorgina Reid from Jackson Heights, New York, asked the Coast Guard if she could test the terrain and the materials at the Point to determine if her method of halting erosion (for which she was granted a patent, No. 3,412,561, on November 26, 1968) would work as well on the south shore as it had on the north. She called her method reed-trench terracing which she describes in her book *How to Hold up a Bank* (New York: A.S. Barnes, 1969). The Cost Guard gave her permission, and Giorgina went to work. Frequently, she worked almost single-handedly with her husband, Donald, but by 1985 she had firmly terraced the entire eastern and northeastern cliff faces owned by the Coast Guard at Montauk Point. Although not an expert in erosion control, after seeing Mrs. Reid's work, Petty Officer W. Gene Hughes, formerly in charge of the light, confidently claimed that her method of reed-trench terracing has halted the erosion at the light permanently. John McComb would indeed be proud of her.

To quote from an article by Giorgina Reid in the *Montauk Almanac:* "To the casual observer, the terracing appears to be a series of steps with wooden risers, but it what goes on underground that does the job of keeping the soil in place. Behind and below each horizontal retainer is a deep trench in which are placed the withered stems of reeds. This leads people to conclude that the reeds are being planted, but such is not the case. The masses of reeds absorb and retain rain water at each level, this forming a barrier which prevents sand from sliding out during periods of drought and preventing rain from forming gullies and carrying off the soil during periods of heavy precipitation. This moist environment creates the condition favorable for establishing the essential vegetation.

"There is no one miracle plant that will work everywhere. It takes a variety of grasses and woody plants to survive on the glacial moraine deposits that form Montauk Point's escarpments, which consist of sand, silt, clay, gravel, bounders and an occasional stratum of iron concentration. On sandy areas, beach grass does well; where some top soil exists, shrubs are good soil grabbers; in dry, gravelly spots, crownvetch is very effective. When the lumber and reeds decay, having done their duty of containment and irrigation, they eventually blend with the roots and grasses and shrubs and furnish nutrients to the plantings as they disintegrate."

The solution to the problem of erosion is, as Giorgina Reid has shown us, containment. This involves both toe protection and terracing. The "toe" is the base of the bluff. Toe protection is necessary for dissipation of wave energy. Terracing is necessary for establishing vegetation to keep the soil in place. "Toe protection comes first. This may take the form of a timber bulkhead, a grouping of precast marine modules, or a riprap revetment consisting of massive boulders interlaced as closely as possible. The boulder installation depends on mass and weight to abosrb energy. This system of riprap revetment is used at the base of the bluff at Montauk Point and was installed by the Army Corps of Engineers during World War II. This type of toe protection has been quite successful and is a definite improvement on rigid installations. However, it is extremely costly and is vulnerable to dislodging or being over-topped during severe storms.

"A fairly recent arrival of toe protection is the gabion installation which the Coast Guard has used between the boulder revetment at the foot of the bluff and the terracing. Gabions are wire cages filled with stone. They are flexible, permeable building blocks from which any number of structures can be built. In addition to their use at Montauk Point, the Coast Guard has used gabions at their nearby station on Star Island. Gabions allow water collecting at the rear to drain through, thus preventing hydrostatic pressure from building up. They can hold their own against the sea, because they do not fight it. They let the storm waves in and out without disturbing the soil behind them. Besides being efficient, they are economical. Until a few years ago, gabions were used chiefly in road cuts and fresh water courses, but now the wire cages are available with a coating to prevent the corrosion of salt water."

The third phase in halting erosion is the reed-trench terracing, invented by Giorgina Reid, on the face of the bluff. This is begun only after the boulder revetment and gabions have been installed at the base of the bluff. One may begin this method either at the toe or bottom of the bluff and work up the slope to·its "lip" or edge, or sometimes one can begin from the top or midway down the bluff. The angle of the slope must not exceed 45° or the terracing will not hold. Mrs. Reid's reed-trench terracing method involves securing cedar planks about 1' x 8' horizontally across the slope and forming trenches in which are placed masses of reeds adjacent to the planks on the upward side, thus controlling bluff erosion by establishing sand-binding vegetation quickly with a minimum of expense and effort.

Controlling erosion on all soils involves the establishment of adapted grasses, shrubs and trees. The reeds entrenched at the base of each terrace prevent sand slippage and stills the sandy soil and other mobile materials. They also provide a stable seed-bed for the establishment of the essential soil-binding vegetation. The reeds (common reed grass or **phragmites communis**) have structural characteristics that make them effective erosion deterrents. They nourish and support the plantings above them, thus creating a flexible, breathing environment for the vegetation whose deep roots go several feet below the cedar nurse barriers, forming a network that firmly anchors the soil and providing absorption during periods of excessive precipitation and protection during long periods of drought. Coast guard officials say that Mrs. Reid's containment system has effectively stopped erosion on the eastern part of the bluff at Montauk Point.

However, in spite of the success at Montauk, all is not completely well. The bluffs to the north and south of the lighthouse are eroding away at a fast pace and little or nothing is being done about it. The property belongs to the State of New York, and the continuing erosion on it threatens the finished work on the Coast Guard property. One of the reasons for this alarming state of affairs is that there has been a lack of awareness by citizens and public officials that an erosion problem exists at the a Point. However, the major problem appears to be the two jurisdictions—state and federal government which both own the land at the Point. "Geographically, Montauk Point is a unit and should be stabilized as such," says Giorgina Reid. But currently, it is not. The bluffs on the north and south and the land to the west of the lighthouse are owned by New York State and are under the jurisdiction of the state's Office of Parks, Recreation and Historic Preservation. Although the Coast Guard has been working with Mrs. Reid to halt erosion on the eastern bluffs, New York State officials are doing little or nothing to halt the erosion on the northern and southern bluffs. They claim they have other priorities, such as capital improvements at Jones Beach on the south shore of Long Island.

Mrs. Reid has graded the steep eastern bluff into terraces. She and her husband estimate that the project cost them between $35,000 - $40,000 since they began in 1970. She needs financial help to finish and maintain it. New York State and local funds are slow in coming, if at all. The Coast

Guard has given over $137,000 to the project but is limited in continued funding, since it is the victim of drastic budget cutbacks by politicians in Washington, D.C. New York State, in comparision, has contributed very little, certainly nowhere near the amount of funds the Coast Guard has given. When it comes to priorities, one wonders if the State of New York has them straight. It is going to ignore an 190-year-old colonial landmark with a charter from President George Washington, a landmark which for almost a century was a symbol of the United States for countless immigrants, in favor of a public beach?

Mrs. Reid blames most of the erosion at the Point on four factors: rain, wind, trespassers and the ocean. Rain is the chief factor, since it creates gullies that wash away the soil. Winds which blow the soil away come next, followed by trespassers who dislodge material as they climb the bluff. Of the four offenders, the ocean is the least to blame; it merely carries off the material that lands at the base of the bluff. It is not a vicious monster which chews away all the land it can get. To prevent people from climbing on the bluffs and thereby contributing to the erosion on them the state and federal government have erected signs warning them to keep off. However, Petty Officer Hughes, the last keeper of the light, claimed the signs are no help. Trespassers ignore them and use them for target practice and beach fires. With the budget cutbacks, Hughes had only three men to help him and could not police the area adequately.

At the present time, erosion of the 65-ft. south bluff causes the most concern. Its edge now stands about 100 feet from the lighthouse. Mrs. Reid estimates that it will cost only $50,000 to terrace and add gabions to the south bluff and has permission to work on this cliff face owned by New York. Donations for plantings, supplies and transportation have come in the past, even from the Coast Guard, and they have seen her through 15 years. At present, however, Giorgina is uncertain how much longer her project will be granted tax-exempt status. But one thing is certain, Giorgina Reid's method of halting erosion by using her invention of reed-trench terracing at Montauk Point has gone a long way in preserving a famous beacon which has guided ships and sailors safely home since 1797.

CHAPTER 28

BLOCK ISLAND SOUTHEAST LIGHT, Block Island, RI (1875)

Light List No.: 635
Location: Latitude 41° 9.2′ N
Longitude 71° 33.1′ W
Height: 67′ (HAW 201′)
Range: 21 miles, Flashing Green every
3.7 seconds
Lens: First Order Classical Fresnel, 1000W lamp
Radio Beacon: 301 kHz, BI (_ . . . . .), 20 miles

High above the Atlantic Ocean on Mohegan Bluffs on the southeast corner of Block Island stands majestically the attractive dwelling and four-story tower of Block Island Southeast Light. It is the 23rd highest light in the United States (the highest is 442 feet at Cape Mendocino, California) and the highest light in New England. There is a magnificent sea view from the balcony that surrounds the tower. Although the light has a geographic range (more of which later) of 21 miles, it is clearly visible under normal conditions for 26 miles and under unusual atmospheric conditions has been sighted as far out as 35 miles.

Block Island Southeast Light is a primary seacoast station. It is made of red brick with quarry-faced granite ashlar foundations, is octagonal and pyramidal. The tower has a 25-ft. diameter at its base and tapers to 15 feet at the base of the lantern. In 1928, when the lighthouse was converted to electricity, its light was changed from a fixed white of 13,000 candlepower to a flashing green of 50,000 candlepower, the flash appearing every 3.75 seconds. It is the only primary seacoast light in New England waters showing a green light.

The lighthouse is about three miles from Old Harbor to the north and was the second lighthouse established on Block Island. The first was Block Island North Light, built in 1829. Unfortunately, the bluffs on which the lighthouse stands are steadily eroding from both ground springs, which are slowly washing away its surface, and from the incessant pounding of the winter seas, as they are at Montauk Point, and may threaten the stability of the structure within 20 years. In addition, the Coast Guard is considering replacing the light with a less expensive, more modern device. Mariners should be aware that at times the fog signal at the light is indistinct and difficult to hear when close-to, yet plainly audible several miles away.

The land near the site of the light is historic ground where the Mohegan Indian invaders from eastern Long Island were driven, kept back and starved by the native Manisses Indians long before the English settled the island. Apparently, the southeast corner of the island, which is triangular in shape, was first discovered by the Frenchman Verrazina

Block Island Southeast Light, Block Island, RI

about 1754. Block Island is about six miles long, and hilly with elevations up to about 200 feet. The shore of the island is fringed in most places by boulders and should be given a berth of over 0.5 mile even by small craft. Shoaling is generally abrupt in approaching the island.

Block Island consists of nearly 7,000 acres and lies in the Atlantic Ocean about 12 miles east-northeast of Long Island and about the same distance from Charlestown, Rhode Island. In July and August maximum temperatures average 74° F. Since the island is too small to build up cumulonimbus clouds, local thunderstorms do not occur. Block Island is famous for fog, however, and it occurs one out of four days in early summer when the ocean is relatively cold. The wind velocity averages 17 m.p.h. for the year, but the mean velocity is 20 m.p.h. in the winter when gales are frequent. Block Island has been called the "Bermuda of the North" and "Manisses Island" after the native Indian tribe.

Early History of the Light

1872. Congress appropriated $75,000 for a lighthouse and fog signal on the southern end of Block Island at the eastern entrance to Long Island Sound.

1873. The plans for the light and a first-class fog signal were prepared, but difficulties in obtaining title to the land on which the lighthouse was to be built, and subsequent delays, prevented building the structure. The site was finally purchased in July, and the erection of the fog signal was begun. The lighthouse proper was placed under contract.

1874. The purchase of the site for the lighthouse was finally concluded, and a steam fog signal in duplicate, except for the boiler, was erected 100 feet east of the site of the proposed tower. On November 4, a keeper, Henry W. Clark, and two assistants were appointed to take charge of and operate the new equipment. Mr. Clark who was paid $600 a year, remained at his post for 20 years and was succeeded by his son-in-law Simon Dodge. A cistern was built for furnishing water for the signals and pipes laid for water supply from an adjacent pond. Contracts were made for the keeper's dwelling and tower, and the first stories of these buildings were completed. The lantern, also made under contract, was completed and made ready for installation. The eight Fresnel lenses (also called "classical" lenses) set in brass frames were made by Henry Lepaute in Paris., France at a cost of $10,000. The plate with the maker's name on it is still attached to the lens.

The expenses for the purchase of land at the site, the district attorney's fees, and the connections for the water supply were greater than anticipated. Also, the exorbitant cost of hauling the machinery for the fog signal, lumber and labor drew heavily upon the appropriation for the station so that no funds were left for the completion of the reservoir or for the fencing of the grounds. Consequently, Congress approved a request for an additional $4,500 by a special act on June 23rd.

1875. Block Island Southeast Light was finally completed in the summer by T.H. Tynan of Staten Island, New York, and a light was first exhibited from the tower on February 1.

Description of the Lighthouse Interior and the Lantern

Passing through the hallway into the tower, one enters first the oil room where, in large tanks with capacities of 900-1000 gallons, refined lard oil was stored, the quantity annually consumed by the powerful lamp before it was electrified in 1928. The ascent from the oil room to the lantern is made by an iron spiral staircase. Immediately below the lamp is the keeper's room where a constant watch was kept during the night to keep the flame at its proper height, to replace broken chimneys and to see that nothing interrupted the working of the light on which depended the safety of thousands of vessels which passed the point each year.

A few steps higher up is the 16-sided lantern which is about ten feet high and 12 feet in diameter. Six persons can stand in it at the same time. The framework is made of cast-iron, contains the magnificent Fresnel lenses, mentioned earlier, which are a marvel of ingenuity in their scientific arrangement. The arrangement of the lenses consists of a cylindrical hoop of glass as a refracting lens. Above and below it are separate triangular prisms placed at proper angles to reflect and refract the light, which would otherwise be uselessly expended in illuminating clouds or the floor of the lantern, so that all the light is made to pass out finally in rays parallel to those of the central lens. No wood is used anywhere in the tower.

The system is arranged in the form of a hollow cylinder, narrowing at the top and bottom, 121 feet in height and six feet in diameter. In the center of this cylinder is the lamp (now electrified) which was provided with an ingenious self-feeding apparatus and had four circular wicks, one within the other, the largest of which was three-and-a-half inches in diameter and the smallest seven-eighths of an inch. The flame was surrounded by a chimney and kept at a certain height constantly. During the long winter nights, the lamp consumed two-and-one-half gallons of oil. During the day, the lenses are covered with curtains to prevent the rays of the sun from striking the lamp and melting the solder on the brass work. As noted previously, the light was converted from oil to electricity in 1928, but it is still magnified by its original Fresnel lenses.

The Fog Signal

During fogs, which seem to hover endlessly about Block Island at times, and storms when the light was of little help, mariners were (and still are) warned to avoid this dangerous island by the piercing notes of the "siren," as it was called. The apparatus consisted of a four-horse-power boiler and a trumpet of cast iron, 17 feet long. The trumpet did not make sound, but directed the sound which originated from a siren, or buzz, in the small end of the trumpet. The larger end was about five feet in diameter. The siren was made of brass, was struck by a current of steam and made to revolve with such a velocity to make a sound that pierced the fog to warn the sailor of his danger. The sound of the fog horn is so loud that it once made a deaf mute, who thought he was immune to its blasts, jump and run for dear life, so greatly did it startle him.

Significance of the Lighthouse

Architecturally, the lighthouse is unique, becasue its ornate design reflects Block Island's taste in building during its popularity as a resort. President Grant visited the light soon after its construction during a visit to the island in 1875. The light is notable today for its Fresnel lenses, once common, but now expensive to maintain when compared to more modern devices. There have been no significant alterations to the structure of the lighthouse itself. On the first floor, for example, the platform that held the reserve barrels of oil for the old lamp are still in place.

The keeper's dwelling is a sturdy example of Victorian Gothic, distinguished by its steep gable roofs. There is an 1873 date-stone in the north gable end. The interior of the dwelling has two symmetrical apartments for the families of the keepers, each consisting of a living room and a dining room with a stair hall on the side. Each apartment has a kitchen in the rear of the first floor and two bedrooms on the second floor. The north apartment is essentially unchanged, while the south apartment was altered on the first floor in the 1960s. Both apartments are still in use by the Coast Guard. Block Island Southeast Light has been recommended for inclusion in the National Register of Historic Places.

The Block Island Historical Society, established in 1942, is working to preserve the two lighthouses on the island. Currently it is trying to raise funds to eventually move, perhaps, the Southeast Light back from the edge of the eroding cliffs. Readers interested in supporting the efforts of the Society are urged to write to its secretary, Block Island, Rhode Island 02807. Annual membership dues are only five dollars.

Marine Disasters—the Wreck of the "Palatine," etc.

As a rule, the salvage from vessels that come from foreign lands with passengers (called "hen boats" to distinguish them from freighters) was highly profitable, because immigrants usually brought along their wordly possessions. Thus, when on a winter's day in the late 1700s a large and disabled ship with many people on board was driven by a storm onto the reefs of the Block Island coast, the wreckers were ready to swarm aboard the hapless craft as soon as it settled. When they climbed up the sides and landed on its deck, they saw a sight they had not bargained for. Instead of finding well-fed passengers, they were confronted by a group of human scarecrows—thin, ragged, pitiful creatures who touched the heart of even the most savage wrecker. Sixteen men and women were taken ashore and cared for. One woman, who had gone mad with fear, vanished into the hold of the ship. Every soul on board was a passenger. What had happened to the officers and crew? This is the story the wreckers were told:

The ship was the "Palatine" which had left Amsterdam, Holland with a group of Dutch families who planned to establish a new Dutch community in Pennsylvania. Bad weather, poor planning and brutal officers drove the crew to mutiny. Once of the sailors had control of the ship, they killed the officers, robbed the passengers, took to the lifeboats and set the "Palatine" adrift. When the ship ran aground on Block Island, the victims of the mutiny had been drifting in the cold Atlantic for many weeks. Children and the elderly died of starvation and exposure. All survivors had given up hope when a storm drove them to land and beached their ship at low tide without breaking it to pieces.

Before high tide set it, the ship was picked bare and set ablaze by the wreckers as the easiest way to get rid of it. Through the vagaries of the elements, it was lifted off the reef by the waves and blown to sea just as the flames began to take hold. By now it was night, and the wind, which had died down at sunset, rose again to gale force. As observers on the beach watched the "Palatine" head seawards, they heard over the roar of the surf the screams of a woman and realized too late that the fear-maddened woman who had vanished into the ship's hold earlier was still aboard.

Local residents say that on nights when the fog is thick and low, the flashing green glare from the light's beam makes it possible for spectators along the shore to see things that may not be there. Among the visions that may appear in the ghastly green light is the burning "Palatine" far off shore. In the dead silence between the unearthly blasts of the light's fog horn, one can hear, so they say, the screams of the mad woman of the "Palatine."

About 0.2 mile southeast of the light is the wreck of another ship, the large tanker "S.S. Lightburne." It is marked by a buoy. The author welcomes any information about this marine disaster. I can be contacted through the publisher, address on title page.

CHAPTER 29

BLOCK ISLAND NORTH LIGHT, Block Island, RI (1829)

Old Light List No.: 134 (Obsolete)
Location: Latitude 41° 13.7' N
　　　　　Longitude 71° 34.6'
Height: 50' (HAW 65')
Lens: Fourth Order, Classical (Fresnel), 2,5000
　　　Candlepower
Rebuilt: 1837, 1857, 1867
Automated: 1955
Deactivated: 1973

Block Island, well offshore, is about six miles long, hilly with elevations up to 211 feet and is bare of trees. The shore of the island is fringed in most places with boulders. Vessels, including small craft, generally give it a berth of over a quarter of a mile. The shoaling is generally abrupt in approaching the island, which is one of the worst places along the southern New England coast for shipping accidents. Of the hundred or so recorded shipping disasters during the past two centuries, it has been estimated that at least half, have been at or near Block Island. For example, between 1819 to 1838, 59 vessels were either stranded or wrecked on the island. These wrecks and strandings included two full-rigged ships, eight brigs, 34 schooners and 15 sloops.

Strategically located near the entrance to Long Island Sound and Narragansett Bay, Block Island is noted also for its fogs and treacherous tides. Sandy Point, which continues several miles out into the water as a sand bar, was particularly dangerous, for here, to quote an account of 1884: "... the swift currents that sweep both shores meet, and struggle for supremacy, the bar in terrible combat being alternately laid bare, and swept by seas towering 50 feet above its surface." Such circumstances, then, showed the danger of navigation near this island and the necessity of maintaining a light of great brightness upon its most dangerous point. Until 1970, when it was deactivated, North Light, or "Old Granitesides," as it is affectionately called, was one of four major lighthouses—others were Block Island South East Light, Montauk Point Light and Point Judith Light—that marked the entrances to Block Island Sound and Long Island Sound.

To mark this entrance and to warn vessels of the long sand bar that extends north into the sea for more than a mile at Sandy Point, a lighthouse was first erected here in 1829 at a cost of $15,000. It was 45 feet high and visible for 12 miles. Despite a protective wall built in 1836, by 1837, the encroaching sea and shifting sands necessitated the building of a new structure. The new lighthouse was constructed a quarter mile farther inland at a spot known as the "blow hole." This new lighthouse was 50 feet high

Block Island North Light, Block Island, RI

Photo by BR1 S.J. Galazzo, U.S. Coast Guard

and built with granite walls. Two fixed lights were shown from towers over either end of the building, in a north and south direction, and each contained several lamps with parabolic reflectors 15 inches in diameter, weighing three-and-a-half pounds each. Lieutenant George M. Bache, U.S.N. reported on November 22, 1838 that these lights were very dim and seen only at a short distance. He noted, "The lights are placed without the foci of the reflectors, so as to produce a divergence in the light reflected of 30° and 40°; but it does not appear brightly when seen at a distance, which is probably owing to the number of lamps in each lantern being too small for the portions of the circle illuminated, as each lamp is required to throw light over a sector of 43°." Enoch Rose, Jr. was appointed keeper on February 23, 19853 at a salary of $400 per year.

This light survived only two decades. The third structure, built in 1857, was located as far out as the first one had been on the Point, but in ten years it, too, was rendered useless by storms. While the location of the first lighthouse is now offshore in water, the foundations of the second and third ones can be seen today at Sandy Point.

The fourth and present lighthouse off the north end of Cow Neck Road was built in 1867. It is a brown tower on a substantial gray granite building, located 700 yards back from the end of Sandy Point. Originally know as Sandy Point Light, its name was changed to North Light in 1875 upon completion of the Southeast Light. Hiram D. Ball, brother of the Honorable Nicholas Ball who had been largely responsible for the promotion of Block Island as a Victorian resort, was appointed keeper of the light station by President Lincoln in 1861. He retained his position at the light for 30 years and thus became the first keeper of the fourth light built in 1867. During this time, the light, reached by way of Cow Neck Road from both Old and New Harbor, was a favorite destination for visitors to the island. By 1900, three life saving stations were also maintained on Block Island: one each at Old Harbor and the West Side, and one at Sandy Point. The rescue station at Sandy Point was in a small frame building located to the north of the lighthouse and was known as the "Skipper's quarters."

In 1867, the light was fixed white and is said to have been visible for 13½ miles. The lantern was a kerosene fourth order classical Fresnel lens, built in Paris and comprised of a complex set of prismatic lenses standing 2' 4" high with an inside diameter of 19-11/16" and shaped like an egg. It used a 60 watt lamp with a four-place lamp changer. In 1894, the light consumed 235 gallons of mineral oil each year. Its one keeper was paid $560 a year. In the 1920s the light showed an occulting white light of 1,1700 candlepower with a group of three eclipses every 13.5 seconds.

Manned by civilians until World War II, the lighthouse was subsequently maintained by the Coast Guard until 1955 when the structure was automated. It was deactivated in 1973. During the 1940s, the lighthouse was electrified, and during the 1950s a flasher was installed. While the French "classical" lenses mentioned earlier remain at the light, the original clock mechanism, turntable and burner have been removed. Their reinstallation is a project of the North Light Commission, appointed by the town of New Shoreham, to whom the responsibility of restoring the lighthouse has been given.

The present light (LLN 18330) is located on a 20-ft. skeleton tower near the old lighthouse and stands 36 feet above the water. Its signal is a flashing white light every five seconds which is visible for 13 miles. This modern light has a 190 mm lens with a 1.15 amp lamp.

In 1973, the United States Fish and Wildlife Service acquired the lighthouse and 28 acres of land as a national wildlife refuge when the Coast Guard declared it was surplus to its needs and could no longer maintain it. Block Island is a major nesting area during spring and fall migrations for many species of small songbirds and some birds of prey. The island is also the site of annual migrations of birdwatchers and members of the Audubon Society who make the trip with the hope of spotting their favorite (or a new) species of birds through field glasses or of capturing their images permanently on photographs. On Tuesday, November 20, 1984, the Fish and Wildlife Service returned the Victorian lighthouse and two acres of land around it to the town of New Shoreham which had originally given the land to the United States Government in 1829.

The two-and-a-half story main block of the building, 30 feet by 33 feet, is constructed of 18 inch granite with handsomely proportioned, heavy Italianate masonry window and entrance treatment typical of institutional building at the time. A single-story kitchen ell is to the rear of the building. Dominating the northern gable over the central entrance is the fireproof tower built of three-quarter inch iron. The building is similar to other lighthouses constructed by the Government and is essentially identical to Great Captain Light, Greenwich, Connecticut (1829) and Old Field Point Light, Port Jefferson, New York (1824).

The town of New Shoreham through its North Light Commission, has repaired the roof, replaced broken windows, and weather-tightened the lighthouse to prevent further deterioration. The Commission intends to complete the restoration of the light as soon as possible. Tax-deductible contributions are always welcome and accepted to help the Commission with its work. The Commission hopes to preserve the structure as a multiuse facility, including, possibly, a maritime museum. The preservation of this fine example of mid-Victorian architecture as a reminder of a passing concept in lighthouse design, among other things, is well worth the effort. Block Island North Light has been nominated for inclusion in the National Register of Historic Places.

•

A Notable Marine Disaster: the Sinking of the "Larchmont"

Off the northwest coast of Block Island on a cold Monday night, February 11, 1907, the schooner "Henry Knowlton" sailed into the steamer

"Larchmont" at about 11:00 p.m. It was one of the worst shipping accidents in the history of Block Island Sound. About 150 persons lost their lives from drowning and exposure as a result of this tragic collision between the Joy Line steamer "Larchmont," bound from Providence, Rhode Island to New York City, and the schooner "Henry Knowlton," bound from South Amboy, New Jersey to Boston, Massachusetts. It was estimated at the time that there were from 75 - 100 passengers aboard the "Larchmont" plus a crew of 50. Of these, there were only 19 known survivors, all of whom suffered terribly from exposure in open boats and rafts in a gale with the temperature below zero degrees. Forty-eight bodies were washed up on the northwest shore of Block Island. Although the "Knowlton" eventually sank despite an attempt to save her, her skipper, Captain Frank T. Haley, and crew of six managed to save themselves by rowing ashore at Quonochontaug, about seven miles north of Watch Hill, Rhode Island. Exhausted and frozen, they staggered into the station to tell what had happened. A complete account of this tragedy may be found on the first two pages of the *New York Times* for Wednesday, February 13, 1907.

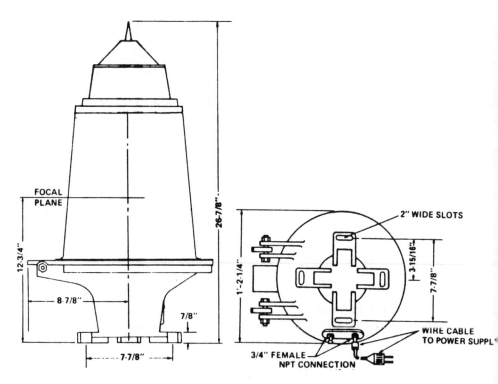

Dimensions of the 250 mm Lantern. Weight 14½ lbs.
Tongue Point, Chapter 15, has one of these lenses. See also page 254

Courtesy U.S. Coast Guard

CHAPTER 30

NEW LONDON HARBOR LIGHT, New London, CT (1760)

Light List No.: 20840
Location: Latitude 41° 19.0′ N
          Longitude 72° 5.4 W
Height: 89′
Range: 14 miles, White Equal Interval White
        11 miles, Red every 6 seconds; Red sector
Lens: Fourth Order, Classical, 500 watt lamp
Rebuilt: 1801
Automated: 1912

At the mouth of the Thames River in Connecticut, the town of New London grew up along one of the best natural harbors in New England. However, dangerous ledges and headlands off the river's mouth were always a shipping hazard, so a beacon of sorts was set up at the harbor's entrance as early as 1750. There is little information to indicate how it was built, where it was located, or how it was supported. But by the end of the decade, the whaling and shipping interests in New London decided that a more substantial lighthouse was needed. They made plans to build the lighthouse on a prominent estate on the western side of the entrance to New London Harbor where the Harris family had lived for generations. At the time, Lucretia Shaw, who was born Lucretia Harris, had inherited the estate and sold part of it, with her husband Nathaniel Shaw, to the colony so that a lighthouse could be constructed on the site.

The money to build the lighthouse was raised by selling lottery tickets, a common and popular practice in those days for raising funds for civic projects like bridges, lighthouses and even churches. History does not record the size of the prize, but it does tell us that the winner had to pay 12% of it as a tax. The tower, finished in 1760, was of stone, 24 feet in diameter at the base and 64 feet high, with the exterior stone hammer-dressed. Its lantern was made of wood. It was the fourth lighthouse to be erected in the young nation. The Colonial Legislature passed various acts which placed taxes on shipping entering and leaving the harbor for the support of the lighthouse, its keeper, and to provide for necessary repairs. During the Revolutionary War, the light served the needs of privateers who sought shelter in New London.

When the federal government was formed in 1789, it assumed responsibility for the few colonial lighthouses then in existence. Consequently, lighthouse work frequently came directly to the attention of the President, whose responsibilities in the fledgling nation were not as vast as they are today. Thus, on Saturday, October 1, 1791, President Washington signed a contract with Nathaniel Richards of New London for supplying oil to the lighthouse:

"... in consideration of which he shall receive Three Hundred & Sixty Dollars to be paid Quarterly .. .the said light consisting of three Lamps of three Spouts each, required annually 800 Galls strained Sperm Ceti Oil at 42 cents per galld dolls. 333.00."

If the lottery was a success, the structure was not. By 1799, the lighthouse was in a state of extreme disrepair. The stone tower had a ten-ft. crack in it, beginning at the top and running down its side. Since there were also many complaints that the light could not be seen to the west because of a promontory of land, the government finally agreed that a new tower should be built. A contract was awarded to Mr. A. Woodward of New London, and construction was begun in 1800. Completed in 1801, the new light was illuminated from a height of 89 feet above the sea, and thus could be seen by all vessels approaching the harbor. It was an octagonal, pyramidal structure, made with freestone, smooth-hammered and laid in courses.

According to early records, the government acquired additional land for its new aid to navigation from:

—Daniel Harris who deeded 19½ rods to the United States on July 18, 1801 for $30.

—Griswold Harris who became a keeper of the light and who deeded 11 rods and 91 feet to the U.S. on September 19, 1814 for $50.

—Charles Harris who deeded two acres and 73 square rods to the U.S. on April 13, 1833 for $650.

—Thomas Fitch who deeded land to the United States on January 27, 1874 for $2,500.

During the War of 1812, at the request of Commodore Decatur, the light in the tower was extinguished, and since there was a regiment of American militia stationed nearby, the British made no attempt to destroy the light. In 1831, the eclipser and lamps were replaced with "patent lamps and reflectors" which in turn were replaced just before the Civil War with a beautiful, efficient (and expensive) fourth-order Fresnel lens.

In 1875, engineers set up two 18 inch fog-signal engines and installed a Daboll fog trumpet which was in operation 553 hours the following year. During 1903, a new fog-signal house was built. Engines were installed the next year, but the fog-signal was discontinued on September 5, 1911, as Race Rock Light and its fog-signal, together with the construction of New London Ledge Light in the harbor in 1908, made the fog-signal unnecessary. On Saturday, July 20, 1912, the light was made an unattended acetylene beacon.

Today, New London Harbor Light is one of the country's most attractive landmarks. The tower remains substantially the same as when it was built in 1801, and is one of the finest masonry lighthouses still in existence. For many years it "pulled a heavy oar" along the Connecticut coast before New London Ledge Light was built in 1908 on a ledge outside the entrance to the harbor. Today, the keeper's house is privately owned by a woman who claims that a former keeper of the light was one of her ances-

New London Harbor Light, New London, CT

tors. Tanks of acetylene gas stored at its base operate the light without attention for several months at a time. A 1500 candlepower red sector from 0° - 41° covers dangerously close shoals to the west and Sarah's Ledge.

Keepers of the Light
Griswold Harris - keeper in 1816; paid $250.

Lyman Reed - appointed May 3, 1853 at $350 year. His salary was increased to $400 on December 22, 1856.

Elijah Bolles - appointed February 1, 1859 at $400 per year.

Description of the Light
New London Harbor Lighthouse stands on a rocky outcrop at the west side of New London Harbor near the mouth of the Thames River. The second lighthouse to have been built on this site, it consists of a tapering octagonal stone tower, presently painted white, with a cylindrical cast-iron lantern painted black, and a circular, cast-iron ogee roof. Contributing to the site is a keeper's dwelling, built of brick in 1863 and englarged in 1900. The foundation of the lighthouse rests directly on the rock of the shoreline. Brownstone, granite and other native stone are laid up on the sloping site to form an uncoursed, rough-faced octagonal foundation topped by a tooled water table. The foundation measures 25' 8" in diameter.

Resting on the water table is the granite sill of the west-facing door. Above the water table, dressed blocks of brownstone laid in courses of varying height form the tapering walls of the tower, each face of the octagon measuring ten feet in width and 19 inches in depth at the water table level. The interior of the tower is lined with brick which supports a cast-iron spiral stair. A six-inch deep, stepped octagonal ring, dating from 1833, projects horizontally from the walls of the tower and supports the cast-iron lantern gallery. A wrought iron lightning conductor, composed of sections and affixed to the lighthouse wall with large staples, extends along the north facade from the lantern gallery to the ground. This feature is unique among Connecticut lighthouses and may be original to this structure.

The lighthouse still contains one of the few remaining Fresnel lamps in Connecticut. A fourth-order lens, manufactured by Henry Lepaute of Paris, France, is set in a bronze mounting. Its focal plane is 89 feet above high water. Light is transmitted through 12 flat glass panes around the occulus in the upper half of the lantern. Beneath the plates are curved cast-iron plates, lined with beaded boards and containing five brass circular ventilators.

The keeper's dwelling, privately owned since 1928, was built in 1863 as a three-bay, gable-roofed house of 2½ stories. The first story, used as both a storeroom and a stormhouse, contained four rooms and a one-story hyphen to the lighthouse. A kitchen wing with a red tin roof was added in 1885. In 1900, shed-roofed dormers were added on the third floor where an assistant keeper and his family were housed.

In former years, other buildings associated with the lighthouse stood nearby. These included: a brick engine room or fog-signal building, measuring 14' x 18' in plan; a barn; and, after 1903, a new fog-signal house measuring 20' x 30' in plan. Each of these structures has since been demolished.

New London Harbor Lighthouse is a primary navigational aid for commercial and pleasure craft entering the Thames River. It is one of the oldest lighthouses on the Connecticut coast and is highly visible to the public from both the sea and land. Its sandstone walls are in unusually good condition. Some sailors rate New London Harbor Lighthouse Connecticut's most beautiful.

Significance of the Light

New London Harbor Lighthouse is highly significant in the history of aids to navigation in Long Island Sound. The first lighthouse on the Sound was established on that site in 1760. In addition, it is the fourth oldest lighthouse in the United States, following the Boston, Mass. (1716) lighthouses. The original light tower was one of the 12 colonial lights taken over by the newly-formed federal government in 1789. George Washington signed the contract with the lighthouse supplier in New London in 1791, indicating both the interest taken in the Lighthouse Service by the leaders of the New Country and the small size of the federal government in that period.

Constructed in 1801 as a replacement for the deteriorated colonial structure, the present tower is the oldest lighthouse remaining in Connecticut and typifies the federal government's standardized format for masonry towers which continued as a model into the mid-19th century. The New London Harbor Light also is significant as the site of numerous tests for improvements in lighting apparatus and fog-signal devices used by the federal Lighthouse Service, from the earliest incorporation of Lewis's parabolic reflector and Argand lamp system in a chandelier, to the thousands of candlepower of the 20th century acetylene gas lamp and electrical equipment.

The original lighthouse was funded through a lottery at a time when lighthouses were built individually by local shipping interests and great stretches of the coast remained unmarked. Prior to the Revolution, the 1760 tower was maintained with funds granted by the state legislature. After the Revolution, taxes on shipping were used to pay for the upkeep of lighthouses. By 1789, when the federal government assumed responsibility for all lighthouses in the young nation, the New London Harbor Lighthouse had developed a crack ten feet long in its hammered stone wall, and at 64 feet, its height was determined insufficient to be clearly visible from the west. On May 5, 1800, Congress appropriated $15,700 for rebuilding, altering and improving the lighthouse. A. Woodward received the contract for construction of the lighthouse, oil vault and cistern for $16,500, eight hundred dollars more than the congressional appropriation. He began construction in the summer of 1800. Completed in 1801, this structure remains unaltered as the present lighthouse.

By 1833, the 1801 lighthouse needed extensive repair. In that year, Charles H. Smith contracted to furnish a new stone deck, lay on a brick arch, and supply the following: a new lantern surrounded with two iron rails one inch square, a new cooper dome and vane, a new flight of wood stairs, and a new outer door and lock. He agreed to cement the the outer points in the tower with hydraulic or Roman cement and white wash the whole. The lantern, deck and dome were to be equal in size to those at Morgan Point Lighthouse in Noank, Connecticut, built between 1831 - 1832. Repairs were to cost $1500. In 1863, a third set of stairs, an iron circular stairway, was installed in the tower. In all likelihood this installation also included the brick lining wall which supports the outer ends of the stair treads.

A remarkable succession of innovative lighting devices have been used at the New London Harbor Light. Oil lamps and an eclipser were installed in the newly constructed light tower only five years after the first use in the United States of such an intermittent lighting device at Cape Cod, Massachusetts. Although Winslow Lewis's patent lamps and parabolic reflectors were adopted for U.S. lighthouses in 1812, New London Harbor Lighthouse was darkened during the war. In 1816, it was among the last of the 49 North American lighthouses to be refitted with the Lewis apparatus. When the new lantern was installed at the lighthouse in 1833, the Lewis apparatus was reinstalled, but by 1850, a visiting inspector had declared the lighting apparatus in poor condition, noting that several arms to the reflectors were either loose or missing.

Within the next decade, a Fresnel lens was installed. The Henry Lepaute fixed lens presently housed in the lantern may be the original equipment. It matches the description of the fourth-order, fixed Henry Lepaute lens in place in the New London Harbor Lighthouse in 1876, 1903, and 1911. In 1909, illumination was furnished by an incandescent oil-vapor lamp. On July 20, 1912, the illumination was changed to acetylene gas. In 1930, the lighthouse had a 2200 candlepower electric lamp.

A lighthouse keeper's dwelling, measuring 36' x 18' in plan, was constructed some distance to the west of the light tower in 1818. A contract for this job for the amount of $1,200 was awarded to Kimball Prince and Lewis Crandall of New London. In 1836, John Bishop of New York enlarged the house with a one-story kitchen wing for the sum of $590. The present keeper's dwelling was built in 1863, somewhat altered from the plans drawn up by the Lighthouse Board's engineers.

Alterations to the dwelling carried out in 1900 reflect a major development in the Lighthouse Service personnel policy. Prior to this time, the assistant keeper's position was available only to single men. However, the Service realized that by providing accomodations for married assistant lighthouse keepers, it could attract and train good candidates for future lighthouse keeper positions. To accomodate a married assistant keeper, the New London Harbor Light's keeper's dwelling was raised one story in 1900, with two shed roof dormers installed on either slope of the gabled roof. A one-story, shed-roofed porch on the south elevation also dates from this general period.

New London Harbor Light is particularly significant in the history of fog-signals. The Daboll trumpet, widely adopted by the Lighthouse Board after the mid-19th century, was named after its developer, C. L. Daboll, a citizen of New London. In 1858, a special commitee was formed to investigate the Daboll invention. At New London Harbor Light a fog-signal engine was in place in 1869, and in 1874, a second-class fog-signal in duplicate was completed and in operation. In 1877, the equipment at the lighthouse was described as a second-class Daboll trumpet in duplicate, operated by an 18 inch Ericson hot-air engine, and housed in a brick fog-signal building. Measuring 18' x 14' in plan, this structure stood 148 feet from the lighthouse. During the first year it operated 1165 hours.

Need for a better signal was expressed, and in 1883 a first-class fog trumpet was installed. Thirteen years later, in 1896, the fog-signal was improved with the installaion of two 3½ horsepower Hornsby-Akroyd oil engines and air compressors to operate the Daboll trumpets. In 1900, the old fog-snal house was converted into an oil storehouse and, in 1904, was moved from its old site to the north side of a new fog-signal house built in 1903. There it was converted into a workshop. The new fog-signal house contained two 13 horsepower engines for the trumpets and siren.

City water pipes were laid to the fog-signal house, as well as the dwelling, also in 1904. In 1911, the fog-signal was discontinued on the site and moved to New London Ledge Lighthouse, a short distance away. Lighthouse inspector reports, early photographs and postcards provide evidence of several structures related to the lighthouse station which no longer remain standing: a barn; an engine room; an oil house; and a privy. Today, only the lighthouse and the keeper's dwelling remain.

The New London Harbor Lighthouse site is significant also in the history of aids to navigation on the Thames River, since a light has been located there continuously since the mid-18th century. This made the light 226 years old in 1986. It is the only lighthouse site in Connecticut to make this claim. It is not surprising, therefore, that this venerable structure has been nominated to be included in the National Register of Historic Places.

CHAPTER 31

NEW LONDON LEDGE LIGHT, New London, CT (1909)

Light List No.: 20825
Location: Latitude 41° 18.3′ N
        Longitude: 72° 4.7′ W
Height: 58′
Range: 17 miles, White
      16 miles, Red
      Group Flashing White (3+1)
      Alternate Flashing Red (3+1), every 30 seconds,
      Horn
Lens: FA-251 Rotating, 150 watt lamp
Automated: Fall 1986

New London Ledge Lighthouse looms on the horizon like a mirage. It looks like a stately house in an old neighborhood that floated away (perhaps in a storm) to become stuck on a submerged reef. Though classified as French Second Empire style, the design is close to Georgian, though it was built in in this century. The light is located at the mouth of New London Harbor, about one mile off shore The structure consists of a square concrete base and a two-story, red-brick house with a white trim, a mansard roof and attic dormer windows; the lantern is located in the center of the roof. The lighthouse is oriented so that its corners face north, south, east and west, but for purposes of clarity, the elevation with the door facing New London is referred to as "north."

The light is highly visible to the public and is one of the best surviving examples of a masonry type lighthouse. An underwater cable from nearby Avery Point provides electricity for the lighthouse. Water used to be shipped to it and stored in an 11,000 gallon tank. Sometimes the winds pick up from the south and fierce storm swells from the Atlantic break through the Race, breaking high on the lighthouse and blowing out the windows on the second floor.

A new lighthouse for the area was recommended in 1890, because New London Harbor Light was ineffective in thick weather in guiding vessels clear of the numerous shoals and ledges at the entrance to the harbor. Black Ledge was selected first for the site, but it was changed afterwards to the west side of Southwest Ledge. Work on the light began in July 1908 and was completed in October 1909; the station was established on Wednesday, November 10, 1909. Mineral oil was used as fuel oil for the light until 1913. The total cost to build the lighthouse was $93,968.96, a considerable sum at the turn of the century.

The original fourth-order classical fresnel lens, removed from the lighthouse in 1984, consisted of hand-crafted crystal encased in brass. It was made in Paris, France. The lamp floated on a bed of mercury and was

New London Ledge Light, New London, CT

turned by a complex clockwork gear system which was counterweighted with an 85 pound dropping pendulum. The clockwork had to be wound every four hours to maintain proper operation of the light.

In the days of the Lighthouse Service (1910-1939), the lighthouse was maintained privately at times. When the Coast Guard took over its operation on July 1, 1939, it provided a yearly budget (recently it was about $15,000) to heat the house, keep it in good repair and to buy any necessary household items. It provided also each member of the new four-man crew with a monthly allowance (about $125 in 1985) for food. The crew, which was surprisingly self-sufficient, did its own shopping and ferried supplies to the lighthouse in the small vessels assigned to it. Larger Coat Guard vessels made the weekly run during the winter. Coast Guardsmen spent off-duty hours at the light watching television, studying correspondence courses or for advancement in rating, working out in the small one-room gym or fishing. One of the last projects at the light before it was automated in the fall of 1986 was the stripping of years and years of six to eight layers of old paint from the interior down to the original wood.

Now that the light is automated, we can only hope that this historic building will not fall prey to the ravishes of mindless vandalism which has been the fate of most of the unmanned lighthouses in the First Coast Guard District. Sadly, however, it seems likely that this will happen unless a close watch of the structure is maintained. When the lighthouse was manned, it was open to the public from 10 a.m. to 6 p.m. as long as visitors furnished their own transportation to and from the station. Project Oceanology has taken over 5,000 school children to the lighthouse during recent years. With automation, this access may be lost and the lighthouse, an integral part of the navigation and maritime history of New London and Connecticut, may become just a memory unless some local organization is willing to assume responsibility for its care and maintenance. The State of Connecticut is working on leasing it from the Coast Guard. If things work out, the State will sublease the light to Project Oceanology.

Description of the Lighthouse

New London Ledge Light rises from Long Island Sound on the east side of the entrance to New London Harbor and marks two hazards to shipping, a sharp ledge of rock and a 200-ft. long shoal on which it rests. The structure consists of a square concrete foundation and pier surmounted by a cubelike brick dwelling with a mansard roof and cylindrical lantern. Presently the dwelling is painted red with white trim.

Standing in 28 feet of water, the foundation was constructed inside a timber crib 52 feet square and 31 feet high. The crib was filled with concrete, riprap and gravel and capped with a three ft. layer of concrete. In 1938, the timber crib was removed and a new boarding ledge created. A riprap deposit, 82 feet square and ten feet deep, forms a bulwark around the foundation. Resting on the foundation is a concrete pier, 50 feet square, rising 18 feet above low water and containing cellar space and two cisterns for the superstructure. On the southwest face of the pier are painted test markings for submarines on their training exercises from the base at nearby Groton. The fog-signal is mounted on top of the pier on the southeast side.

The superstructure measures 32 square feet. Blocks of smooth-faced granite are used for trim. Rising from the center of the mansard roof is the upper half of the octagonal brick watchroom and a cast-iron lantern. the more imposing of the two doorways is located on the southeast facade, facing the Sound. Above this double-leafed door the date "1901" is carved into the lintel, the numerals presently highlighted with black paint.

Walls of the octagonal watchroom, presently painted white with black trim, contain alternating port hole windows and ventilators. A cast-iron lantern gallery, surmounting the watchroom and extending beyond its walls, is edged with a single pipe rail carried by plain cylindrical stanchions. Curved glass panes measuring 24 inches on a side are fitted in the top half of the lantern walls. The panes are separated by diagonal astragals and are set above curved cast-iron plates containing ventilators of two styles. Interior space was utilized, until the fall of 1986, for both living quarters and aids to navigation, following the original intent of the design.

The structural system includes the use of concrete in what was the state-of-the-art technology for 1906, before flat slab construction was widely used. Drawings from the New Jersey Foundry and Machine Company labelled "Second Floor Steel Plan" show that the floors are supported by steel I-beams. The basement contains the base of a central cast-iron column which rises to the lantern. Unlike those in earlier lighthouses, this column has no structural function, but served only as a channel for the clockwork mechanism weight drops for the Fresnel lens.

The original fourth-order Henry Lepaute Fresnel lens, operated by clockwork and rotating on ball bearings, was furnished with a thirty-five millimeter double-tank incandescent oil vapor lamp. The present light was installed in 1984 when the Fresnel lens was removed. It's a somewhat smaller automated light (SA-251 rotating with a 150 watt lamp), emitting three white flashes and one red flash every 30 seconds.

A Ghost Story

Local legend has it that New London Ledge Lighthouse is haunted by the ghost of a jilted husband. In 1936, when the lighthouse was operated privately by one family prior to the Coast Guard take-over in 1939, a keeper named Ernie discovered that his wife had run away with a Block Island ferry captain. Ernie was so distraught at this turn of events that he climbed to the top of the lighthouse, opened the curved steel door in the lantern gallery and leaped from the catwalk which encircles it, dashing to his death on the riprap below.

Subsequent keepers claimed that the heavy curved door, which is bolted from the inside, opened mysteriously at times. "The wind can be blamed for many of the strange noises we hear, but I know the sound of that door opening up and no wind ever did that," a Coast Guardsman recently said. Some crew members claimed to have heard the decks being swabbed in the early hours of the morning. Others have said they heard footsteps or felt cold spots in the rooms of the lighthouse. Still others claimed that boats were mischievously untied and allowed to float away with the currents. Ernie is blamed also for the occasional unexpected switching on and off of the light signal and the fog horn.

None of the electronic devices the Coast Guard has added to the lighthouse have been able to detect Ernie's tortured ghost opening the catwalk door or swabbing the decks in the dead of night. And there is no guarantee that Ernie will leave New London Ledge Light just because it is automated.

Significance of the Light

New London Ledge Lighthouse is a significant landmark in the history of navigational aids in New London Harbor, marking a major hazard to navigation at the harbor entrance and replacing functionally the New London Harbor Light, constructed in 1801, long considered inadequate. In the history of lighthouse architecture, New London Ledge Light presents a rare example of a turn-of-the-century lighthouse on a wave-swept site which is not of pre-fabricated cast-iron construction. The light is an unusual example of French Second Empire style applied to a lighthouse long after the style had been popular in the period 1860-1890.

There is a remarkable similarity between the light and a building called the "Chateau" on Green Street in New London, built about the same period. It seems likely that the lighthouse inspired the owner of the "Chateau" to imitate a style quite out of fashion. Nevertheless, perhaps because the Congressional appropriation followed the initial site survey by 14 years, the design of the superstructure combines 19th century ideas and styles with those of the 20th century in an unusual way. Original working drawings of the lighthouse, dated 1906, show the use of steel beams and cinder slab construction to support the wood floors, an early use of this technology in the United States.

New London Ledge Lighthouse is a rare example of a combined light tower and keeper's dwelling, built during the 20th century in a revival style and emphasizing the domestic model. This type of lighthouse design had flourished in the United States during the 1860s and 1870s. Stylistically, it reflects the influence of early 20th century Colonial Revival in a variety of features, such as red brick and white trim, small paned rectangular windows, prominent quoins, pedimented dormers, and a "hipped" roof with dentiled cornice. The flooring system consisted of cinder, concrete and steel I-beams, innovative materials and building technique when the lighthouse working drawings were drafted in 1906. The proportions and the scale of details, however, reflect the taste of the late 19th century and the period's enthusiasm for and appreciation of early American architecture. In general, Colonial Revival buildings of the late 19th century lacked the sophistication of later, more authentic re-creations.

The lighthouse type appearing as a house with cupola was begun in the United States in the 1830s with structures of frame construction. The idea of combining living and lighthouse functions in one structure, emphasizing the dwelling function, was a design practice which flourished under the Lighthouse Board from 1852 to 1910. After mid-century in Long Island Sound, the country's enthusiasm for revival styles was reflected in such lighthouses as Penfield Reef and Stratford Shoal Middleground. The practice continued into the period of pre-fabricated, cast-iron construction and included metal houses-with-towers, such as Southwest Ledge Light, New Haven, Connecticut and Fourteen Foot Bank Light in Delaware Bay.

Beginning in the early 1870s with the development at Hunting Island, South Carolina of the pre-fabricated, cast-iron lighthouses of truncated conical shape, the combination of house and lighthouse lost its domestic emphasis. During the 1870s, tubular cast-iron foundations were developed for erecting lighthouses on difficult sites, such as reefs, shoals and ledges in northern waters where ice floes during the winter months made the screwpile lighthouse impractical. These foundations could be fabricated in sections and assembled at the site of installation by bolting together flanges molded around each section. By changing the number of sections or rings, the height of the foundation could be adjusted. The development of superstructures which also were circular in section and constructed in the same economical way followed naturally. For wave-swept site such as Southwest Ledge, upon which New London Ledge Light rests, a cast-iron, tubular foundation would have been the common choice from the late 1870s until the 1920s.

Instead, a square foundation of timber, 52 feet square and 31 feet high, was constructed by the Thomas A. Scott Company of New London on the banks of the Thames River in Groton, Connecticut. Tom Scott, a master diver, was also the builder of the famous Race Rock Lighthouse in 1878. His friend, F. Hopkinson Smith, engineer, painter and author, worked with him to build the two lights. Their stories are told later in this book, in Chapter 33. Towed into position over the Southwest Ledge Shoal, a timber crib was filled with concrete and riprap and sunk into the 28 feet of water to the bottom. On the concrete top layer of the foundation which extended three feet above the water, the Hamilton R. Douglas Company of New London erected the lighthouse. The company also built the Groton Town Hall.

In the history of aids to navigation in the Thames River area, the site of New London Ledge Lighthouse was early marked as a hazard. The state of Connecticut ceded rocks and ledges off the harbor of New London to the federal government in 1790, as well as the lighthouse on the western shore, New London Harbor Light. In 1794, Congress acted to establish a buoy on Southwest Ledge and other rocks to be funded by import duties and tonnage fees. Lobbying for a lighthouse on the site began in 1890, when the fog-signal and light at the old lighthouse in the harbor were believed to be inadequate in thick weather. In addition, the light was difficult to discern against the illumination of arc lights on the shore. The first site chosen for the new lighthouse, Black Ledge, was later abandoned for Southwest Ledge, which otherwise would have presented a hazard between a Black Ledge Lighthouse and the ship channel. Since a Southwest Ledge Lighthouse already existed near New Haven, the name was changed to New London Ledge Light.

Construction of the 11-room lighthouse was delayed for more than a decade after initial consideration by Congress. In 1908, the contracts were awarded. Upon completion of the structure in October 1909, the fourth-order Fresnel lens, manufactured by Henri Lepaute in Paris, France, was installed, and the lighthouse was illuminated for the first time one month later. Its 22,000 candlepower beam supplemented the weaker beam of New London Harbor Light. In 1911, the fog-signal apparatus at New London Ledge Light replaced that of the older lighthouse. The valuable and beautiful Fresnel lens was removed in 1984 and replaced with a somewhat smaller modern lighting apparatus. Serving both as a hazard marker and entrance beacon to a major harbor and river, New London Ledge Lighthouse is a priceless rarity, a 20th century east coat lighthouse which fulfills a function usually carried out by an early 18th century lighthouse or its replacement on site. Is it any wonder that this unique and handsome structure has been nominated for inclusion in the National Register of Historic Places?

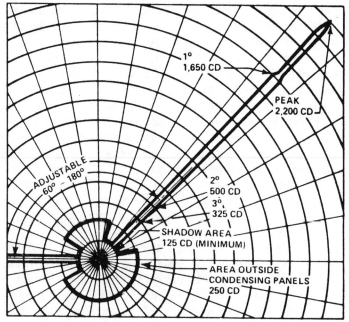

Horizontal intensity distribution of a 250 mm lens with two condensing panels and a 12 volt d.c. 0.77A Lamp. Refer to Chapter 42

CHAPTER 32

LITTLE GULL ISLAND LIGHT, THE RACE, between Long Island Sound and Block Island Sound, NY (1806)

Light List No.: 18665
Location: Latitude 41° 12.4′ N
Longitude 72° 6.5′ W
Height: 81′ (HAW 91′)
Range: 18 miles, Fixed White, Horn
Lens: Second-order Classical, 1000 watt lamp
Radio Beacon: 306 kHz, J (. _ _ _) II, 20 miles
Rebuilt: 1868
Automated: May, 1978

Little Gull Island Light is a tall, slim gray-granite lighthouse located seven miles northeast of Orient Point, New York. It warns mariners of The Race and the shoals south of it and has a much used radio direction finding station, synchronized for distance finding. Vessels sailing from the east to Long Island Sound pass it and another unusual lighthouse Race Rock Light. The two lights are 3.3 nautical miles apart off the shores of New London, Connecticut.

Its erection in 1806, at a location known as the "Key to Long Island Sound," gave mariners hope that shipwrecks in the vicinity would diminish, for year after year vessels attempting to run The Race met with disaster. However, the original 50-ft. tower brought no such result. Accordingly, the Lighthouse Board decided that an additional light would be needed in these waters and eventually erected a second lighthouse northeast of it on Race Rock in 1878. The deed to the island is dated 1803. Benjamin Jerome received $800 for about 17 acres of land which included Little Gull Island. In 1883, mineral-oil lamps were substituted for those burning lard oil.

Little Gull Reef, with little depth over it and foul ground, extends 0.3 mile east-northeastward from Little Gull Island. Deep-draft vessels should avoid this locality. Craft passing south of Valiant Rock should hold a course about one mile northeast of Little Gull Island Light. Fishing boats frequently ply close to the reefs around Great Gull and Little Gull Islands. Stay away. Many wrecks have occured there.

Description of the Lighthouse and Site

Little Gull Island is a rock outcropping about two acres in area. It lies between Long Island Sound to the west and Block Island Sound to the east. The channel between the two Sounds is about 3.5 miles wide and is known as The Race; it is subject to varying and violent currents due to the confluence of the two bodies of water. For example, the average flood velocity is 2.9 knots and the average ebb velocity 3.5 knots. Velocities can reach 5 knots. There are always rips and swirls in the wake of all broken ground in The Race, except for about one-half hour at slack water. The rips are exceptionally heavy during heavy weather, and especially when a strong wind opposes the current, or the current sets through against a heavy sea. It was this condition which led to the initial establishment of a lighthouse on Little Gull Island as early as 1806.

The granite base for the second (1868) lighthouse is a circular structure about 19 feet in diameter, rising to 12 feet in diameter at the top. The door to the tower faces north and presents a vaguely Italiante appearance with the granite blocks brought forward on either side of it to suggest pilasters. The lintel above the door is a single piece of granite with the date "1868" carved in the center of it. At one time, the tower had a keeper's dwelling attached to it; that dwelling has been replaced by a modern brick building, which holds the generating equipment, and two small fiber glass-walled storage sheds which do not abut the tower. There are four windows in the tower, one on the entry level facing south and three others staggered around the tower to light the landings inside. The lantern surmounts the watch deck. Twelve-sided in plan, the walls feature three tiers of glazing in cast-iron frames. Sheet-metal covers the ogee-shaped roof which has a ventilator ball at its peak.

Inside, the tower is lined with brick. Total wall thickness, including brick and stone, is 5½ feet at the base and 2 feet at the parapet. A cast-iron column rises through the center of the tower. The cast-iron stairs which ascend in spiral fashion, hang from the central column. Resting atop the central column is the footing for the cast-iron floor of the watch deck. The lantern retains an old Fresnel lens, probably dating from the early 20th century. Made in Paris, France by the firm of Henry Lepaute, the drum-shaped lens consists of round prisms stacked atop one another in brass retainers.

Gone from the site are a boathouse and privy which stood south of the tower and a wharf which extended westward from the island. The site retains a measure of historic integrity because of the lighthouse and the base upon which it stands. Although there are some cracks in the tower lining and the interior metal elements, the lighthouse and its base are essentially sound.

Keepers 1805-1909

Israel Rodgers, July 1, 1805. Resigned November 18, 1809
Giles Holt, December 6, 1809. Resigned September 16, 1816
John Rodgers 2nd, September 24, 1816. Removed
Frederick Chase, March 8, 1826. Resigned August 27, 1836
Horace B. Manwaring, September 5, 1836
William S. Gardiner, May 29, 1849. Removed. Paid $400 year
William Ross, March 23, 1855. Paid $400 year
James Warner, February 1, 1859

Little Gull Island Light, Little Gull Island, NY

195

Wallace Reeves, April 16, 1861. Removed August 9, 1861
John H. Conkling, August 9, 1861
William W. Reeves, May 13, 1869
George S. Tooker, April 24, 1874
Henry P. Fields, May 3, 1875
Henry P. Fields (Perm.), September 18, 1875. Resigned
George H. Adams, July 25, 1901
Peter M. Peterson, September 1, 1906
William J. Murray, December 19, 1909

Assistant Keepers 1854 - 1857
Shubael Bogue, October 10, 1854. Resigned. Paid $300 year
James Wilcox, April 21, 1855. Resigned. Paid $300 year
Shubael Bogue, October 24, 1855. Removed. Paid $300 year
James Warner, February 1, 1857. Paid $300 year
Elisha G. Beebe, March 3, 1857. Paid $300 year

Historical Significance of the Light
The second light on Little Gull Island illustrates a distinctive episode in the development of United States lighthouse design. It was among the last masonry lighthouses built on the East Coast in the 19th century. By the time of its construction in 1868, lighthouse building had been influenced by a trend towards stylization and a growing use of new materials such as cast-iron. Little Gull Island Light is thus an example of lighthouse technology in transition during the 1860s.

The lighthouse also has significance within the maritime history of the eastern Long Island Sound region. While the present lighthouse represents a period of increased shipping to and from the ports of New York City and the towns along the Connecticut coastline, its location was important to the more local sea-going interests as far back as 1806, when the first lighthouse was erected on Little Gull Island. Fishing and coastal trade ranked among the most prominent economic activities in the communities around eastern Long Island Sound from the days of their earliest settlement. The hazardous condition at the confluence of Long Island and Block Island Sounds had long been recognized, and the first lighthouse on Little Gull Island was among the earliest projects completed by the federal government upon its assumption of responsibility for aids to navigation.

In the 18th and first half of the 19th centuries, masonry provided the only available means to satisfy the stringent requirements of lighthouse construction. The lighthouse had to be stable and relatively tall. Even when architects participated in lighthouse design, as with the 1850 tower at Execution Rocks, New York, the masonry techniques of vernacular builders formed the structural scheme. Even internal elements, notably stairways, consisted of masonry. In the mid-19th century, many of the early masonry lighthouse were refitted with cast-iron stairways, but the iron stairs of Little Gull Island Light appear to be the original, indicating that the introduction of iron as a structural material for lighthouses, begun in the early 1850s, had an impact on the design of the site.

For the most part, the early masonry towers have scant sign of ornament or stylization. By the 1860s, however, many new lighthouses embodied fully realized architectural statements. For example, the door of Little Gull Island Light has a stylish, Italianate-inspired appearance, suggesting that the movement toward aesthetic consideration had an impact on even those towers that followed long-established structural schemes. In the use of iron and its stylized door, then, Little Gull Island Light portrays two elements which differed from prior practice, while the overall design, nevertheless, falls squarely in the realm of traditional techniques. By the early 1880s, iron towers had supplanted masonry ones, so Little Gull Island Light represents the final stage of masonry lighthouses construction in the United States.

The lighthouse also gains significance by virtue of the old Fresnel lens, mentioned earlier, which remains in the lantern. The lens probably is not original to the lighthouse, but it is important as one of the decreasing number of such devices still in service. Little Gull Island Light has been nominated deservedly to be included in the National Register of Historical Places.

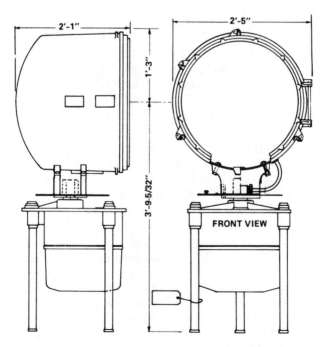

FRONT VIEW

Dimensions of a DCB-24 Lantern. See page 255

CHAPTER 33

RACE ROCK LIGHT, The Race, near Fishers Island, NY (1878)

Light List No.: 18650
Location: Latitude 41° 14.6' W
Longitude 72° 2.9' W
Height: 67'
Range: 19 miles, Flashing Red every 10 seconds
Horn
Lens: DCB-24, 1000 Watt lamp
Automated: November 1978 (Fresnel lens removed)

The Challenge

Race Rock Lighthouse will stand forever as a monument to the courage and skill of two indomitable men. Francis Hopkinson Smith (1838-1915), its engineer, and Captain Thomas Albertson Scott (1830-1907), his construction foreman. They successfully attempted the formidable task of building a lighthouse at a location that others said was impossible. Their engineering challenge was monumental.

As we shall see, just establishing basic acceptable working conditions proved difficult, requiring thousands of tons of riprap to secure the work-in-progress from the violent water conditions. These tons of materials were ferried to the site occupying several vessels for weeks at a time during the construction which was to last for seven years. Storing and handling these materials required the erection of temporary piers, cranes and inclined planes. Masons had to work underwater frequently. And at all times the builders were subject to the whims of nature with her winds, waves and sudden storms. It was not an easy task. We must remember that most lighthouses were built on land with the notable exception of Minot's Ledge Light (1850-1860) at the southern entrance to Boston Harbor, which was also a remarkable engineering feat.

Race Rock, in general, is a ledge of some extent, composed of one 12 by 4-ft. rock and several smaller spurs of rocks rising above the surface, but it is chiefly submerged at low water. It lies eight miles southeast of New London, Connecticut and 0.6 mile southwest of Fishers Island in Long Island Sound. It was not, as Smith and Scott first supposed, one gigantic "bowlder." On the principal spur, Race Rock proper, the least depth at mean low water was three feet, whereas the greatest depth in the 69-ft. circle prepared for the lighthouse foundation, was 13 feet.

The mean velocity of the tidal currents at strength through the Race is about 3.5 knots, although at times it is much greater. Nearly always there are strong rips and swirls in the wake of all broken ground in the vicinity, which is similar to the neck of a bottle, through which most of the tidal

Race Rock Light, off Fishers Island, NY

water races (hence the name) as it enters and leaves Long Island Sound. The rips are unusually strong in heavy weather, especially when a strong wind opposes the current, or when the current sets through against a heavy sea. Thus, it was upon Race Rock proper in from three to 13 feet of water that the lighthouse was to be built. Such was the challenge to Smith and Scott.

F. Hopkinson Smith was a remarkable man. He was the partner in the firm of Smith and Symington which won the contract to build the light. In addition to being an engineer, Smith was a good painter and writer. Perhaps his best known novel is *Caleb West, Master Diver* (Boston: Houghton Mifflin company, 1898), which tells the story of the construction of Race Rock Light and is a personal tribute to his friend, Captain Scott. His other novels of interest are: *The Tides of Barnegat* (1906) and *Kennedy Square* (1911). As a water-color and black-and-white painter, he illustrated his own travel sketches in Spain, the Netherlands, Italy and Mexico and his own *Charcoals of New and Old New York* (1912), *In Thackeray's London* (1913) and *In Dicken's London* (1914). Besides his artistic accomplishments, Smith built the government sea wall at Governor's Island, New York and a similar one at Tompkinsville, Staten Island, New York. He later constructed the foundation for the Statue of Liberty in New York Harbor. Earlier, in 1874, he built the foundation for Penfield Reef Light, Bridgeport, Connecticut.

Captain Tom Scott, the Captain Joe of Smith's novel, *Caleb West*, was head of the Scott Wrecking Company until his death. He met F.H. Smith accidentally during the 1860s in New London, Connecticut, and they became friends. Smith once described Scott as "a bifurcated sea dog." Scott was a master diver and, as such, did the submarine work on many of the lighthouses that Smith built. During his career, he performed many acts of heroism which were recounted in Smith's novel. He received citation after citation for his bravery during the building of Race Rock Light, since in its early stages much dangerous work had to be done under water. Scott and Smith returned to the scene of their triumph many years later and were pleased to note that the fine joints in the masonry of the pier and the lighthouse structure were as true as the day they had placed them. John Floherty has a good account of Race Rock Light and its builders in his book *Sentries of the Sea* (New York: J.B. Lippincott Company, 1942), pages 110-122.

Preliminary Efforts

Race Rock Lighthouse was built, as I have said, under great difficulties, both physical and financial. At times one wonders that it was ever built at all. Not only was it in an extremely dangerous location upon which to build a light, but it took also forty years to persuade Congress to provide the necessary funds for its construction. Between 1829-1837, eight vessels were lost on Race Point Reef. Accordingly, the first plan was to erect a light station at Race Point on the southwest end of Fishers Island where so many of the wrecks had occurred. This portion of the coast was examined by Lieutenant George M. Bache, U.S.N. in 1838. In his report, he mentioned the accidents at Race Point and wrote:

... much benefit might be derived from a light upon Race point, if the navigation in its neighborhood were free from obstructions; but in addition to the reef which extends for some distance off from Fisher's Island, the dangerous rock, called Race Rock, lies at a distance of nearly three-fourths of a mile from it. It is difficult, in hazy weather particularly, to form an accurate estimation of the distance of a light; and vessels judging from the bearings of one on Race point, that they had given it a sufficient berth to clear all dangers, might be decoyed upon the rocks; its erection therefore is not recommended.

Bache's observations apparently settled the matter temorarily as far as Race Point was concerned. Even though Congress appropriated $3,000 for a lighthouse to be built at Race Rock, no further action was taken at this time. It was not until a dreadful marine tragedy took place, the sinking of the steamer "Atlantic" in 1846, that the entire subject was brought back into sharp relief. However, it was not until 1852 that the Lighthouse Board reported, "Various attempts have been made, and numerous appropriations expended in endeavoring to place an efficient and permanent mark on this point. Buoys cannot be kept on it, and spindles have only remained until the breaking up of the ice in the spring." Within the preceding 50 years, two different spindles had been placed on the rock. Each was about three inches in diameter and set eighteen inches into the ledge, and each had been carried away. As a result of the recommendation of the Lighthouse Board, an examination of Race Rock was made with the view to erecting a third spindle. The Board believed that a whole season might be required to set a spindle seven inches in diameter four feet into the Rock.

In 1853, $7,000 was appropriated "for a beacon on Race Rock." This took the form of a day beacon, completed in 1856. Nothing further was done along this line, but the question of a lighthouse at Race Point was revived, the proposed site was examined, and in 1855, another $8,000 was appropriated for the station's establishment. But troubles and delays arose in obtaining valid titles, and Race Rock itself was finally chosen as the site. Developments were slow. On July 28, 1866, after the comparative quiet which reigned in new lighthouse ventures during the Civil War, Congress appropriated yet another $90,000 for the erection of a "beacon" on Race Rock, but without a dwelling. At that time, the rock was supposed to be a big "bowlder." On it was proposed to erect a tower, and the keeper's dwelling was to be at the south end of Fisher's Island. After a careful survey of the rock, however, which disclosed its true dimensions, the plans were modified to build a concrete base instead of the riprap formerly planned.

Between 1838 and 1870, Congress appropriated a total of $108,000 for the lighthouse project at or near Race Rock, and in 1871 an additional

$150,000 was provided after surveys indicated that $200,000 would be required to build the lighthouse. Smith and Scott began work at last in April 1971. *The Annual Report of the Lighthouse Board* for 1872 reads: "The proposals for the construction of the foundation and the pier of this structure were so excessive in rates, and so much above the amount of the appropriations on hand ($95,539 had been expended out of $261,000 appropriated to June 1872), that no more than the landing and the encroachment of the foundation, the two courses of the pier would be contracted for. This embraces 8,000 tons of dimension-stone weighing eight to ten tons each for the encroachment alone. The landing has been commenced, and good progress made upon it." It was estimated that $75,000 would be required to continue the construction of the pier and dwelling. In 1873, Congress appropriated additional funds, and in 1878 the lighthouse was completed at a cost of $278,716, a considerable sum in its day.

Construction

Due to the peculiar structure of the ledge at Race Rock, Smith and Scott decided first to make it level by laying small broken stones and riprap upon it. Then they built a wall of ten thousand tons of riprap in an oval around the rock. The stones were irregular in shape and weighed on the average about four tons each. Next, they cleared a circular space of 60 feet in diameter in the center of the oval, and a wood and iron framework was lowered into this space around the rock. Captain Scott and his divers then built an artificial concrete island and foundation around and on the rock. It is nine feet thick and is in four concentric layers, like a wedding cake, the lowest layer being 60 feet across and three feet thick. The concrete was held in place as it was being laid by large one-half-inch iron hoops of the desired diameter and width for each layer. The completed foundation projected just eight inches out of the water at mean low tide. Smith and Scott apparently completed this phase of their building by November 1871. On top of this cement foundation, they began laying the granite-block foundation for their lighthouse. This foundation projects out of the water to a height of 30 feet. It is round in plan with a base diameter of 57 feet and a diameter at the coping of 55 feet.

Work proceeded slowly due to bad weather, disputes over the building contract and, at different periods, because of lack of cement of the proper quality and stones for the pier. In the fall of 1876, for example, the quarters occupied by the workmen were damaged twice by the sea during storms. On November 21, 1876, the crib at the end of the temporary landing wharf was carried away by high seas. Two workmen lost their lives during the construction of the light. Finally, the pier was completed in December 1877.

The pier is conical in shape, 57 feet in diameter at the base and 30 feet high above the foundation. Large granite blocks form a thick outer wall, the center is filled with concrete, and the whole is surmounted by a projecting coping 55 feet across. In the center of the concrete portion of the pier are spaces for cellars and cisterns. A jetty 53 feet long and 25 feet wide are built on the northerly side to provide a landing place. The entire pier and jetty are surrounded by riprap.

Plans for the keeper's dwelling and tower were approved in March 1878. A preliminary examination was made, and measures were taken for erecting a temporary pier for landing material and a building for housing the working party and storing supplies. In April, the temporary landing pier was completed at the depot and taken to the station by the lighthouse tender "Mistletoe;" the crib was then sunk in place and filled with stone. The materials were conveyed to the lighthouse pier over an inclined railway about 75 feet long, extending from this temporary landing crib to the pier. During April, the cut stone for the facing of the keeper's dwelling and tower was delivered to the lighthouse wharf at New London, Connecticut, but work was delayed in May, because the "Mistletoe" was in use at Sandy Hook, New Jersey.

Operations were resumed on June 11, and the tower was finally completed in December 1878. Of note is the fact that it took only nine months to build the tower and keeper's dwelling but seven years to build the foundation upon which it rested, a further indication of the difficulties that Smith and Scott had to face when building on water rather than on land.

Description of the Lighthouse

The two-story keeper's dwelling built on the pier was, like the tower, built of granite. The tower rises in front of the dwelling on the south side. It is square at the base and octagonal at the top. The light first shone from the tower on the night of New Year's Day 1879. The lantern was (and is) 67 feet above high water, and the illuminating apparatus was a revolving fourth order classical Fresnel lens giving alternate red and white flashes every ten seconds. The light at that time was visible for 14 miles. The power of the white flash was 18,000 candles and that of the red flash 16,000 candles. In 1979, when the lighthouse became automated like so many others, the classical lens was removed and a rotating twenty-four inch beacon (DCB-224) installed in its place.

To this day, to the credit of its two little-known builders, F. Hopkinson Smith and Captain Tom Scott, Race Rock Lighthouse has a high degree of historic integrity of which they would be proud. The structure itself is virtually unaltered, and its foundation, walls and rock retain their original forms and, with the possible exception of the roof, original materials as well. The sash and door are new, but most of the interior window frames and doorways are the original. The stone elements show no substantial cracks or missing pieces, although a century of exposure to the elements of nature has left substantial pitting in the walls. The lighthouse has been nominated to be included in the National Register of Historic Places and rightly so.

The new lighthouse immediately proved a very great value to commerce in the Race and surrounding waters, but no provision had been made for a fog signal, and its lack was much felt. Vessels in clear weather found the Race well-marked and could approach the light to within a short distance, but in thick or foggy weather, they often had a great deal of difficulty in sailing through. Finally, in 1895 a fog signal was officially recommended and, as a consequence, a second-class siren and an auxilliary bell were established on October 20, 1896. The signal was unsatisfactory, however, due to the poor operation of the engines, so the siren was discontinued on June 8, 1897. The bell was used until February 21, 1898 when a new siren apparatus was installed. In 1929, the fog signal was a first-class siren which gave a group of two blasts every thirty seconds.. Mariners should be aware that today the fog signal is reported at times to be inaudible when a vessel is approaching from eastward and is close southward of Fishers Island.

Wrecks

Race Rock was a killer until, incredibly, Smith and Scott managed to build their lighthouse upon it. For example, on August 4, 1837, Captain Andrew Mather of the United States revenue cutter "Wolcott," wrote to Secretary of the Treasury Woodbury: "Since I have commanded the revenue cutter on this station (1829), I have assisted eight vessels ashore on Fisher's Island, six of them were on Race point; all of them on nearly the same place, or within a space of not more than a hundred yards; and during that period have known several more to go entirely to pieces, and in some instances with loss of life, and a great deal of property."

Captain Mather believed that the danger in passing through the Horse race, as it was first called, appeared to arise from vessels mistaking the tides; the flood, when not allowed for, cut them so much to the northward that they ran upon Race Point. Accordingly, in the *New York Journal of Commerce*, he made some observations which present-day mariners would do well to heed:

Vessels bound eastward in the night generally run down near Plum island and the Gull islands; and when abreast of the latter, they steer the sound course, which is E. by N.; and too many of them are not aware of the strength and course of the flood tide. The first half-flood sets NW., the last half about W. NW.; consequently, when steering E. or E. by N., they have a strong tide on the starboard bow, which cuts them over to the northward; and, instead of making, as they supposed, an E. or E. by N. course, they are making a NE. by E. or NE. course, which often carries them on Race point, from which runs far out a reef of rocks under water.

Throughout the history of Connecticut, the perils of The Race were well known. For instance, a terrible marine tragedy occurred shortly after midnight on November 26, 1846, when Captain Isaac K. Dustan sailed the steamer "Atlantic" from New York Harbor. A stormy night had caused many of the passengers, including Daniel Webster of Marshfield, Massachusetts, to cancel their passage. However, there were 59 people aboard, including crew, when the shrill whistle of the "Atlantic" echoed through the cold November air. All went well until the "Atlantic" was nine miles off Fishers Island. A steam pipe burst, disabling the steamer. She anchored at once, but since the seas were heavy, the passengers began to fear for their safety.

At five o'clock in the afternoon of the following day, the gale increased, and the steamer began to drag her anchor toward the dangerous shores of Fishers Island. At about two o'clock the following morning, the "Atlantic" was forced into the breakers. At abut 4:30 a.m., the ship hit a treacherous ledge with a sickening thud. Both anchor cables parted instantly, the ship broached to, and she began to break up almost at once. Terrified, the passengers clung to whatever they could. The gigantic seas swept in and over them, and the icy surf dashed them into eternity, one by one. Of the 39 passengers and 20 crew, only 14 made it to shore alive. 45 perished. Among the survivors was Varnham Marsh of New York, who told a sad story of suffering and death.

A strange aftermath of the wreck was revealed when the storm went down and the local inhabitants on Fishers Island were able to visit the scene. They heard the weird sound of a bell tolling in the surf and found on reaching the wreck that a beam which supported the ship's bell was jammed between the rocks in such a fashion that the bell sounded whenever the waves broke over it. As long as it remained, the wind and sea tolled a meloncholy reminder of the 45 departed souls.

Race Rock was to claim still another victim. Thomas A. Carroll was appointed keeper of the light in 1880. During his service at the tower, he carved many beautiful corner shelves, boxes and picture frames which his niece, Mrs. A.T. Ryan, inherited. Whenever he left the lighthouse, Carroll rowed across the Sound to his home in Noank, Connecticut on the mainland and returned in the same manner. During a severe storm in January 1885, he was marooned ashore and, after several days had elapsed, believed it was his duty to attempt to row out to the lighthouse even though the waves were high and dangerous. Keeper Carroll started out manfully but was soon lost to sight in the great waves. He was never seen alive again. The following spring his body washed ashore at Groton Long Point, Connecticut.

How rough the weather can be at Race Rock, and the consequences of such heavy weather—and also a little about the men who guarded the lighthouse—may be gathered from the official report of George H. Tooker, keeper-in-charge of Race Rock Light Station, April 27, 1931:

To Superintendent of Lighthouses, Staten Island at 2:30 p.m. on the 26th, the Barge "Victorious," one of a tow of four, was carried ashore on this station at the east side by the wind and high seas and broke up in one hour. The Captain of the barge, the only man on her, was in a serious position. We had a hard job getting him off, being unable to throw a line against the gale, so the 1st Assistant and the 2nd Assistant tied ropes to themselves, and with the Keeper, crawled over the rocks through the seas that washed over them, and got close enough to reach a large rock and fasten a small line to a long pole that the Captain passed down to them ... He then lowered himself to the rock and we worked ourselves back to the dock, and it was some job ... We gave the man dry clothes and took care of him until today. We lost three hundred feet of two and a half inch manila rope and forty feet of heaving lines ... The 1st and 2nd Assistants deserve great credit for crawling through the seas as it took nerve to do it, as they were washing over them all the time they were on the rocks and both did not hold back for an instant when we had to do the job ...

Significance of the Lighthouse

Race Rock Lighthouse ranks among the most significant of American lighthouses not only because of the formidable odds against which it was built and the great expense in its building, but also because it represents the last period of masonry construction for wave-swept or water-bound sites. The enormous difficulty of the construction project illustrated the Lighthouse Board's motivation in developing the iron caisson foundation, a technique which, by the end of the 1870s, had superceded masonry in marking such sites. The lighthouse also represents one of the last 19th century aids to navigation projects to follow closely a contemporary architectural style, in this case the Gothic Revival.

In addition, Race Rock Light has significance in the history of the eastern Long Island Sound region. Proximity to the abundant fisheries off the New England coast, as well as the location between the early centers of population in New England and the Middle Atlantic States, had resulted in rich maritime heritage for this region.

Race Rock figures largely in that heritage, because the dangerous winds, tides and currents around the submerged rock formed a major navigational problem. Dozens, and perhaps hundreds, of ships were lost at Race Rock before the erection of the lighthouse, with wrecks averaging one per year during the 1830s, the peak of wind-powered transportation. The stories of the "Wolcott" and the "Atlantic" have already been told. The imposing lighthouse, and the prodigious effort that went into building it by F. Hopkinson Smith and Captain Thomas A. Scott, testify both to Race Rock's navigational importance and to the extraordinary demands of this difficult site.

Race Rock Lighthouse marked the climax of 19th century masonry lighthouse construction. Through the third quarter of the century, such massive stone foundations offered the only means to mark permanently wave-swept sites such as rocks and shoals. Timber obviously would not have sufficed, and lightships were less then fully reliable. The increase in trade after 1850 caused a rise in potential losses at Race Rock, leading to agitation for a suitable beacon. The engineering challenge was monumental.

Ironically, between the time that work on Race Rock began in April 1871 and completed in December 1878, the Lighthouse Board had developed the cast-iron caisson foundation for use at such sites. Made of pre-fabricated iron plates bolted together on site, the caisson formed a shell that was then filled with concrete, creating a rigid, heavy footing. The oldest caisson-based aid presently in service in the former Third Coast Guard District is the Ship John Shoal Lighthouse in Delaware Bay, completed in 1877, one year prior to the completion of Race Rock Light. Thus, Race Rock Lighthouse not only illustrates the condition which led to the development of the caisson foundation, but also marks a technological cusp as one of the last masonry-based navigational aids to be built.

The lighthouse at Race Rock has yet another claim to fame. It is significant as an example of the stylized lighthouses built in the 1860s and 1870s. Before that time, masonry lighthouses generally assumed an unadorned, utilitarian appearance. In the 1860s and 1870s, however, new lighthouses often followed a contemporary architectural style.

This change reflected the newly established solidarity of the Lighthouse Board in the 1850s. Before that time, there was no central administration of lighthouse construction or operation. In the 1850s, with the founding of the Federal Lighthouse Board, the government's aid-to-navigation function gained a national, administrative identity. While local contractors were still engaged for lighthouse construction, the centralization permitted nation-wide control of design. Thus, the stylish lighthouses of the 1860s and 1870s were an early expression of this national stability and centralized planning.

Most of the lighthouses from this period followed the Second Empire style. The Gothic Revival styling of Race Rock Light was an exception. The lighthouse presents a somewhat more monolithic appearance than the customary Gothic Revival house. Nevertheless, the picturesque quality of the roof treatments, notably the carved rafter ends and pent roofs, truly represent the style. The most characteristic Gothic features are the pointed-arch openings in the entry pavilion and lower tower. Along with the handsome stonework, which is another tribute to its builders Smith and Scott, these details form a striking image of the Gothic Revival style, and identify the lighthouse clearly as the product of a unique period.

It is interesting to note that the centralization of design, which first led to stylization in lighthouses, eventually resulted in the standardized iron towers of the 1880s and after, such as Old Field Point Light (1899), Port Jefferson, New York. Race Rock, therefore, was one of the last lighthouses to portray the influence of contemporary architectural style. It also remains over 100 years after its construction, mute testimony to the heroic efforts of two men, F. Hopkinson Smith and Captain Thomas A. Scott, who accomplished the impossible.

CHAPTER 34

NORTH DUMPLING LIGHT,
Fishers Island Sound, N Y (1849)

Light List No.: 18990
Location: Latitude 41° 17.3′ N
        Longitude: 72° 1.2′ W
Height: 31′ (HAW 91′)
Range: 9 miles, White Fixed White Red Sector

Lens: 300 mm plastic, 2.03 amps
Rebuilt: 1871, 1980

Besides having the most powerful light in Fishers Island Sound, North Dumpling Island, located about one-half mile off the north shore of Fishers Island, has the distinction of having only five owners since 1639. In that year Governor John Winthrop of Massachusetts Bay Colony purchased it from the Indians, and it remained in his family for 208 years until they sold it to the United States Government in 1847. In 1848, the Government surveyed the island, and one year later erected a lighthouse on it. The new beacon proved to be a welcome guide to mariners who sailed Fishers Island Sound during the Civil War. Engineer's drawings for 1867 show that the island had a dwelling with the lighthouse attached to the roof, a bell tower a short distance away to the north and connected by a covered walk, a hen house, and two gardens. The 1906 *Light List* shows that in that year the lighthouse had a fifth-order classical (or Fresnel) lens with a fixed white light and a fixed red sector between W¼S through southward to NNE7/8E. Various keepers maintained the light until the Coast Guard automated it in May 1959 by erecting a 60-ft. skeleton tower on the southwest part of the island.

With an automated light, the Coast Guard transferred its maintenance personnel elsewhere and offered the 2.3 acre island for sale. In August 1959, the third owner of North Dumpling Island, George Washburn, a New York City investment manager bought the island at a government auction for $18,000 and soon began to regret his purchase when he took possession of his property in December. The new owner, not a yachtman who admittedly bought the treeless island as an investment venture, received countless telephone calls from the news media and numerous letters from happy island owners far and near who "welcomed him to the club." However, since Mr. Washburn spent more time at his home in Manhattan than at his island retreat, he had serious difficulty with with vandalism, always a problem with absentee island owners. Consequently, the old lighthouse and its buildings fell into disrepair.

In 1980, the island got its fourth owner, David Levitt, who, for better or for worse, gave the light and island a face lift. The new owner, also a New

North Dumpling Light, Fishers Island Sound, NY

York City businessman, bought the island for $95,000. Unlike the third owner, Mr. Levitt was an avid yachtsman who sailed a forty-ft. Hinckley ketch and used the island as a retirement hideaway. With the help of architect Howard Leonard, he remodeled the red brick, two-story keeper's house, built additions to the kitchen and living room, constructed a caretaker's cottage, and had a new wooden pier built beside a refurbished boat house which orignally was designed as a marine laboratory for Dowling College, Oakdale, New York. Planted landscaping included Japanese black pines, azaleas, beach plums, Russian olive, weeping willows, forsythia, red and white Rosa Rogura, blueberries, roses, rhododendrons, mountain laurel, daffodils, tulips, dwarf peach, pear and apple trees, bayberry and cotoneaster. In addition, the new owner had the Coast Guard remove, "for aesthetic reasons," the steel skeleton tower it had erected in 1959 near the house. The light was moved back into the tower atop the mansard roof of the house where it had been originally. Although the "renovation" of the lighthouse was impressive, one cannot help wishing that its owner had not modernized it quite so much, for in doing so he practically destroyed every original detail of this old, historic Second Empire-inspired structure. The new modern design construction seems incongruous with the beautiful original construction.

North Dumpling Island and its lighthouse was sold to its fifth owner, Dean A. Kamen, in November 1986 for over one million dollars. Mr. Kamen, a thirty-five-year-old bachelor from Long Island, New York, is president of DEKA Research and Development Corporation based in Manchester, New Hampshire. Highly successful, his company designs artificial organs and other high-tech medical devices.

North Dumpling Light, ·along with Race Rock and Penfield Reef Lights, have always been for me "castles in the Sound."

●

Lighthouse Dogs

The keeper's life was, for the most part, monotonous and lonely. Occasional jaunts to town or the mainland, in the case of offshore stations, highlighted his schedule. Otherwise, save for the occasional wreck of a ship, the occasional visitor, or the crash of stormy seas over his lighthouse, the keeper's days were made up of repetitive log entires, trudging up and down the spiral staircase, and daily housekeeping chores like polishing brass or cleaning the glass panes of the lantern gallery.

For obvious reasons, companionship became a desperate need for many keepers. Even keepers whose wives and children lived with them at the light often kept pets as additional companions. Most interesting are the stories of famous dogs and their masters who lived at the lights. The careers of these faithful dogs, although often as colorful as the keepers', were rarely documented in log books or lighthouse records. Yet, without them, more lives might have been lost, and the keepers and their families would certainly have led a drearier existence.

210

Probably the best known dog of lighthouse lore was a huge, friendly Newfoundland-St. Bernard mix named Milo. His fame came more from a painting than from his feats of life saving. Entitled *Saved*, its artist skillfully captured the security and protection Milo was known for at Egg Rock Light, one mile southeast of Nahant, Massachusetts. The light was discontinued on April 17, 1922.

Milo came to the rock in September 1855, with the first keeper of the Egg Rock Light, George B. Taylor and his family. Workers were still finishing the tower when the Taylors arrived, and they liked Milo so well that they left a small hole in the stone entry way to the lighthouse to give the dog his own private entrance. Milo's strength and determination was first exhibited shortly after arriving at Egg Rock. Keeper Taylor had tried to shoot a large loon but succeeded only in wounding it. Milo jumped into the ocean on the east side of the island and began swimming after the bird. The loon took off when Milo neared it and flew a quarter of a mile before landing on the water again. Milo continued to swim after it.

As he reached the loon a second time, it again took flight. The chase continued this way until both Milo and the loon disappeared from the keeper's sight. Milo was gone all that night, and the Taylor family was certain he had drowned, since he had paddled east—away from the mainland. Late the next day, however, Milo was sighted swimming toward Egg Rock—from the west. Apparently, he had attempted to return to the rock after dark the night before and had missed the island. He then swam all the way to Nahant and rested on shore during the night. The next day, he swam back to Egg Rock.

Milo's fame as a rescuer came later and prompted a local artist to paint *Saved*. Details pertaining to his rescues are sketchy, but he is known to have saved several children from drowning at the rock. Keeper Taylor's son, Fred, is pictured in the famous painting resting safely between the giant dog's paws. Sadly, Fred Taylor later drowned on a trip through Shirley Gut. Had Milo been with him at the time, he too, might have been saved.

CHAPTER 35

LATIMER REEF LIGHT, Mystic, CT (1884)

Light List No.: 18930
Location: Latitude 41° 18.3' N
         Longitude 71° 56.0'W
Height: 49' (HAW 55')
Range: 9 miles, Flashing White every 6 sec. (2 sec. Flash), Horn
Lens: 300 mm, 2.03 amp lamp

Latimer Reef Light is the oldest cast-iron lighthouse still in service in the First Coast Guard District. In 1884, it replaced the lightship at Eel Grass Shoal, about 0.8 mile northwest of the present lighthouse. Coming from the west, the light is the most important one in this area and a prominent mark in this end of Fisher's Island Sound. Mariners should use it as a gauge of when to turn into Stonington Harbor. The main channel through Fisher's Island Sound lies south of the light, though you certainly can pass north of it. Although Eel Grass Ground, Ram Island Reef, and other shallows are well buoyed, the safest course coming from the west in poor visibility is to head for the lighthouse, departing for the Stonington breakwaters just before you reach it. Your editor has twice used Latimer Reef Lighthouse in this manner coming into Stonington Harbor in blind fogs. Stonington Breakwater Light is northeast ¼ east, 1½ miles, and Watch Hill Light is east 3⅜ miles of Latimer.

Latimer Reef itself, about 0.6 mile south of Noyes Shoal, is a very broken and rocky area of 0.4 mile. It is marked by the lighthouse at its west end and a buoy at its east end. The eastern end of the reef has a least depth of six feet. A detached 11-ft. spot, marked by a buoy, is about 0.4 mile northeast of the light. The reef is located about four miles southeast of Mystic, Connecticut and about one mile north of Fishers Island's east end.

The lighthouse is a brick-lined, cast-iron tower on a cement-filled cast-iron foundation. It was constructed in this way, because on sheltered sites in the water where a masonry tower would be impractical or too expensive, and where a structure of moderate size would serve the needs of navigation, cast-iron caissons or shells could be easily sunk and firmly secured. Besides the lighthouse, the site includes the remnant of a masonry dock and a protective band of riprap which encircles the foundation and extends northward for some 50 feet.

Attempts to Mark the Reef

Recorded accounts of attempts to mark Latimer Reef with navigational aids go back to 1804 when the *Coast Pilot* noted: "Latimer Rock... has an iron spire on top of it, about 13 feet high, with a white vane." The iron spindle was carried away by ice on numerous occasions. By 1867, it was

Latimer Reef Light, Mystic, CT

Photo by Julius M. Wilensky

213

replaced with a can buoy with red and black horizontal stripes. Eleven years later, the reef was marked by two navigational aids. A spar buoy, painted red and black in horizontal stripes was placed in 15 feet of water "close to the seaside of the ledge." The dry part of the reef was marked by an iron spindle painted red and black in horizontal stripes and surmounted by a square cage.

The *Coast Pilot* for 1888 listed the lighthouse as an "iron pier, painted red surmounted by a brown iron tower with a black lantern, flashing white every 10 secs., distance visible in nautical miles 13. Fog signal, bell struck by machinery every 15 secs." By 1899, the light had been painted in the colors mariners know so well today, white with a brown band about midway of its height on a brown cylinder foundation. The lantern is still black.

Keepers

Charles E.P. Noyes was appointed keeper on June 12, 1884 at an annual salary of $600. Assistants at the light included: Samuel G. Gardiner, George W. Friend, and Manuel E. Joseph (from the Azores). They were paid $400 a year. There were nine other assistants to the keeper to August 12, 1898, who were paid $420 a year.

Description of the Light

The foundation of Latimer Reef Lighthouse rests directly upon the rock-bottom of the reef. Its cast-iron shell is composed of curved and flanged cast-iron plates, bolted together on the inside. The prefabricated plates were assembled on the site and then filled with Portland cement, creating a heavy stable footing, 30 feet diameter and 25 feet high. The inside faces of the foundation plates are corrugated, probably to insure that the cement would not shift once it hardened. In the center of the foundation's top, an area was left unfilled to provide a basement storage area.

The tower takes the form of a truncated cone, 21 feet diameter at the bottom and 18 feet diameter at the top. Walls are curved cast-iron plates connected by bolts through internal flanges. Unlike most lighthouses, Latimer Reef Light is missing its brick lining in two stories. The space between the edge of the foundation and the base of the tower form a gallery which has a single pipe rail. The plain, rectangular door faces west.

Three stories held living quarters when the light was manned, and the fourth story served as the watch deck. Each of the living quarters' stories has three windows, arranged irregularly to light the quarters but not the interior stairway. Round ports light the watch deck. Both the watch deck and the octagonal lantern which surmounts it have galleries with pipe railings featuring ornate, cast-iron stanchions. The overhanging watch deck gallery is supported on cast-iron brackets which also serve to anchor these stanchions. The peaked metal roof of the lantern is surmounted by a spherical ventilator.

The interior of the tower contains only back-up generating equipment, although its structural features remain. Chief among these are a central cast-iron column which supports the cast-iron floor plates, and the brick lining which is 18 inches thick at the bottom and tapers to a smaller thickness above. The cast-iron stairs ascend around the periphery of the tower and are set into the brick lining for support.

An interesting feature, reflecting the need to conserve interior space in such structures, is the use of round-arched niches in the lining. Fitted with shelves, these niches served as storage spaces. Narrow-board hardwood flooring covers the cast-iron floor plates. Where brick lining is missing, markings on the individual plates such as "2J," "8J," etc. illustrate how the prefabricated plates were assembled on-site.

A Capsizing

The weather was cold and clear on Monday morning, November 8, 1982. Wind was west at 20 knots. Seas were four to six feet and running west southwest. Two contractors working on Latimer Reef Light observed two men in a 16-ft., V-bottom, white fiber glass boat drop anchor about 200 yards east of the light. They soon dropped fishing lines over the side of their boat.

The morning became somewhat warmer. Workers at the light saw several waves hit the boat broadside. It broached, capsized and sank within three to four minutes, according to the two witnesses. One of the fishermen, a 69-year old man from Brooklyn, New York, apparently became entangled in the lines in the boat and went down with it when it capsized. He never came up. The second man, 48-years old from Pawcatuck, Connecticut, managed to jump clear of the boat as it went over and clung to her hull briefly until she sank.

Two lobster boats, which were checking their traps in the area, arrived at the scene of the accident within 20 minutes and picked up the drowned body of the fisherman from Pawcatuck. The Coast Guard, notified by the lobstermen by radio of the capsizing, conducted an intensive search of the area for the missing body of the second fisherman and the debris of the sunken boat. They found neither, and to this day the missing person has never been found or seen again.

Historical Significance of the Light

Latimer Reef Light is a relatively well-preserved example of a late 19th century lighthouse. One of its major losses is the roof that once protected the gallery at the tower's first story. The roof's absence alters the distinctive profile of the lighthouse. The roof recalled the days of manned operation when such amenities were part of the lighthouse design.

A second major loss is the light's fourth-order omni-directional Fresnel lens which was removed in 1983 when the signal equipment was modernized. The classical lens was transferred and installed in the Elbow of Cross Ledge Light in Delaware Bay, New Jersey. Made in Paris by the French firm of Barrier, Benard and Turrenne, the lens consisted of glass prism rings set in brass retainers. The lens at Latimer Reef Light is due for yet another change shortly. Within a year, it will be replaced by a more economical, more efficient, and easier to maintain solar lighting system.

Despite these losses, the light's concrete-filled iron foundation, cast-iron tower and architectural details such as hoodmolds and railing stanchions are still present at the light and represent characteristic elements of the period. Latimer Reef Light also has historical significance as part of the Lighthouse Board's efforts to assure safe shipping in eastern Long Island Sound and Fishers Island Sound, a region where ship-borne commerce and commercial fisheries have long been important. The Connecticut communities of Mystic and New London and other area communities have a strong interest in and an awareness of their area's maritime heritage.

Prior to the late 1870s, lighthouses were commonly constructed of brick and stone, but by 1875 structural iron had begun to replace masonry. Not only was iron becoming cheaper and more readily available as the iron industry matured, but also it was in some respects a superior material. The cast-iron plates which form the walls of the light's tower, as well as the foundation shell and the interior floors, provided a superstructure which was in large part pre-fabricated and therefore easily assembled under the difficult conditions of a water-bound site. When lined with a layer of brick several feet thick, the tower offered stability equal to that of masonry construction.

Thus, iron towers such as Latimer Reef Light are historically significant, because they exemplify the increased standardization of lighthouse design in the United States during the 1880s and 1890s. The same basic scheme, even including virtually identical details such as brackets and woodmolds, can be found all along the East Coast. The cast-iron towers were suitable in a variety of situations, including shoals, reefs, and even atop breakwaters. This enabled the Lighthouse Board to reuse the same plans and contract specifications for each new light. This economy of time and expense in design effort was especially important in view of increased shipping in the late 19th century and consequent need for more lighthouses. Latimer Reef Light has been nominated to be included in the National Register of Historic places.

CHAPTER 36

MORGAN POINT LIGHT, Noank, CT (1831)

Old Light List No.: 139 (Obsolete)
Location: Latitude 41° 18′ 57″ N
          Longitude 71° 59′ 03″ W
Height: 52′ (HAW 60′)
Range: 12 miles
Lens: Sixth Order, 160 candlepower
Rebuilt: 1867-68
Discontinued: 1922

During the American Revolution and the War of 1812, there was neither spindle nor beacon to mark the mouth of the channel of the Mystic River. American frigates, clipper ships, schooners, and smacks depended upon the skill, and often luck, of their crews to get them in and out of the harbor safely. Since that time, however, two lighthouses have been built at Morgan Point (as it was originally called), one in 1831, the other in 1868. During the 91 years their lights flashed a warning to mariners on dark and stormy nights, a host of men and ships have passed up and down the channel beside them. The light was the last to bid farewell to the brave and aventurous fishermen bound for Georges Bank off New England, and the Grand Banks off the coast of Newfoundland. It was also the first to welcome them home again.

Noank was not extensively settled until the middle of the 19th century. In 1712, the land was drawn through a lottery by James Morgan. Although farm lots were laid out as early as 1713, there were only 13 homes there in 1825, and it was not until 1841 that a meeting house (Baptist) was built. Poor soil, Pequot Indian fishing privileges, and more convenient locations in Mystic or Groton have been cited as contributing to the late development of the peninsula. The village grew quickly thereafter, however, with the economy resting on fishing and shipbuilding. The Noank fishing fleet once numbered over 60 vessels. As many were owned in shares, a large number of residents were involved in fishing. Captain Ebenezer Morgan made one of the most lucrative whaling trips on record in the 19th century.

Noank is the Mohegan Indian equivalent of "naiag" meaning "a point." Until 1665, it was also called "Naiwayonk," "Nowayunck," and "Naiwayuncke."

On April 19, 1831, the land for a proposed lighthouse was purchased from Roswell Avery Morgan, a great grandfather of Mary Virginia Morgan Goodman of Noank, descended from an original settler of the penninsula, James Morgan. A Special Act of Cession by the State of Connecticut to the United States Government was required at this time for any property transaction.

The original lighthouse built in 1831 was a white circular granite tower separated from the keeper's dwelling by 80 feet. It was located a few feet from the present building built in 1868, and its foundations are still there. In dry weather the outline of the circular tower may be distinctly seen. The whale oil for the light was kept in a separate brick house, parts of which are still in use. The first light also had a barn on its property.

Keepers and History of the Lighthouse

The first keeper of the 1831 lighthouse was Captain Ezra Daboll, and his duties were many. For example, he had to be constantly alert to see that the whale oil did not run out, and it was necessary for him to go out several times a night to trim the wicks of the ten lamps then used. To get to the village in those days, the keeper and his family had to wade across the narrows at high tide. In winter, they were frequently cut off. Every Sunday, the family walked to Fort Hill where the church was located. Daboll built a beacon at the mouth of the channel of the Mystic River.

When Captain Daboll died in 1838, his wife, who had six small children to support, received the appointment as keeper. Her letter of appointment from Washington, D.C. noted, "Mrs. Daboll belongs to that class of citizens whose standing in society is of the first respectability." Once, while Mrs. Daboll kept the light, it went out and, fearing she would lose her job, she walked to the ferry in Groton to report the situation to authorities in New London before anyone else reported the light's failure. She got to New London in time and kept her job.

Mrs. Daboll's eldest daughter used to help her mother tend the light. Legend has it that when winter storms raged and the girl had to leave her warm home to clean the wicks at the lighthouse 80 feet away, she used to sing at the top of her voice to keep up her courage, startling mariners who passed close by on such unfortunate nights. She never lost her interest in the light even in later years, when another keeper was in charge of it. One night when the light failed, she saw that it had gone out, put on her bonnet and rushed to the lighthouse to warn the keeper.

About 1850, Captain Silas Spicer became the new keeper of the light. A single lamp was installed in place of the old ten lamps, and a more refined oil used to keep the wicks clean for a longer time. In the winter, when snow and hail packed itself against the glass of the lantern, Spicer had the difficult task, as did other keepers of other lights, of keeping the glass clear during heavy storms.

Frequently, vessels in distress needed the lightkeeper's assistance. On one occasion, Spicer looked out over Fisher's Island Sound and saw a ship on fire. It had run aground on the hummocks and was loaded with burning hay. Spicer promptly climbed into his small boat, rowed out to the stricken vessel and rescued her skipper, wife and child. They stayed at the lighthouse for several days with Spicer and his family while they recuperated from their ordeal.

Lightkeepers were required to keep a record of all vessels which passed

Morgan Point Light, Noank, CT

their lighthouse and had to submit the records to the federal government. In one year, Spicer recorded almost 400 schooners which passed at the light until the outbreak of the Civil War in 1861.

At the beginning of Spicer's tenure at the lighthouse, shipbuilding began in earnest in the village of Noank. The Palmer Shipyard was founded on the site of the present Noank Shipyard. The Palmer Yard grew to be quite extensive and built vessels of all sizes. The railroad was important for bringing in material for shipyards, as well as for carrying Noank's seafood to market.

The fourth keeper of the light, a Mr. Barber, succeeded Spicer in 1861 and served until 1867. In that year, the Lighthouse Board decided to tear down the old tower built 30 years earlier and build a new lighthouse, combining in one building the tower and living quarters for the new keeper. The present building was completed and put in operation in 1868. Numerals of that year, engraved on the front of the building, are still there. It was constructed by Captain Henry Davis of Noank. The lenses of the new light were brought from Germany. The lamp burned lard oil instead of the old whale oil. The lard came in butts or barrels like ordinary lard. Before it could be put into the lamp, it had to be heated so that it would not congeal after it was put into the lamp. Late in the 19th century, a benzine or kerosene lamp was installed. It was said to have 2,000 candlepower and to give out a light that could be seen for 20 miles.

During the interim period (1867-68), while the present building was being constructed, a temporary light was installed on the roof of the old keeper's house. Alexander McDonald, a disabled Civil War veteran, was appointed keeper of the light. He served for a little over a year until ill health forced him to retire. After he died, his wife was appointed keeper and served until 1871, when Thaddeus Pecor, a well-known and highly regarded resident of Noank, was appointed keeper. Pecor had to clean and fill the lamp each day and check it several times during the night to make sure the light was burning.

During Pecor's long tenure as keeper, there was a shipwreck off Seaflower Reef on a cold, winter night. The shore was bordered with ice and the crew, rowing to Morgan Point in their lifeboat, had to break the ice and wade part of the way to shore. When they reached the lighthouse, they were nearly frozen to death, and Pecor had to cut their shoes and part of their clothing off of them. During World War I, the public was forbidden to visit Morgan Point and, although Mr. and Mrs. Pecor did not like to tell Noankers to stay away, they obeyed orders and did so. Pecor retired from the lighthouse service in 1919, after having served an astounding 48 years as keeper of the light at Morgan Point.

A Mr. Riley was appointed keeper to replace Pecor in 1919. Riley was apparently the last keeper at Morgan Point until it was discontinued in 1922. During its 91 years of warning seafarers with its beacon, the lighthouse had only eight keepers, two of them women.

Discontinuance of the Lighthouse

About 1900, Noank began to receive summer residents from New York and other urban areas, although to this day vacationers are much less evident than in nearby villages. Partly due to the 1938 hurricane, there are few visible physical remains of the summer visits by business and literary figures. Theodore Dreiser found inspiration in Noank and in his book *Twelve Men* (1919), he descirbed the village as " . . . a little played-out fishing town." Publisher George Putnam also frequented the town and married Amelia Earhart in the house at 43 Church Street. Most of Noank's residents of the past are unknown outside of the area or the ports they visited. An exception is Hubbard Chester whose house was 25 Main Street. He played a key role in the 1872-73 "Polaris" arctic rescue mission, and his boat is at the Smithsonian Institute, Washington, D.C. Captain Chester also patented a folding anchor for the Navy.

In 1922, the lighthouse was discontinued in favor of an automatic electric beacon erected on a foundation at the entrance to the channel of the Mystic River. This beacon was discontinued eventually in favor of a smaller one several years ago. The original iron beacon may now be seen at the entrance to the Noank Shipyard at the foot of Pearl Street in Noank. The eight-ft. octagonal lantern and its works were removed from the top of the tower of the lighthouse leaving it looking like the headless horseman of Washington Irving's tale. The building was sold at a public auction as a private residence to Mr. and Mrs. Huett. The Huetts sold the light about 1965 to Mr. and Mrs. Woodruff Johnson who added a wing to the back of the lighthouse.

The regret on the part of the residents of Noank at the discontinuance of the old lighthouse was nostalgically expressed in the early 1920s by Professor Everett Fitch (1869-1936) in the following poem:

> Good-by, old friend, old friend, good-by.
> For me you held the light up high.
> Through all the years I sailed the sea,
> But now you are no more to be.
> Alas! I miss thy kindly beam
> That from your tower did nightly stream,
> And can but heave a heavy sigh.
> Good-by, old friend, old friend, good-by.
>
> The sister lights are bowed with grief.
> From Latimer to Bartlett's Reef;
> The little island seems to shout,
> The rocky hummocks, all about,
> The buoys and sea-gulls circling round,
> The edge of Fisher's Island Sound,
> United in one pathetic cry,
> Good-by, old friend, old friend, good-by.

Noank Today

The shipyards in Noank have been replaced by modern marinas, yet much remains in the village of life in the past century. The town is significant for its architecture because of the concentration of Greek Revival and Gothic—and Eastlake—detailed dwellings which line its narrow streets. Only a few of them date from before 1840 or after 1910, accurately reflecting the growth of the village in the second half of the last century. A few of the houses have ropeknot bargeboards or wave-like bargeboards on crestings, like that on the porticos of 26 Main Street. The small size of most of the houses, particularly the Greek Revival dwellings with the four-bay facade, may in part be accounted for by the fact that many residents spent much of their time at sea.

Noank offers today, in a relatively small area, an opportunity to see a wide and imaginative variety of architecture and architectural ornament. The decorative pilasters, bargeboard, peak ornaments, porches and fences, the ecletic borrowing of details, and the concentration of old houses are grouped along narrow, winding streets. A comparable group of buildings can be found in no other area of Connecticut. One is tempted to label these dwellings as "maritime picturesque." There were large numbers of woodworkers and carpenters in Noank's shipyards.

Significance of the Lighthouse

The Morgan Point Lighthouse is one of several of the same type built by the federal government in the 1860s. Others are located on Block Island, Old Field Point, New York, and Great Captain Island, Greenwich, Connecticut, all described in this book. They were constructed of granite ashlar with extremely thick walls, approximately two feet, and all have slate gable roofs.

The wisdom of this solid construction is apparent 117 years later the lighthouse is in much of its original form, and practically no work has had to be done on its walls. The same holds true for the other lights mentioned above. Morgan Point Lighthouse survived the devastating hurricanes of 1938, 1944 and 1985, as well as the many storms of the 1950s without difficulty. In the 1938 hurricane, everyone on the Point went to the lighthouse as the one safe place to be. When first built, there were (and still are) on the first floor an entrance hall and four rooms: kitchen, dining room, living room, and, just off the entrance, a small room used by the keeper as an office where charts and records were kept. The original desk and bunk in that room are still in use. The remains of the 1831 oil shed may still be seen, 2½ stories high. Today, the lighthouse is significant both as a reminder of the importance of the sea in the lives of the residents of Noank and as an example of the standardization of lighthouse design after mid-19th century.

The "headless" lighthouse at Morgan Point has been included in the Noank National Register District for inclusion in the National Register of Historic Places.

CHAPTER 37

STONINGTON HARBOR LIGHT, Stonington, CT (1823)

Old Light List No.: 163 (Obsolete)
Location: Latitude 41° 19' 43" N
          Longitude 71° 54' 21" W
Height: 32½' (HAW 59½')
Range: 11 miles, Fixed White
Lens: Sixth Order, Classical (Removed)
Moved and Rebuilt: 1840
Discontinued: 1889

Stonington Harbor is three miles northwest of Watch Hill Point and is protected by breakwaters, marked by lights, on each side. Although the harbor can be approached from the southeast and west, the southeast approach has fewer hazards, with excellent navigational aids along the way. In daytime with clear weather, no difficulty should be experienced in entering the harbor by either of these approaches. The town of Stonington is on the east side of the harbor as you enter it, as is its famous lighthouse, the first one operated by the federal government in Connecticut.

Stonington Harbor Light is situated at the south end of Stonington Borough, and inland a short distance. From this strategic position, it served in the 19th century as a beacon for ships navigating Fisher's Island Sound, and Stonington Harbor. This area was heavily involved in shipbuilding, whaling, fishing and commerce, and the maritime traffic generated by these activities depended upon this small but sturdy lighthouse. The structure is of more than local significance, however, for in many ways its history is representative of Federal lighthouse policy.

The first lighthouse on Stonington Point was erected in 1823 by the federal government. The station consisted of a small stone dwelling for the keeper and a stone cylindrical tower, 30 feet high, and was built by Benjamin Chase at a cost of $2,500. The non-rotating white light was 47 feet above sea level and could be seen for 12.25 miles. It was generated by ten whale oil lamps arranged in an arc so as to be visible from all directions except due north which was land. Each lamp had a silver-coated parabolic reflector, 13 inches in diameter, placed behind it to concentrate its beam. However, the choice of the site proved to be a poor one.

In 1838, an official inspector, Lieutenant George M. Bache, U.S.N., made his report on the Stonington light facility. He found that the light's reflectors were practically useless, because so much of the silver coating had been worn off. This condition was probably the result of too much scouring with the officially sanctioned abrasive mirror cleaner, tripoli powder. Also, the wooden staircase inside the tower had been apparently in danger of collapsing, since it was reported that repairs had solved serious problems. Finally, Bache reported that the entire light station was in danger of being washed away. It had been farther south down the Point than the present light, and this proved to be too close to the sea. Storms, especially southeasters, had, in the 15 years since the establishment of the light, eroded much of the beach, and high tide in 1838 was fully 22 feet closer to the lighthouse. The Government was forced to choose between building a seawall or replacing the $2,500 structure. It chose replacement.

Work was completed on the second lighthouse in 1840. Many of the stones from the original tower were hauled up the Point to its present site. The new structure was built by John Bishop for $2,840 plus $168 for the overseer of the work. The new lamps and reflectors, including the plate-glass lantern housing them cost $1,933.30 and were supplied by I.W.P. Lewis, an engineer who was the foremost critic of the federal lighthouse establishment of his day. The lighthouse probably was painted white, but this finish has long since been removed.

The new lighthouse was in many ways an improvement over the old. This was the result of greater professionalsim and competence in the federal bureaucracy. The eight lamps had larger parabolic reflectors, 16 inches across in diameter instead of 13 inches, and they were formed with greater precision than the previous ones. The tower itself was higher (32½ feet) and stood upon a higher elevation, raising the focal plane of the fixed white light to 59½ feet above sea level. Because of the additional 12½ feet of height, the light could been seen at a greater distance, 15 miles. The tower is about 10 feet in diameter both at its base and its top. It is surmounted by a cylindrical plate-glass lantern, about six feet in diameter, which in turn supports a weather vane.

The design of the structure combined the keeper's dwelling with the tower, perhaps to facilitate maintenance and more frequent trimmings of the lamps. The spiral staircase inside the octagonal tower was constructed from granite blocks, thus avoiding the failings of the pervious wooden stairs. This time, the light was located far enough up the Point to be out of danger from the sea. Even the architecture of the light seems calculated to convey a sense of solidity. The tower is trimmed with corbelling, like a Norman fortification, and the attached keeper's dwelling, also built of massive granite rocks, has no windows on its sides, as if it were its own sea wall. It is 1½ stories tall and about 30 feet square.

Despite these improvements, the expenditure of nearly $5,000, and the employment of Lewis, a nationally known engineer, the federal government still did not have a completely modern lighthouse. For example, the type of lamp installed in 1840 was already obsolete. In addition, the new reflectors were prone to the same kind of deterioration which affected the first light. The official reflector polishing powder wore off the silver coating very quickly. However, there is an explanation for this state of affairs.

The period between 1820 and 1850 was one of tremendous expansion in the number of lighthouses in the United States and a large number of these, such as Stonington Light, were intended to guide local coastal traffic and serve as harbor markers. There was very little professional input

Stonington Harbor Light, Stonington, CT

Photo by Julius M. Wilensky

into key location or construction decisions, however, and fully 40% of the nation's lighthouses were found to have structural problems, and even more had inadequate lighting. This is the reason that Stonington Light had the problems it did. The light, then, with its early problems and long-delayed solutions is representative of the many lighthouses of this period.

In 1822, Augustin Fresnel (1788-1827), a Frenchman, had perfected a system for concentrating light which greatly intensified the beam. The Fresnel lens was a drum-shaped piece of glass with prisms cut near the ends which refracted or bent the light so that it came from the center of the lens in a bright, narrow beam. At the same time, the problems of reflectors and multiple lamps were elminated, since there was but one lamp in the center of the glass drum.

United States lighthouses were slow in adopting the Paris-made Fresnel lenses, because the official in charge, the Fifth Auditor of the Treasury, Stephen Pleasanton, was unconvinced of their value. Also, they were very expensive, about $10,000 each, depending upon their size. His judgement was undoubtedly influenced by his close friend, Winslow Lewis, the major supplier of the old system of lighting. At last, a Congressional investigation in 1851 exposed the deficiency in the old lights and demanded an immediate conversion to Fresnel lenses for all United States lighthouses. With few exceptions, all lighthouses in the United States were converted to Fresnel lenses in a decade.

In 1856, a sixth-order (or smallest) Fresnel harbor light was installed in Stonington lighthouse and remained in the gallery until the facility was discontinued in 1889. The light, with a range of 11 miles, originally fueled by whale oil and later probably by lard oil, is on display inside the lighthouse which was bought by the Stonington Historical Society in 1910 and opened as a museum in 1925.

Captain B.F. Pendleton, a former whaler and sealer, became the keeper of the light in 1872 and served until November 1, 1889, when the Lighthouse Board decided that the light on Stonington breakwater which had been maintained privately for some years, should be taken over by the Government and the somewhat redundant lighthouse discontinued. The keeper of the breakwater light continued to live in the stone dwelling attached to the tower of the Stonington Light until 1908, when a wooden house costing $6,000 was built one lot down from the light. Shortly after the Stonington Historical Society acquired the light, it completely remodeled the interior but limited external changes mainly to the installation of diamond-paned windows in the front.

Because it served as a sentinel for Stonington Harbor for 66 years, the lighthouse is important in preserving the town's past. As noted earlier, the major activities in 19th century Stonington were shipbuilding and refitting whaling and sealing vessels. These produced a large amount of commercial activity, and hence the life of the town depended upon its harbor. The significance of the lighthouse is increased by its location at the south end of Stonington Borough, a mile-long peninsula rich in 18th and 19th century buildings. Its fortress-like construction and detailing are unusual for a lighthouse. Its thematic unity, solidness which befits its function, makes the Stonington Harbor Light an architectural resource. Thus, the light is significant historic propery, because it typifies the history of United States lighthouse policy and because it is an essential element in the physical preservation of Stonington's maritime heritage. It is fortunate that its future is secure by being included in the National Register of Historic Places.

The museum at the lighthouse consists of six room which display 19th century portraits, whaling and fishing gear, swords, a children's room and doll house, articles from the Oriental trade, decoys, local stoneware and items from the Battle of Stonington in the War of 1812. One can view three states from the tower. The museum is open to the public from May to October, Tuesday to Sunday, 11:00 a.m. to 4:00 p.m., or by appointment. Admission is $1.00 for adults, children under 12 years, 50¢. The museum telephone number is (203) 535-1440. Stop by for a visit! It's a great place for kids.

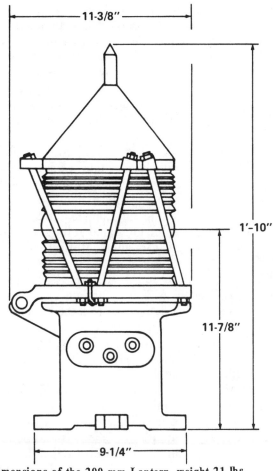

Dimensions of the 200 mm Lantern, weight 21 lbs.
Peck Ledge Light, Chapter 9 has one of these. See page 253

Courtesy U.S. Coast Guard

CHAPTER 38

WATCH HILL LIGHT, Watch Hill, RI (1807)

Light List No.: 18635
Location: Latitude 41° 18.2' N
　　　　　Longitude 71° 51.5' W
Height: 45' (HAW 61')
Range: 16 miles, White
　　　　15 miles, Red
　　　　Alternate Occulting and Flashing (2) Red every
　　　　15 seconds
Lens: FA-251
Radio Beacon: 306 kHz, WH (. _ _　　. . . .) V,
　　　　10 miles
Rebuilt: 1856
Automated: August 31, 1986

The strategic importance of Watch Hill as a natural landmark has long been recognized, a fact indicated by its name. The Colony of Rhode Island and Providence Plantations established a watch tower and beacon in the vicinity during King George's War (1744-1748), meant to serve as a warning of naval attack rather than as a strictly navigational aid. This early colonial beacon was totally destroyed by a gale in 1781 and was not replaced until Congress provided for the erection of the present structure in 1807.

Watch Hill Light was one of the last manned stations maintained by the men and women of the United States Coast Guard. It was manned until August 31, 1986. It is about 17.5 miles west of Point Judith and is located on a high bluff overlooking Block Island Sound and the eastern entrance to Fisher's Island Sound and Long Island Sound. Mariners should note that it is reported that the fog signal at the station is not easily heard eastward of the light, but from the southwest can be heard nearly to Montauk Point, 18 miles away.

From Watch Hill to Point Judith, the shore is low and for the most part consists of sandy beaches which are broken by several projecting rocky points and a few shallow inlets. Back from the immediate shore are areas of cultivation interspersed with rolling grass-covered or wooded hills. Except for Point Judith Pond, pond inlets are used by small local craft only. The coast is fringed by broken ground and boulders in places which should be avoided by deep-draft vessels.

As early as May 22, 1794, Jeremiah Olney, Collector of Customs at Providence, received an inquiry from Tench Coxe, Commissioner of Revenue, on the advisability of erecting a lighthouse on Watch Hill Point or on another site near the mouth of Fisher's Island Sound and The Race. The skippers of vessels sailing out of Providence favored Little Gull Is-

Watch Hill Light, Watch Hill, RI

land for the location of the proposed lighthouse as evidenced by a letter dated December 8, 1794 to Jeremiah Olney, Esq. from John Updike and signed by 54 other skippers and owners of vessels. On the other hand, the Watch Hill location was defended in a letter to Collector Olney from George Stillman, Surveyor for the Port of Pawcatuck.

The controversy raged, each faction declaring and trying to prove that its respective location was the best suited for the proposed light until Congress passed "An Act to provide for lighthouses in Long Island Sound; and to declare Roxbury, in the state of Massachusetts, to be a port of delivery." The Act was approved and signed by President Thomas Jefferson on Wednesday, January 22, 1806. It provided for the erection of two lighthouses, one located on Watch Hill Point in Westerly, Rhode Island, and the other at Sand's or Watch Point in North Hempsted, Long Island. Little Gull Island Light (LLN 18665) was erected also in 1806, so both factions won out in the end.

On Saturday, May 3, 1806, George and Thankful Foster of Westerly, Rhode Island, sold about four acres of land on Watch Hill Point for $500 to William Ellery, Superintendent of the United States Lighthouse Service. Work on a lighthouse soon began on the property. This first light was a round, shingled, wood tower built by Elisha Woodward of New London, Connecticut, and had a bank of ten whale-oil lamps to cast the lighthouse beam. This structure stood until 1855, when construction began on the present tower, 50 feet northwest of it. The gradual wearing away of the Point by the action of the waves made it necessary to construct a light farther back from the shore. Legend has it that local Indians helped in the construction of either the first light or its successor.

The builders of the new, second tower used gray granite to build the square tower and fitted it with a single Fresnel fourth order lens, which was more efficient that the whale-oil lamps, to send its strong, steady white beam out to sea. The area surrounding the lighthouse was reinforced with large granite blocks to resist the wave action around the Point. Even so, in his *Annual Report* for 1876, the writer noted: "The seawall on the east side of the station is exposed to the forces of the sea and shows signs of giving away. It is recommended that it be protected by riprap at its base and for some distance out, which could break the shock of the waves." The new light was first shown on Friday, February 1, 1856.

In later years when the use of bright street lights became prominent, mariners found that they could not easily distinguish the familiar Watch Hill beacon from the electric street lights. To offset this confusing situation, the beacon was adjusted to the characteristics which it uses to this day, one 15-second white light followed by two brief red flashes. The fog signal was added to the station about 1909.

Early Keepers of the Light

Jonathan Nash was the first lightkeeper and looked after the station with his numerous sons for 27 years. He lost his job in 1834 when the

Jackson spoils administration turned him out. During his tour of duty, Nash reported 45 vessels wrecked on the rocks near Watch Hill. At one time in his career as keeper, he took a few summer boarders into his house to augment his keeper's salary which was about $300 a year. However, the Government frowned upon such activities, so he had to stop the practice. Nash was succeeded by Enoch Vose, Gilbert Pendleton, Daniel Babcock, Ethan Pendleton, Nelson Brown (appointed August 13, 1853 at $350 a year), then Daniel F. Larkin, Jared S. Crandall, Mrs. Crandall (his wife), Joseph Fowler and, finally, Julius Young about 1915. The last keeper of the light at Watch Hill was William I. Clark, who retired in the 1960s.

Watch Hill Light Today

The Watch Hill Light Station comprises a three-story, square, granite light tower topped with a cast-iron and glass lantern. A two-story, brick keeper's dwelling is attached to the tower. Also as part of the station is a one-story stuccoed oil house, a one-story, brick signal house, and a one-story, brick garage. All of these building are painted white except the light tower and stand on a grassy 2.4-acre tract of land at the tip of Watch Hill Point, a rock-bound promontory extending southerly from the Atlantic coastline between the sandy shores of East Beach and Napatree Point, marking the juncture of Block Island and Fisher's Island Sounds. The property also contains two steel-frame towers, one supporting a pole for signal flags, the other as a radio beacon transmitter.

The light tower is the focal point of the group. Measuring about ten feet square, it is constructed of rock-faced gray granite blocks about 12 inches thick, 18 inches high, and in different lengths, eight and ten feet. The orientation of the blocks creates a quoined effect at the corners. Windows are on the east side at the second-and-third-story levels.

The gallery surrounds a cylindrical lantern of black-painted cast-iron and glass, with helical glazing bars and a conical roof topped with a pipe-like chimney that originally served as a vent for the oil-burning lamp within the lens. The interior of the tower is cylindrical with white-painted brick walls. A cast-iron spiral staircase leads to a second-floor landing with a door that opens into the attached keeper's house and continues up to the lantern.

Until it was automated on August 31, 1986, the lantern contained a fourth order Fresnel ("classical") lens with its glass components set in brass mountings. The lens floated on a mercury bath that allowed it to be easily rotated. A fixed white beacon produced by the oil lamp was shown originally from the lantern. The lens was illuminated by a 1000 watt electric lamp. Two panes of red glass were fitted side by side over the outside of the lens.

The keeper's house, constructed at the same time as the tower, is a cubical mass of white-painted brick. The interior of the house is irregular in plan, the result of numerous alterations over the years. The original floor plan is not recorded in any documents discovered to date, so it is difficult to determine what it might have been from existing structural evidence. Extensive remodeling since 1964 has led to the removal of nearly all traces of 19th century interior finish in the keeper's house.

East of the keeper's house is a smaller, square, white-painted stuccoed oil house dating from the construction of the tower and a keeper's house in 1855-56. South of the oil house is a one-story, rectangular, white-painted brick bulding erected in the late 19th century to house the fog signal equipment. A fog horn is mounted on a concrete slab south of the house. Finally, north of the keeper's house is a one-story, square, white-painted brick garage with two bays, probably built about 1940 when repairs were made here following the 1938 hurricane. None of these buildings has noteworthy interior features. The transmitting tower for the radio beacon stands north of the garage and was erected about 1980.

Today, the buildings and grounds of the Watch Hill Light Station are kept in excellent condition through the efforts of a local organization known as the Watch Hill Light Keeper's Association, an affiliate of the Watch Hill Improvement Society, which assumed care of it with the Coast Guard and signed a 20-year lease when it became automated on Sunday afternoon, August 31, 1986. Two members of the organization live at the light to protect it from vandalism.

The Association plans to maintain the lighthouse in top condition and keep it open to the public. Eventually, it will establish a muscum containing various items of local history. The centerpiece of the museum will be the station's rare Fresnel lens. This was replaced by an FA-251 lens in August 1986, with its hand-made crystal and brass work. The Association hopes also to accurately restore the lighthouse to its 18th century condition. Upkeep of the grounds and buildings costs $20,000 a year; part of which is funded by yearly membership drives and private donations.

Commander David Lyon of Coast Guard Station New Haven said at the time of automation that full automation of the light will decrease maintenance costs. The station is now equipped with two fog-sensor beams that can detect fog at a distance of five miles, as well as a timer to activate the light beam at night. Upkeep of the automated equipment is the responsibility of the Aids to Navigation Team, a Coast Guard unit based on Woodward Avenue in New Haven.

Shipwrecks

The lightkeepers at Watch Hill have seen many ships battered by storms, rammed, stuck upon the rocks, sunk, and some just disabled. Curiously, the records indicate that most ship disasters have occurred while traveling southwestward along the coast and not often to eastbound shipping. Some of the more notable marine disasters in Watch Hill history are:
1812. Oliver Hazard Perry, while commander of the coastal patrol vessel on route from Newport to New London, with a pilot on board, ran upon the Watch Hill rocks in a dense fog. Young Perry was exonerated after an investigation revealed that the fault lay with the pilot and not him.

1872. The only life-saving apparatus at the station was an old whale boat which was manned by a volunteer crew when the occasion demanded its use. This volunteer crew was of great help in saving lives from the steamer "Metis" which was rammed by the schooner "Mattie Cushing" at 4:00 a.m. on a stormy Thursday, August 29th. The "Metis" sank quickly between Block Island and Watch Hill Point. Even though 33 persons were rescued, 20 passengers lost their lives. The following February, Congress passed a resolution authorizing President Ulysses S. Grant to make and present each rescuer with a gold medal in appreciation of their heroic efforts.

1907. The steamer "Larchmont" collided with the schooner "Henry Knowlton" four miles southwest of Watch Hill Light during a violent February blizzard while en route from Providence to New York City. One hundred and fifty persons lost their lives in this disaster, many of them unknown, since the passenger list went down with the ship and no other copies were available. The "Larchmont's" story is told in connection with Block Island North Light, Chapter 29.

1917. The "Onandago" struck a reef just southwest of Watch Hill and sank. Today the wreckage is a rendezvous for local scuba diving clubs.

1928. The British freighter "Ellaston" went aground in a fog. She was later refloated.

1930. The "Storm Petrel," laden with coal, went to the bottom in December with a loss of seven lives.

1962. The 3,192-ton "Leif Viking" landed on rocks just a few hundred feet off Watch Hill Light. The crewman on watch, John Bullis, informed the keeper, William I. Clark (the last keeper of the light), that they had a ship in their front yard. The Coast Guard buoy-tender "Mariposa" was sent to aid the stricken vessel. Thousands of sightseers flocked to Watch Hill for a view of all the activity. After nine days, the ship was pulled free by a McAllister tug and towed to New York City.

Significance of the Lighthouse

The Watch Hill Light Station is significant for its association with the history of commerce and transportation in Rhode Island. For 129 years it has served as an aid to navigation, helping to ensure safe passage of goods and travelers, primarily for vessels plying the coast between eastern New England ports and New York, but also for vessels destined for Little Narragansett Bay and the port at Westerly/Pawcatuck. It is arrchitecturally significant as a handsome and well-preserved example of a 19th century lighthouse complex of simple vernacular design, especially notable for the distinctive form and masonry work of the light tower. As a visually prominent man-made element of the coastline, Watch Hill is an important cultural artifact. It stands also as a symbol of the maritime heritage of the town and state.

The tower, keeper's house and oil house are fine examples of 19th century vernacular, and the signal house, although erected in 1909, has very simple Italianate detailing typical of the ornament used on Victorian industrial and commercial buldings. The light tower is unusual for its square, straight-sided shape and its rugged granite work. The tower is identical in form and construction to the lighthouse at Beavertail Point, Jamestown, Rhode Island, which was also completed in 1856.

These two structures differ markedly from other New England lighthouses. At the same time, their stonework makes them part of a particular southern Rhode Island architectural tradition. The availability of granite from the quarries of Westerly led to the construction of many buildings of rock-faced granite ashlar throughout the area in identifiable concentration found only in this part of the state. Although the specific shape of the blocks and the method of assembling them at the Watch Hill Light and its counterpart, Beavertail Light, is unique, the general character of the masonry places both structures within this southern Rhode Island granite-construction tradition.

The visual impact of the light tower at Watch Hill makes it an important landmark with value as a monument intimately associated with the landscape as perceived by generations of local residents, visitors and mariners. Today, Watch Hill Light still serves as an important navigational aid to maritime traffic past it and the reefs offshore. Its historical associations, architectural quality, and scenic character make it a cultural resource worthy of preservation. In 1984, the lighthouse was nominated to be included in the National Register of Historic Places.

Watch Hill Light, Watch Hill, RI

Photo by BR1 Rusty Merritt, U.S. Coast Guard Officer-in-charge, Watch Hill Light Station

CHAPTER 39

POINT JUDITH LIGHT, Point Judith, RI (1810)

Light List No.: 18280
Location: Latitude 41° 21.7'N
          Longitude 71° 28.9'W
Height: 51' (HAW 65')
Range: 16 miles, Group Occulting White every
    15 secs., Horn
Lens: Fourth Order, Classical, 1000 Watt Lamp
Radio Beacon: 325 kHz, PJ (. _ _ .   . _ _),
    10 miles
Rebuilt: 1816, 1857

Point Judith Lighthouse, the last light to be described in this book, marks the entrance to Block Island Sound and Narragansett Bay. Established in 1810 on the western side of the entrance to Narragansett Bay, Point Judith Light is, next to Block Island Southeast Light, the most important lighthouse in Rhode Island. It marks, as all mariners know, one of the most dangerous spots along the Atlantic coast which has been referred to at various times as the "Graveyard of the Atlantic." Even during the American Revolution, a tower beacon was maintained on the point to warn vessels away from its treacherous shoals. Deceptively tame on calm days, "Point Jude," as it is frequently called, has been the scene of many shipwrecks. Only when high winds roll up huge breakers does the Point impress landlubbers with its threatening character. However, the light itself is quite sturdy. In the hurricane of 1938, Whale Rock Light, only six miles north of Point Judith, was completely destroyed and never rebuilt. Point Judith remained unscathed.

The bottom around Point Judith is irregular with many rocks and boulders. Caution is advised to avoid the shoal spots, even with a smooth sea, and to exercise extra care where the depths are not more than six feet greater than the draft of a vessel. The land surrounding the Point is flat, sandy and nearly treeless. The Point Judith Harbor of Refuge on the west side of the Point is formed by a main V-shaped breakwater and two other breakwaters extending to shore. It is of easy access for fishing boats, ferries, power and sailing vessels but is little used by tows. The ends of the breakwater are marked by unattended lights.

Many stories are told about the origin of the name "Point Judith." Some people say the Point was named for the wife of John Hull, a Boston goldsmith and mint master, while others claim that it was named for Judith Stoddard, his mother-in-law. Also, legend has it that the name was given by a Boston churchman who took the name from the Bible. On some of the earliest maps, the name is printed "Point Juda Neck." Another story has it that a Nantucket sea captain was lost in the fog and did not know in which direction to steer. His daughter, who was a passenger on the ship, cried out that she spied land. The old captain, whose eyes were not what they used to be when he was younger, commanded her anxiously, "P'int, Judy, p'int!"

In May 1793, the State of Rhode Island apparently ceded to the United States Government five acres of land on what is known today as Point Judith in South Kingston. On May 25, 1809, Mary and Hazard Knowle, who had somehow acquired the property, deeded 4.8 acres to the United States, and the next year a lighthouse was erected on the site. Daniel S. Way was the contractor for the construction of the light. Its first keeper was paid $350 a year. This first lighthouse was a crude wooden structure and used 12 single stationary lights as a lamp. It was blown down in the great gale of September 17, 1815.

A second lighthouse was erected in 1816 by William Ellery. It was built of rough stone coated with cement, was 35 feet high and showed a revolving light 74 feet above the sea. Its beam was visible for 14 miles. At its base it was 23 feet, ten inches, tapering to 13 feet at the top. The revolving light, made in Paris, France, consisted of ten oil lamps, each having an eight-and-one-half inch reflector with plano-convex McBeth-Evans lenses made of green glass and supported by two copper tables which had the machinery producing their revolutions. The lamps were arranged in two clusters of five. Mineral oil was used in the lamps and continued to be used in lamps as late as 1922. A 288 pound weight provided power that turned the table. The light revolved once every 144 seconds. A keeper reported that the light stopped only once: on the night of November 20, 1837.

Gilbert Pendleton, an early keeper, was appointed to the light on July 11, 1843 at an annual salary of $350. The light was distinguishable from Newport Light, which was stationary, and from Watch Hill Light, by it not entirely disappearing when within nine miles of it.

In his report made in Washington City (Washington, D.C.) on November 22, 1838, the ubiquitous Lieutenant George M. Bache, U.S.N., made the following observations about the lighthouse at Point Judith:

> The lamps are in bad order, and not firmly fixed upon the tables; some of them have screws, and others small wedges of wood under their tube barrels, which, the lightkeeper informed me had been placed there to elevate that part of the lamp, in order to prevent the overflowing of the oil. The reflectors are attached to the lamps by their hooks of sheet iron or tin, and are moveable in every direction; their axes make different angles with the horizontal line. Each reflector is 8½ inches in diameter, and weights from 9-12 ounces; the silver is so much worn from the concave surface of three of them that the copper is exposed in spots ... The keeper was under the impression that the light should be shown every one minute thirty seconds, but he had no watch or other means of measuring time accurately.

Point Judith Light, Point Judith, RI

U.S. Coast Guard Photo

The tower is damp, and in cold weather the moisture frequently condenses and freezes upon the glass of the lantern. The lightkeeper informed me that, occasionally, the ice formed in this manner has been of such thickness that he has been obliged to permit it to remain on the lantern for some days, until the wind should come from the southward and enable him to take it off without danger of breaking the glass.

The dwelling house, containing seven rooms, is of frame; it requires painting and a new kitchen floor. there is also belonging to this establishment a stone oil-vault, detached from the other buildings; it is so much out of repair that oil is stored in the tower.

In calculating the distance at which lights in this district should be seen, the height of the eye of the observer is supposed to be fifteen feet above the level of the sea, which is generally the case when the observation is taken from the deck of a coasting schooner.

The present, and third, lighthouse at Point Judith was built in 1857. It is an octagonal, granite block, pyramidal structure. It had an improved single revolving light also made in Paris. This was simply a brass lamp with a wick one-and-one quarter inches in diameter. It consumed one quarter of a pint of oil an hour. The framework of the lamp was made of 120 lenses which so reflected the rays of the light as to magnify its power many times. A fog horn 26 inches in diameter and a four horsepower engine were connected with the keeper's house. Joseph Whaley was keeper of the light for many years. His son, H.A. Whaley, succeeded him.

In 1869, a new lantern and deck plate were fitted. A first class steam fog signal was erected in 1873 and was replaced in 1903 by a 16 horsepower engine. A new fourth order, 24,000 candlepower light was installed in 1907. The intensity of the light was also increased by changing it from illuminant oil to incandescent vapor. In 1899, the color of the upper half of the tower was changed from white to brown. The ten-sided lantern, painted black, is covered with cast iron panels on the bottom half with large sheets of rectangular glass above, and is topped with a spherical ventilator with a lightning rod spike. A solid iron door on the west side opens to a granite-stepped spiral stairway leading to the lantern.

The nine-room brick keeper's dwelling was painted white and was connected to the tower by an enclosed gallery. It was torn down in 1954. At one time, the lighthouse inventory also listed an oil house, privy, barn, two fuel houses, a signal house, and a hen house on the site. In a 1922 "Description of Light Station," the keeper said the station was an unhealthy, old brick house, which was very damp. He said that rheumatism was common at the station, particularly in cold weather. He thought that a new wooden house might alleviate this condition.

Shipwrecks

As I mentioned earlier, "Point Jude" has been the scene of many shipwrecks. Here is a partial list: The "Normandy" in 1864 and the "C.B. Hamilton" in 1866. The "American Eagle" foundered there in 1870, and in the same year the steamer "Acusionet" was wrecked nearby. Other vessels include: "Henry W. Scavery," 1875; "Catherine W. May," 1876; "Venus," 1877; "Cucktoo," 1882. In 1885, the "Amon Bacon" went down, followed the next year by the "Allen Green." The "Harry A. Barry" went to a watery grave in 1887 as did the "Anita" in 1888, "Mars" in 1892, and "Blue Jay" in 1896. The "Agnes" foundered there in 1898 as did the "Edward M. Laughlin." At the turn of the century, the "Swallow" sank, followed by the "Amanda E." in 1902. Most recently, the "M/V Comet" sank off the Point in 1973.

Significance of the Lighthouse

Established as the third lighthouse in Rhode Island (Beavertail Light, 1749, was first; Watch Hill Light, 1807, was second), Point Judith Light has served continually since 1810 as the primary navigational aid for all shipping entering Narragansett Bay, as well as an important mark on Block Island Sound. Smallest in size of all the states in the Union, Rhode Island, the "Ocean State," is, however, one of the most important states in lighthouse history. Many of her old beacons, such as Point Judith, have been vital to the development of Newport and Providence. Point Judith Light has played an important role in the state's maritime economy by assisting early coastal freighter, whaling and merchant ships, fishing vessels, passenger steamers, as well as modern cargo ships and oil tankers, to the major ports of Newport, Providence, Fall River, Massachusetts, and the smaller towns along the Bay. The light is also significant as the site of the first radio beacon to be established at a Rhode Island lighthouse.

Although the light is an important mark on the Rhode Island coast, much of its historical significance also relates to the operation of its fog signal, a Daboll's trumpet sounded by a Wilcox hot-air engine which was established in 1867. Because of problems with its sound being lost in the noise of the surf offshore, it was replaced in 1872 by two first-class steam whistles. The earlier signal was kept as a spare in case of a failure of the new one. The amount of time needed to operate and maintain the fog signal required the hiring of an assistant keeper in 1874 and building quarters for him. During the following year, the signal operated a total of 777½ hours.

On November 11, 1931, the first radio beacon at a Rhode Island lighthouse was established at Point Judith. This marked an important event in this history of lighthouses that would have a far-reaching effect on the aids to navigation system. With the help of a radio beacon, ships could, for the first time, navigate at night and in fog without the assistance of a light or fog horn.

In addition to the light, a number of other structures were built on the station grounds during the last half of the 19th and beginning of the 20th centuries. Most of these no longer survive. The largest structure was a nine-room, one-and-one-half story brick keeper's dwelling connected to the tower by a short enclosed gallery. Built in 1857, it was torn down in 1954. A second dwelling, constructed in 1874 for an assistant keeper who was needed to operate the fog signal, has been torn down as well. Also no longer standing is a one-story clapboard fog signal building, constructed south of the tower in 1872 to house the whistle's steam engine and boiler, and a 1931 wood frame radio beacon house. Finally, the light's two 60-ft. high radio towers were taken down in 1974, because they were unsafe.

Although a United States Life-Saving Station was established in 1876 only about 50 yards east of the light, there was little interaction between the station's crew and the lightkeepers. The Life-Saving Service·and the Lighthouse Service were administered separately until 1939, at which time the Lighthouse Service became part of the U.S. Coast Guard. The Life-Saving Service had been part of the Coast Guard since 1915. The light was automated in 1954 when the keeper's dwelling was torn down. Since then, the light and-fog signals have been maintained by personnel from the Coast Guard Station. The light is the only manned station mentioned in *Lights & Legends*. Point Judith Light has been nominated in the National Register of Historic Places.

Point Judith Light, Point Judith, RI

Photo by Julius M. Wilensky

CHAPTER 40

LIGHTHOUSE TECHNOLOGY AND DEFINITIONS

Automation of the Lights

The romance of lighthouses has been extinguished in most of the nation and the world as new scientific technologies emerged in the second half of the 20th century and automated electronic lighting equipment took over the job of the old keepers, or "wickies" as they were sometimes called. Coast Guard officials began automation of the lighthouses on Long Island Sound in the mid-1960s. Eatons Neck Light at Northport, New York, became the first automated light in the nation on Monday, February 7, 1966, and became the prototype for the modernization process which followed.

The move to automate the nation's lighthouses was motivated primarily by budgetary considerations. It is cheaper to run a lighthouse with automatic equipment at a time when the Coast Guard has increasing pressures in other service areas, such as the prevention and cleanup of oil spills and drug intervention patrols. Fisheries patrols have also represented a large expenditure in terms of manpower and equipment deployed among foreign fleets since the enactment of the 200 mile limit off the east and west coasts. Also, as a branch of the Department of Transportation and not the Department of Defense, the Coast Guard is strictly limited in its funding.

However, despite all this, Coast Guard officials are confident that the automated lights will provide the same efficient services that the manned stations formerly provided as navagational aids to recreational and commercial boats traversing the Sound. Race Rock Light, for example, where the power supply comes from a submarine cable extending from and monitored by the New London Coast Guard station on shore, is backed up by batteries and an emergency diesel-powered generator capable of keeping the light and fog horn operating for more than two weeks.

While critics argue that the black boxes and other electrical gear are unable to render emergency assistance that the old light keepers of earlier days could, the Coast Guard maintains that really is not necessary any more. Today, emergency aid is available from a number of small boats, 21 feet to 44 feet in length from search and rescue stations up and down the coast, or dispatched from the Coast Guard helicopter base in Brooklyn, New York. Many Long Island Sound communities have police patrol boats that answer distress calls. Nassau and Suffolk Counties on Long Island both have police patrol boats that can come to the rescue. The Coast Guard Auxiliary does this in some other communities. Private companies also render aid for a fee when the Coast Guard cannot do so. The Coast Guard continues to respond to life-threatening situations.

As I have noted repeatedly in this book, one of the sad effects of automation is the mindless vandalism which invariably occurs once boaters discover the a lighthouse is unmanned. It is for this reason that local organizations should be encouraged to take over the lights if they are to be preserved as a vital part of our maritime history.

The Lighthouse Board

If one had to indicate the most important year in the history of the nation's aids to navigation, it would have to be 1852, the year the Lighthouse Board came into being. At that time, the United States' lighthouses and other aids to navigation were third-rate. The lighting system that illuminated the lighthouse towers were not only out of date, but in its last days did not come up to the quality of other nations with similar systems. Many towers had been poorly constructed, and many aids to navigation had not been placed in locations to be of maximum help to the mariner. The nation's coasts were inadequately marked, lights were poorly maintained by poorly trained keepers, many of whom were political hacks. Moreover, the administration of aids to navigation, known as the Lighthouse Establishment, could be termed as being at its best, inept.

The new Board consisted of three officers of the navy, three officers of the engineer corps of the army, and three civilians, one of whom was the Secretary of the Treasury; the remaining two were persons of high scientific attainments.

Such a composition placed its members beyond the pale of political appointment and enabled them to lay plans which they hoped to see carried out.

The Board divided the Atlantic and Pacific coasts, the Gulf of Mexico, the Great Lakes, and the great western rivers into districts. To each, an inspector, who was an officer of the Navy, and an engineer, who was an officer in the Army, was assigned. The inspectors, under direction of the Board, kept up the lighthouses and were charged with the discipline of the lighthouse keepers. They made constant visits to the lights and reported the condition of them and of the behavior of the keepers to the Board so that the system was as nearly perfect as it could be when we consider the exposed location and solitude of many of the lights.

The Lighthouse Board lasted until 1910. After that, it was known as the Lighthouse Service or the Bureau of Lighthouses. On July 1, 1939, it was transferred to and consolidated with the Coast Guard where it has remained ever since.

The Lighthouse Board took over the nation's aids to navigation, and over the years brought order to them. They instilled dedication among the service's employees, and added lighthouses, beacons, fog-signals, buoys and lightships so that this country's shores were fully illuminated and hazards to navigation were clearly marked. Efficiency, reliability and quality came to have meaning in the lighthouse service. By the time the Lighthouse Board had become outmoded as an administrative organization in 1910, it had so firmly set the lighthouse service on the path to being among the world's best that its successors, the Lighthouse Service and the Coast Guard, became imbued with the same spirit of quality. They also retained the same dedication to progress in maintaining a first-class system of aids to navigation.

The feeble light of the 1716 Boston Lighthouse, the nation's first, gradually grew brighter. Now lighthouses are far more efficient, reliable and effective than they have ever been in their long history. Powerful lights glow brightly from them so that the mariner does not have to peer into the dark seeking a dim beacon from a weak flame. Indeed, the mariner has a veritable cornucopia of aids to help him safely navigate the waters of the United States. This state of affairs stands as a monument to the Lighthouse Board. They first set this country on the path to systematically providing adequate and technologically advanced aids to navigation to bring a measure of safety to mariners.

Outline of Lighthouse Administration
1789-1844   Established under U.S. Treasury Department; known as the Lighthouse Establishment.
1845-1902   Shifted to Revenue Department, Marine Division; on Tuesday, August 31, 1852, Light-House Board established by Congress.
1903-1938   Under the Department of Commerce; in 1910, Lighthouse Service or Bureau of Lighthouses formed.
1939-now   Coast Guard assumed responsibility for all aids to navigation in the United States. The Coast Guard was recently transferred to the Department of Transportation.

Keepers of the Light
The key figure in a lighthouse was the keeper. Early keepers used to pilot ships into port and also serve as health officers. Each ship had to pass health inspection before being allowed to pass the lighthouse on its way into the harbor. Since 1939, the keepers of the light have been men of the Coast Guard. Before that, the Lighthouse Service attracted a motley crowd of men and women, united by a devotion to their jobs that was almost incredible. On a light, where the slightest mistake can mean catastrophe at sea, attention to the endless chores of keeping the light going was unflagging.

True tales of heroism have become almost legendary. Many lighthouse keepers stuck to their posts for years without being relieved, such as Captain Brooks of Falkner Island Light. Others made heroic rescues at sea, or went down in storms with their lights, such as the two assistant keepers who perished when their light at Minot's Ledge, southeast of Boston, Massachusetts, toppled into the sea during the early morning hours of Tuesday, April 17, 1851. Women such as Ida Lewis of Lime Rock Light, Newport, Rhode Island and children tended lights valiantly against enormous physical odds while their men were away. Some of their exploits were related in this book.

Yet, with all the hardships of that life, cramped living quarters, semi-isolation from the world, constant exposure to danger, the job of lighthouse keeper had always held a strange fascination for people. When the Lighthouse Service was under Civil Service control, there was never a shortage of applications, even in boom times, although keeper's salaries were meager. One man, Francis Malone, a bachelor, was so eager for the keeper's job on a light at Lake Superior, that when the inspector told him only a married man would do, he found a wife within a week. New inspectors were appointed every two years, and the Malones got into the habit of naming their new babies after the inspectors. This system worked all right twelve times, but the Spanish American War proved to be too much for even the Malones. That year, three new inspectors were appointed.

Lighthouse keepers had an amazing record of tenure. Ten years at a light was considered nothing. After 25 years, a man was still to be watched. He might turn out to be a restless drifter! Only after a half a century of service did the other "wickies" really consider a keeper as one of them, a man who had settled down to a steady occupation. In this book, the keeper with the longest tenure was Eli Kimberly of Falkner Island Light, serving 33 years, 1818-1851. Another keeper, who had seen 38 years of of service on a light, in perfect health, remarked, "the secret of my good health is that I have been where the doctors could not get to me."

There was bound to be friction between men who had to stay in close quarters for long periods of time. At one station, two keepers who could no longer stand the sight or sound of each other, simply stopped talking. An inspector learned the reason for their disagreement. One of them wanted his potatoes mashed, the other, fried.

In the old days, lighthouse keepers were men of the sea who, for one reason or another, found themselves ashore for good. Some were married men who moved their wives into the lighthouse as they began a new way of life. Together, the couple tended the lonely light, enjoying, we suppose, a certain peaceful solitude which must have called for complete compatibility. When the man died, frequently his wife or daughter carried on his work, doing a surprisingly good job. For example, Elizabeth Smith took charge of Old Field Point Light, Port Jefferson, New York when her husband died in 1830, and remained on the job for 26 years. When the Coast Guard took over the lights in 1939, no women were dismissed. Those assigned to lights needing only one keeper were allowed to remain on duty if they so desired.

Mrs. Maggie R. Norwell, keeper of lighthouses in Louisiana, held her position for 40 years before retiring in 1932. The last woman to leave the service was Mrs. Fannie Salter, whose appointment by President Calvin Coolidge was the last given to a woman. "Too hard on the feet," was her explanation when she retired in 1948 after spending her final 23 years in Upper Chesapeake Bay at Turkey Point Lighthouse, after her husband died in 1925.

Since the Coast Guard became the keeper of the lights in 1939, the romance and danger of the job are practically gone. Men are stationed at whatever few manned lights are left for a definite hitch, then transferred elsewhere. Modern improvements make tending the lights easier, and radio and television break up the tedium of isolation. With almost all of the lights being automated, keepers of the light are fast becoming a vanishing breed. One of the two civilian ones left I know is Frank Schubert who signed on with the U.S. Bureau of Lighthouses in 1937. Later he served as keeper of the Coney Island Light Station for 25 years. Now in his 70s and still on active duty, Mr. Schubert still lives in Brooklyn and has many interesting tales about the life of a keeper. The other keeper, Norman Boyd, is also in his 70s and lives in Old Saybrook, Connecticut. At one time he served as keeper of the Lynde Point Light.

Ancient Lighthouses

Motives other than safety were probably the reason for building the first lighthouses. For example, the motive for the lights of ancient Egypt was religious and the worship of fire. The towers of the Libyans and the Cushites, topped by iron and bronze braziers in the shapes of sea creatures, held blazing wooden fires. Mariners used the towers as temples by day and as navigational aids at night. In turn, the priests, the ancient keepers of the lights, engraved nautical charts on the walls of the temples.

The Egyptians were responsible, too, for the most notable lighthouse of antiquity, the Pharos of Alexandria. Designed by Sostratus of Cnidos and built on the Island of Pharos at the entrance to Alexandria Harbor, it stood about 500 feet high, cost $2,500,000 and took 20 years to build. Completed about 300 B.C., it was of "such wonderful construction," according to Caesar, that it was considered one of the Seven Wonders of the World. The flames from its top, which were visible for 30 miles, burned on the Egyptian coast for 1400 years. Today, pharology is still the name given to the branch of engineering dealing with lighthouses.

The first modern type lighthouse, built on a submerged foundation, was the famed Eddystone Light, built near Plymouth, England in 1698. In 1664, when people first began talking about building a light on the dangerous reef that juts out into the English Channel near Plymouth and had become a graveyard for hundreds of ships, the idea was considered preposterous. An eccentric English country gentleman, Henry Winstanley, went to work and built an equally eccentric lighthouse, a carved and guilded wooden structure. One wit at the time commented, that it would have looked more at home in a Chinese cemetery than in the English Channel. People laughed, but the builder claimed it would stand the fiercest gale, and he hoped to be on hand if such an event occured. His wish was granted. In 1703, on an inspection trip to his lighthouse, a violent storm broke out and swept Winstanley, five keepers and Eddystone Light into the Channel forever.

Another wooden tower was built and burned before an engineer named John Smeaton solved the problem of keeping a light on the terrible reef. Huge interlocking stones, held together with a horizontal and vertical network of iron bars, formed a massive tower. Smeaton's methods were copied all over the world. In time, his original scheme was improved upon through the use of caissons and screwpiles, but his construction of Eddystone Light remains a milestone of progress in man's battle with the sea.

Early American Lighthouses

In our own country, progress in lighthouse building was slow, partly because of the "Moon Cussers" mentioned elsewhere in this book. Throughout the entire 18th century, only 24 lighthouses were established on the Atlantic Coast. North America's first lighthouse was built on Little Brewster Island in Boston Harbor in 1716, but it met a sad fate as the defeated British fleet returned to England in 1776. As a last gesture of defiance, the British blew up the lighthouse, and it was not rebuilt until 1783. The second Boston Lighthouse, a 200 year-old white, stone tower 89 feet tall, still operates today in a remarkable state of preservation.

Its beacon is as necessary to Boston marine traffic now as in colonial days when its predecessor warned of the treacherous ledges in Boston Harbor. A crew of five Coast Guardsmen maintained the light with two men in residence at all times. Its first-order lens is visible 27 miles at sea and exhibited from the 1783 tower with only slight modification in height and intensity of beam. Unfortunately, only seven of the 20 odd colonial masonry towers built before 1900 remain today. Of these, the oldest surviving colonial lighthouse in the United States is Sandy Hook Light on the New Jersey side of the entrance to New York Harbor. The white, octagonal, stone tower, built in 1764, rises serenely 85 feet into the air. It was built with money raised through two lotteries.

It was called New York Lighthouse when it first went into service, but later took the name of the small neck of New Jersey land on which it stood. Taxes levied by tonnage on passing vessels were used to maintain the nine-story structure with its 48 oil lamps. The tower originally rose to 103 feet, tapering from a 29 foot diameter at its base to a 15-foot diameter just below the lantern. The fighting between British and American troops during the Revolution resulted in the destruction of Sandy Hook's lantern, but no damage could be inflicted on the sturdy tower itself. The lantern was replaced after the war, and Sandy Hook Lighthouse survives today, a tribute to its builder, Isaac Conto.

The Structure of Lighthouses

The principal purpose of a lighthouse is to support a light source and lens at a considerable height above water. The same structure may also house a fog-signal, radio beacon, equipment and quarters for the operating personnel. In many instances, however, the auxiliary equipment and personnel are housed in separate buildings nearby. Such a group of buildings is called a light station. Eatons Neck, New York, is an example of a light station.

Lighthouses vary greatly in their outward appearance, determined in part by their location, whether in the water or on shore, the importance of the light, the kind of soil on which it is constructed, and the prevalence of violent storms. The essential features of a light structure where operating personnel are not in residence are: best possible location as determined by the physical characteristics of the site, sufficient height for the requirements of the light, a rugged support for the light itself, and proper shelter for the light source.

Lighthouses are marked with various colors for the purpose of making them readily distinguishable from the backgrounds against which they are seen and to make possible the identification of individual lights among others that are in the same general area. Solid colors, bands of colors, stripes, and various other patterns are used in marking lights.

The United States Coast Guard, in its *Aids to Navigation Manual* for 1964, defines a lighthouse so:

> A lighthouse structure is an enclosed edifice which houses, protects, displays, or supports visual, audible, or radio aids to navigation. A lighthouse structure is complex in design and construction and usually requires a significant amount of individual engineering site analysis. It can be manned or unmanned and is usually made of granite, brick, cast-iron plate, monolithic stone, concrete or steel. The structure can be located in an offshore, wave-swept, exposed environment, on a coastline as a landfall object, or at any location where a large support structure is required.

Great Captain Island Light, Greenwich, CT

Wave-Swept Lighthouses

Wave-swept lighthouses occupy more exposed positions than any other class of structures and are obliged to resist a greater variety of strains. To be most helpful for ships running the gauntlet of rocky shores and hidden reefs, a guiding light must often be placed far out from land in extremely exposed positions. Thus, the problem of lighthouse building has been, from the first, to build a structure which could resist the enormous force of the wind and waves. In early times, the lighthouse builders were unable to solve the problem, and evaded it by building only on solid land well out of the reach of the sea. In this book, there are three notable examples of wave-swept lighthouses which rise from ledges of rocks or hard bottoms: Race Rock, New York (Chapter 33); New London Ledge, Connecticut (Chapter 31); and Stratford Shoal (Middle Ground), (Chapter 16).

The force of the waves lashed by the wind seems incredible. The following table, which indicates the pressure according to the velocity of the wind, gives some idea of the problem:

Velocity of Wind, Miles per Hour	Pressure in Pounds, per Square Inch	Description
1	.005	Hardly perceptible
15	1.007	Moderate breeze
50	10.000	Gale
80	26.000	Hurricane
108	46.000	Destructive hurricane

When the lighthouse is designed, the maximum force exerted by wind and waves is first calculated. To design a tower which will be stable under all attacks from wind and wave, the common center of effort of all these forces is first determined so that the net weight falls within the outer edge of the base. Something of the same problem is encountered in building towers and chimneys, but the lighthouse must have greater stiffness and rigidity than these, because the vibration set up in a great storm will interfere with the lamps and the complicated clock devices and lenses of the lights.

These wave-swept towers are built if possible on rocks, well above the water, which offer a secure foundation. It is often necessary, however, to build upon rocks which lie below the water except at low tide. In designing these foundations and bases, the center of gravity is kept as low as possible. The base is built of stones of high density ingeniously dovetailed together. Even a base of solid masonry, in which the stones are laid in concentric circles, has not proved strong enough to withstand the stroke of the waves. The dovetailing of the stone suggests some Chinese puzzle. They are cut in advance and fitted together and secured with concrete.

The lighthouse is built in its familiar circular form, because that shape offers the least resistance to the wave stroke and wind pressure, no matter from which direction they may be directed. The lower portion of the lighthouse is exposed, of course, to the direct horizontal stroke of the water and is made vertical. The upper part of the tower is built in a continuous curve in a vertical plane. The curve is designed with great care. The wall recedes at such an angle that the waves striking its base will be carried quickly upward and thrown back on themselves, thus averting the full power of the stroke. The surface of the walls is kept smooth in order that they will offer as little resistance to the water as possible. Even the lantern gallery, built on top of the tower above the reach of the water, is designed to offer as little resistance as possible to the wind. The height of the lighthouse is determined largely by the force of the waves which rise about its sides. The light must be kept above the broken water and even the sea spray of the severest storms.

In some localities where the water is very deep, cribs have been laboriously filled with stone and capped with concrete and other masonry to serve as a foundation. When the bottoms are hard but not rocky, lighthouses have been built on piers. The foundations are often secured again by being bolted securely to the rocks on which they stand, even at considerable depths. In building at the entrance to harbors, it is often possible to utilize the end of breakwaters, as at Old Saybrook, Connecticut (Chapter 22), or pierheads. The lighthouse must, as a rule, be as compact as possible.

When a caisson is used for supporting a lighthouse, a cylinder is constructed from 20 to 35 feet in diameter, composed of iron plates. This is sunk by dredging or by a pneumatic process in shallow water until a firm foundation is obtained. Then its interior is solidly filled with concrete. In some cases, as at Race Rock, New York (Chapter 33), caissons have been placed on rocks or ledges. Today there are 46 lighthouses standing on caisson foundations, located for the most part on the North and Middle Atlantic coasts. The first one was built at Fourteen Foot Bank in Delaware Bay.

American engineers often follow a novel design in building wave-swept lighthouses. Instead of cutting foundations in the rocks in exposed positions and raising towers of solid masonry to battle against the waves and wind, they evade the problem by building an open-work steel base which offers the minimum amount of resistance. These lighthouses are known as screwpile lights. The support is obtained by drilling into the floor of the sea and forcing down steel rods and screwing them into the ocean bed.

The pile or steel rod is made with a broad flange at its end which makes the rod virtually an auger. This is bored into the sea bed until it has reached a sufficient depth to fix it securely and rigidly in place. The pile can, of course, be bored into the bed of the sea at any angle. The foundations are elastic, so in case one of the steel beams should be broken, it may be easily replaced. The first screwpile lighthouse in the United States was built in the Delaware River in 1850. There are none in the area covered by this book, where ice formation could preclude their use.

CHAPTER 41

LENSES

Introduction

The first really efficient light was created by Englishman William Hutchinson in 1763. The idea came to him at a meeting of scientific gentlemen in Liverpool. One of the men there wagered he could read a newspaper by the light of a candle at a distance of 200 feet away. He lined a wooden bowl with pieces of mirror stuck into putty. This created a reflector producing a beam of light strong enough to read the newspaper. Hutchinson's refinement of this idea used oil lamps placed in the center of a reflector. Reflectors were first used in the United States in 1810, made of silvered glass or sheet copper, silver plated.

Unprotected lights were given glass covers. These, highly unsatisfactory, gave way to catatropic and diatropic lenses, which, while they focused the light in a solid flow, let a great deal of light escape up, down, and to the sides. The problem remained until the 1820s, when Augustin Fresnel, a member of Napoleon's Lighthouse Board, succeeded in uniting both the catatropic and diatropic approaches into one lens. His remarkable device, frequently referred to today as a "classical" lens, is still in use all over the world. Refracting prisms and glass rings surrounding a central reflecting bullseye direct the beam of light into a solid column seaward to the horizon. With a Fresnel lens, the glare of a match can be magnified into a column of flame. This lens entered use in the United States in 1841.

The lens itself rests on a platform that floats in mercury. To achieve flashing or occulting effects, which give each light its identifiable characteristic, the lens is usually revolved in conjunction with flash panels.

The French in the early 1800s refined the reflectors to a parabolic shape that gathered the rays into a concentrated beam (similar to automobile headlights). By the mid-19th century, both systems of reflectors and lenses were used to provide the best light of all. The ultimate success of both systems was dependent on the discovery in 1780 of the Argand Burner which became the first modern light source. Invented by Aimé Argand, a Swiss, the Argand Burner consisted of an oil lamp with a cylindrical wick enclosed with two concentric tubes and a glass chimney producing the brightest light known until that time.

By the late 19th century, sweeping lights and flashing lights came into existence. Sweeping lights were visible to all ships regardless of their position. Flashing lights made recognition by mariners of one lighthouse from another by the frequency and duration of the flashes. Today's lights are capable of producing as much as 14 million candlepower.

The Fresnel or Classical Lens

Development of increased illumination seems to have been one of the lighthouse engineers' chief problems since the days of the Pharohs in ancient Alexandria, Egypt. Many devices were tried, but no real progress was made in creating an intense light beam until 1822, when the French physicist Augustin Frensel (1788-1827) developed his revolutionary annular or ring-like lens which became standard equipment in all primary and secondary lighthouses throughout the world. The Fresnel lens solved the problem of intensity and control of the beam. Contemporary Fresnel lenses differ little from those first used in 1822.

Many of the early colonial lights in the United States sent forth fixed beams whose length had never been correctly measured. The amount of their illumination in terms of candlepower was unknown. The few that were equipped to send a rotating beam pivoted at random. Their keepers (known as "wickies") had no accurate way of timing the revolutions and no orders to make a check. Skippers back from European voyages reported in detail about the lighthouse system there and how much better it was than our own.

During the early 1800s, the research of Fresnel in France in the field of optics led to the development of lighthouse lenses of a truly scientific pattern. These lenses were quickly put into use in the principal lighthouses in France, Great Britian and other European countries. They were much brighter than lights in service in the United States, resulting in fewer shipwreck losses. However, Fresnel lenses were not officially adopted by the Lighthouse Board in the United States until 1852, largely due to the successful lobbying efforts of Winslow Lewis in behalf of his own lamp system.

By 1859 practically all reflectors in the United States' lighthouses had been replaced by the superior Fresnel lenses. These priceless lenses are rapidly disappearing from the galleries of many lighthouses as the Coast Guard continues to remove them and replace them with more economical modern plastic lenses. Hopefully more historical societies will acquire them so the public can enjoy their beautiful gem-like quality.

Fresnel's principles revolutionized lighthouse technology and optics science. His discoveries resulted in design and construction of a glass optic or lens which reflected or refracted 65%-70% of all the light emitted from a central single light source. These aggregations of beautiful cut-glass prisms of the dioptric, catadioptric and catoptric types set in brass frames collected and concentrated a high percentage of the light emitted by the lamp and directed it out along useful horizontal beams. The beam became primarily a function of intensity per unit area, horizontal width of the light source, and the projected vertical height of the lens.

Fresnel lenses are known as classical lenses. Although no longer being purchased by the Coast Guard, they are still found in some lighthouses in the First Coast Guard District such as Stepping Stones and Montauk Point, New York. Regretfully, mindless vandals on occasions have used the lenses as objects for target practice. damaging these priceless and irreplaceable prisms. The classical lens apparatus may be fixed, in which case a flasher must be used to produce a characteristic other than steady, or it may revolve to produce a flashing characteristic.

The Order of Lenses

In addition to inventing the principle of the lenticular system of lenses, Fresnel designed orders or sizes for his lenses. The largest is the 1st Order, a brass and glass structure six feet in diameter and standing over 18 feet high (including the metal base clockworks). The "Orders" extend down through a tiny 6th Order that is 18 inches high and one foot in diameter; Tongue Point Light has one of these. In later years, a 3½ Order and a hyper-radial lens were added. The giant hyper-radial lens is 8½ feet diameter, over 22 feet high and weighs ten tons. The optic was designed by Messrs. Barbier of Paris, France in 1885 and was also manufactured by the Chance Brothers in England. The only hyper-radial lens in this country is in the Makapuu Point Lighthouse on Oahu, Hawaii.

The largest orders (1st and 2nd) were installed in major landfall lights, the mid-range of orders (3rd, 3½, and 4th) were designed for coast and harbor entrance lighthouses, and the smallest lenses (5th and 6th) served in structures located in bays and estuaries. This is only a general overview, since many lighthouses served dual functions. A major seacoast lighthouse might be a warning of a reef or low island as well as serving as a landfall aid to navigation. A seacoast light could assist a navigator fix his position and also serve as a harbor entrance light.

In *Lights & Legends*, the following lighthouses have or had Fresnel lenses of different orders:

> 1st Order - Block Island Southeast
> 2nd Order - Little Gull Island
> 3rd Order - Eatons Neck, Horton Point, Sheffield Island
> 3½ Order - Montauk Point
> 4th Order - Most (26) of the lighthouses discussed in this book used this order of lens
> 5th Order - Black Rock Harbor, Lynde Point, North Dumpling
> 6th Order - Tongue Point, Stonington, Cedar Island, Morgan Point

The small museum attached to Montauk Point Light has some of these lenses on display. The Coast Guard keeps unused lenses in storage until they are solicited by a museum or historical society. Then they are loaned out for ten to 20 years so the public may view them.

A number of small maritime museums containing Fresnel lenses and lighthouse memorabilia exist from Maine to Maryland. Among them are:

> Shore Village Museum, Rockland, Maine
> Old Lighthouse Museum, Stonington, Connecticut
> Maritime Museum, King's Point, New York
> Twin Lights Historic Site, Highlands, New Jersey
> Chesapeake Bay Maritime Museum, St. Michaels, Maryland.

As mentioned previously, when lighthouses use Fresnel or classical lenses, the lenses were ranked according to the distance from the center of the lantern, where the lamp is located, to the lens which surrounds it. There are eight classifications of lenses.

1. The rare **hyperradial lens** is the largest ever made, with a distance be-

tween the center to the lens being 52.3 inches. None of the lighthouses in this book has this lens.

2. Next comes the **first-order lens** with a distance or radius between the center and lens of 36.2 inches. This lens was used extensively in important United States' lighthouses. Block Island Southeast Light still uses one of these.

3. A **second-order lens** has a radius of 19.7 inches from the center of the lantern to the lens. One of these lenses may still be found in the lantern of Eatons Neck Light, Northport, New York.

5. A **3½-order lens** has a radius of 14.8 inches. Historic Montauk Point's Lighthouse has one of these lenses.

6. A **fourth-order lens** has a radius of 9.8 inches. Picturesque Stepping Stones Light, Great Neck, New York still has one of these beautiful prisms.

7. A **fifth-order lens** measures 7.4 inches along the focal plane from the source of the light in the center of the lantern to the lens. Such a lens may be found in the lantern at Lynde Point Lighthouse, Old Saybrook, Connecticut.

8. Finally, a **sixth-order lens**, the smallest, has a radius of only 5.9 inches. Tongue Point Light in Bridgeport has one of these lenses.

MODERN LENSES

190-mm Lens

The 190-mm rotating lens (or lantern) is used only on structures not subjected to noticable vibrations. This lens is used only where battery power is available and when the required nominal range for a white or colored light exceeds eight or six nautical miles respectively. Orient Point and Block Island lighthouses have this lens.

Some of its features are:
- Requires precision focusing and leveling
- Replaceable clear, green or red lens cover
- Can dissipate 60 watts of heat continuously
- Requires relamping every 230 days
- Selection of rpm and number of flashpanels (up to six)
- Cannot be used with color sectors in the lens cover
- The 190-mm lens must be equipped with 12-volt lamps.

The flash characteristic of the lens depends upon the beam pattern and the rotation speed selected. The rotation speed of the lens stays within six percent of the rated rpm for motor voltages above 8.0.

The optic rotates twenty-four hours a day.

200-mm Lens

The 200-mm lens (or lantern) provides an omnidirectional light where light-to-moderate icing is expected on exposed bars and jetties subject to breaking water. A maximum nominal range of eight nautical miles is obtained with 12-volt lamps. Peck Ledge lighthouse has one of these lenses.

Some of its features are:

- Aluminum base
- Glass lens
- Aluminum lid
- Uses a 12 volt lamp

250-mm Lens

The 250-mm lens (or lantern) is for use only on stable platforms. It is not used on buoys or on wooden single pile beacons located in the water. It is installed only on steel or concrete beacon structures in a hard bottom and not subject to collisions. Omnidirectional nominal ranges of up to nine nautical miles can be obtained with standard twelve-volt equipment. Tongue Point lighthouse has one of these lenses.

Some of its features are:
- Optimal color sectors and pencil beams
- Requires precision focusing and leveling
- Requires azimuth sighting of beams and sectors
- Replaceable clear, green, red or yellow acrylic lens covers
- Ventilated version can dissipate 75 watts of heat continuously
- Aluminum base with four 1/16 inch drain holes
- Requires a 12 Vdc lamp

300-mm Lens

The 300-mm lens (or lantern) can be used only on stable platforms. It cannot be used on buoys and single pile beacon structures located in the water. Omnidirectional nominal ranges up to ten nautical miles can be obtained with standard twelve-volt equipment. Lloyd Harbor, Latimer Reef and North Dumpling lighthouses have these lenses.

Some of its features are:
- Requires precision focusing and leveling
- Replaceable clear, green, red and yellow acrylic lens
- Can dissipate 250 watts of heat continuously
- Plastic base with four 1/16 drain holes
- Uses a 12 Vdc lamp

FA-251-AC Lens

The FA-251-AC rotating optic is a 120-volt AC version of the 190-mm 12-volt DC optic. The FA-251-AC lens (or lantern) must be mounted on rigid structures and provides a maximum nominal range for a white or colored light of 17 or 15 nautical miles respectively. Greens Ledge, Southwest Ledge, New London Ledge and Watch Hill lighthouses are equipped with these lenses.

Some of its features are:
- Requires precise leveling
- Replaceable clear, red or green lenses and lens cover
- Forced air cooling
- Selection of rpm and number of flash panels (up to six)

- Cannot be used with color sectors in the lens cover
- Uses 150 watt tungsten-halogen lamps. The 120-volt, 250-watt lamp cannot be used in the optic, because the lamp is physically too large.

The rotation of the optic is daylight controlled. The flash characteristics of the optic depend on the beam pattern and rotation selected.

DCB-10 Lens

The DCB-10 rotating optic produces an omnidirectional light with a maximum nominal range of 18 nautical miles. It provides light intensities between those obtained from standard fixed optics and the standard Coast Guard optics for a landfall light—the DCB-24 and DCB-224. Old Field Point lighthouse has one of these lenses.

Some of its features are:

- Two pencil beams of light separated by 180 degrees
- Clear, green or red lenses
- Large angular divergence of the light beam
- Easy access for maintenance and lamping
- Lamp adjustment in the horizontal plane
- Uses two 120 Vac, 500 watt, CC-8 filament tungsten-halogen lamps with medium bipost bases.

DCB-224 Lens

The DCB-24 and DCB-224 are the Coast Guard's standard landfall lights. These rotating optics are used for lights that must have a nominal range greater than 18 nautical miles. The DCB-224 emits two pencil beams which sweep the horizon. Race Rock, Stratford Point, Montauk Point and Penfield Reef lighthouses have this lens.

Some of its features are:

- Two drums with variable beam separation in the horizontal plane
- Requires precision focusing and leveling
- Replaceable clear, green or red drum covers
- Available without motor drive and gear assembly for use as a sighted pencil beam light
- Uses a 120 Vac, 1000 watt tungsten-halogen lamp with a CC-8 filament and a mogul bipost base.

The DCB-24 lens rotates 24 hours a day when daylight controlled unless precautions are taken to protect the lamp changer from solar heat.

CHAPTER 42

Forms of Illuminant in Lighthouses

1. **Fire** - Until the first application of electricity to lighting late in the 19th century, all artificial light was produced by fire. The earliest form of illuminant used as a navigational aid was a burning pyre of wood and later, coal set in a brazier or grate erected on top of a tower. Because of the huge flame area, sufficient light was evolved to be seen at a distance of several miles. The useful candlepower to the mariner was limited by the low intensity per unit area of the flame and its total projected area. Until the end of the 18th century and even into the 19th century, these primitive illuminants continued to be almost the only ones in use.

2. **Oil Lamp** - Oil wick lamps were used in the lighthouses of Liverpool, England as early as 1763, when Argand, the Swiss physicist, perfected his cylindrical wick lamp which provided a central current of air through the burner, thus allowing more perfect combustion of the gas issuing from the wick. Fresnel produced burners having two, three and four concentric wicks.

(a) Multiple Wick Burner - It was not until 1868 that a burner was devised which successfully consumed hydro-carbon oils. A multiple wick burner, invented by Captain Doty, was quickly adopted by lighthouse authorities. The "Doty" burner, and other patterns involving the same principle, remained practically the only oil burners in lighthouse use until the last few years of the 19th century.

(b) High-Pressure Type - Mineral oil, heated under high-pressure air to a vapor, was first used in 1898. This process resulted in a sixfold increase in candlepower over oil wick lamps. From time to time, sperm oil, olive oil, lard oil, and coconut oil have been used for lighthouse purposes in various parts of the world.

3. **Gas Burner** - Gas burners were introduced in 1837. The invention of the Welsbach mantle placed at the disposal of lighthouse authorities the means of producing a light of high intensity combined with great focal compactness.

(a) Oil Gas - In 1870, the Pintsch oil gas burner first came into use. It was used for both buoys and beacons. High-pressure containers (nine to ten atmospheres) were used to recharge large storage tanks connected to the lights.

(b) Acetylene - Generated from calcium carbide, acetylene was first shown to be a possibility by Thomas M. Wilson in 1892. The lights, which were open flame burners, were first used in Sweden in 1904, and assumed wide-spread use in 1906. The gas was placed in cylinders (accumulators) under pressure of from ten to 15 atmospheres. The brightness of this flame was about equal to that of the mantle oil vapor burners. The high illuminating power and the brightness of the flame of acetylene make it a very suitable illuminant for lighthouses and beacons, providing certain difficulties attending to its use can be overcome.

4. Incandescent Oil Vapor - The introduction of kerosene or coal oil was another important step resulting in more brilliant lights, and from kerosene the incandescent oil vapor light was developed. This lamp, placed within a carefully designed lens of great size, produced the most powerful light known up to the time of the general introdution of electricity, which, in lighthouse work, was undertaken about 1916.

5. Electric Lamp - The first arc lamp, known as the Wright arc, was patented in England in 1845. This arc light, used only in the larger English lighthouses, was the first experiment with electricity as an aid to navigation. The first attempt to electrify buoy lights through cables in New York Harbor was made in 1888, but proved unsuccessful. The beginning of widespread use of electricity at both attended and unattended stations occurred in 1928. By this time, electricity had been proven to be an economical and a reliable source of power and made available a light source having a greater intensity per unit area.

Electricity is the illuminant now used in most of the larger lighthouses. Electric incandescent lamps placed inside the larger sizes of lenses can produce beams of several million candlepower.

Light Characteristics

Lights are given distinctive characteristics so that one light may be distinguished from another as a means of conveying definite information. This is achieved by employing lights of various colors, by fixed lights, and by lights flashing of various duration with varying periods of intervals. In this manner, a great variety of characteristics may be obtained.

Lights are referred to as "flashing" when the light period is shorter than the dark period, and as "occulting" when the light period is equal to or longer than the dark period. At short distances and in clear weather, flashing lights may show a faint continuous light. The period of flashing or occulting light is the time required to go through the full set of changes. The limiting basis for the period of light characteristics has been set up as 60 seconds, since it is considered that the mariner cannot always safely watch the light to the exclusion of everything else for a longer period.

Light characteristics which are so similar as to require careful timing in order to differentiate between them are not established in close proximity. While the mariner may wish to use a watch with a second hand or a stop watch to make identification as certain as possible under some circumstances, in normal practice it should be possible to identify primary and secondary lights by their characteristics without instruments of any sort.

Although infrequently used today, rotating opaque shutters and colored glass screens are a means of producing certain phases of light characteristics. Such shutters or screens are arranged to pass between the light and the observer's eye at certain regular intervals, either cutting off the light or changing its color. They may be mounted upon a ring or chariot rotated by an electric motor or weight-driven clock mechanism. Adjustment of the width of the shutter in connection with the speed with which it rotates controls the length of the dark period or colored flash.

Flashing lenses which must be rotated to produce the desired results are composed of various elements of panels designed to produce a given characteristic. The number of flash panels, the width or arc of the fixed lens sections or of the dark sections, and the speed with which the entire lens assembly is rotated determine the exact length of the various parts of the characteristic. In such lenses, the light, whether it is electric, acetylene or kerosene oil, burns steadily. Other flashing characteristics are obtained by interrupting the light source.

The flashing characteristics which distinguish many of the lighthouses are produced by revolving the entire lens. Electric flashers provide the characteristics in the drum lenses, such as a DCB-224.

Types of Lights

To the navigator, one point of lights looks just like another. Unless he can positively identify each light he sees, he is no better off than if there were not lights. After years of trial and error, the flashing light was adopted as the surest means of lighthouse identification. The term "flashing light," however, is really a misnomer, since the light source remains steady. The lens that surrounds the lamp revolves at a fixed speed. One or more areas of its surface is blocked off by an opaque screen so arranged that it obscures the light for a determined period during the passage around the lamp.

There are 11 types of lights that stand watch along our coasts today. They are known to the navigator during the day by their physical appearance and at night by the character of their lights. Some of the more common lights are:

1. A **fixed light**, as its name implies, is one that shows a continuous and steady light.

2. A **flashing light** is one that shows a simple flash at regular intervals or one or more flashes of greater brilliance. The flash is usually preceded and followed by a dimming of the light or by an eclipse.

3. A **group flashing light** shows groups of flashes at regular intervals.

4. An **occulting light** is a steady light that is suddenly and totally eclipsed at regular intervals.

5. A **group occulting light** is suddenly and totally eclipsed by a group of two or more eclipses.

6. An **alternating light** is when a light changes color, showing red and white alternately in varying combinations.

The "period" of a light is the time required to go through its characteristic changes, flashing and occulting.

When in doubt as to the identity of a light, the mariner is urged to consult the latest *Light List*, published by the United States Coast Guard (CG-158). The *List* is for sale by the Superintendent of Documents, U.S. Government Printing Office, Washington, D.C. 20402, Stock Number 050-012-00195-6. It sells for $12.00 a copy (paper cover).

Types of Beams

1. **Fan beam** - one in which the light is concentrated in and about a single plane. The angular spread in the plane of concentration may cover either 360° or a smaller angle. This beam is the most widely used.

2. **Pencil beam** - one in which the light is concentrated symmetrically about a single direction. The rays of light from revolving systems and range lights are of this category.

3. **Converged beam** - a form of fan beam in which the angular spread of a fan beam is decreased by diverting a part of the light literally to increase the intensity of the remaining beam over its full arc or over a limited arc. This type of beam is used in a few large Fresnel lenses.

4. **Diverged beam** - a form of fan beam in which the divergence of a pencil beam is increased in a plane containing the axis of the beam (usually either horizontally or vertically) so that the angular spread of the fanned beam is greater than that of the original beam. This type of beam is used in many range lights and in the latest revolving apparatus.

5. **Diverted beam** - one whose axis is changed from the original direction in which it issued from the projection apparatus by means of diverting prisms placed in its path which do not change the beam divergence. This is frequently done to **only a portion** of a pencil beam to provide asymmetrical lateral spread.

The Colors of Lights

The three standard colors, white, red and green, are used for navigational lights in order to provide greater distinctiveness and easier identification. Other colors are not used as they might readily be confused under certain atmospheric conditions with those mentioned above. The light source in all illuminating apparatus is white. However, due to the increase in shore illumination along navigable waters, the usefulness of fixed white lights is limited to areas where the usable range is short or where the natural background includes few other lights. Color is produced by the addition of colored glass shades or screens.

When approaching a light of varying intensity, such as fixed varied by flashes of alternating white and red, due allowances must be made for the inferior brilliance of the less powerful part of the light. The first-named light may, on account of distance or haze, show flashes only, and the true characteristic will not develop until the mariner comes within range of the fixed light. Similarly, the second-named may show as occulting white until the mariner comes within range of the red light.

Color sectors are employed to mark special areas, such as shoal spots, in shoal areas, or channels through foul ground. In some cases, a narrow sector may mark the best water across a shoal. A narrow sector may mark also a turning point in a channel. Sectors may be but a few degrees in width, marking an isolated rock or shoal, or of such width as to extend from the direction of the deep water toward shore. Bearings referring to sectors are expressed in degrees as observed from a vessel toward the light.

Colored sectors, where the light is to appear either red or green over a certain arc of the horizon, are produced by mounting appropriately colored sheets of glass next to the glazing of the lantern. The exact width of the colored screen and its position are adjusted to produce the desired result. A sector changes the color of a light when viewed from certain directions but not the characteristic. For example, a flashing white light having a red sector, when viewed from within the sector, will appear flashing red.

In some conditions of the atmosphere, white lights may have a reddish hue. Therefore, mariners should not trust solely to color where there are sectors, but should verify their position by taking a bearing on the light. On either side of the line of demarkation between white and colored sector, there is always a small sector of uncertain color, as the edges of a sector cannot be cut off sharply. In addition, the mariner must be aware of the difference in visibility between white, red and green lights. Red and green lights will only show one fifth as far as a white light. This difference is caused by the absorption of light from the colored lens. For this reason, white is used for almost all the landfall lighthouse beams.

The Visibility of Lights

The theoretical visibility of a light in clear weather depends upon two factors, its intensity, and its height above water. The intensity of the light fixes its **nominal range** or the maximum distance at which the light may be seen in clear weather. Clear weather is defined as a meteorological visibility of ten nautical miles. Height is important because of the curvature of the earth. It determines what is known as the **geographic range** or the maximum distance at which the curvature of the earth permits a light to be seen from a particular height of eye without regard to the luminous intensity (power) of the light.

As a rule, the nominal range of major lights is greater than the geographic, and the distance from which such aids can be seen is limited only by the earth's curvature. Such lights are often termed "strong." Conversely, a light limited by its luminous or detection range (i.e., the maximum distance a light can be seen in the existing visibility) can be called a "weak" light.

Often, the glare or "loom" of strong lights may be seen far beyond the stated geographic range. Occasionally, under rare atmospheric conditions, the light itself may be visible at unusual distances. On the other hand, and unfortunately more frequently, the range of visibility may be lessened by rain, fog, snow, haze or smoke.

The Coast Guard's *Light Lists* show the nominal range when such is five miles or more. Instructions are given for conversion of nominal range to luminous range. Both nominal and luminous ranges take no account of elevation, observer's height of eye, or the curvature of the earth.

For lights of complex characteristics (such as Group flashing white, alternating flashing red with three white and one red flash in each 40-second period), nominal ranges are given for each color and/or intensity.

The geographic range of lights is no longer given in the *Light Lists* but may be calculated from information in the front pages of each volume. Mariners should know their height of eye when at the helm of their vessels and should be aware of the greater range obtainable from a greater height above water.

The Range of Lights

The following table shows the geographic range of lights:

Height in Feet	Visible Nautical Miles
5	2.4
25	5.7
50	8.5
75	9.9
100	11.4
150	14.0
200	16.2
500	25.6
1000	36.2

It is extremely difficult to judge the distance a light will carry at sea. As a general rule, the visibility of a light depends upon its height and intensity. The distance a light is visible because of its height is known as its geographic range. The distance due to a light's intensity is known as its iluminous range. The luminous range is usually greater than the geographic range. The relation of height and visibility is expressed roughly by the equation:

Distance (in nautical miles) $= 8/7 \sqrt{\text{Height (in feet)}}$.

BIBLIOGRAPHY & REFERENCES

Introduction
Adamson, Hans Christian. *Keepers of the Lights.* New York: Greenberg, Publisher, 1955, p. 5.

Holland, Francis Ross, Jr. *America's Lighthouses: Their Illustrated History Since 1716.* Brattleboro, Vt.: Stephen Greene Press, 1972, pp. ix, 212.

Development of Lighthouse Construction
Clouette, Bruce and Roth, Matthew. *Historic Lighthouses in the Third Coast Guard District: New York. National Register of Historic Places Inventory—Nomination Form.* Prepared for the United States Coast Guard, Third District, Governor's Island, New York 10004. Hartford, CT: Historic Resource Consultants, April 30, 1983.

A Few Notes on Modern Lighthouse Practice. Birmingham, England: Chance Brothers & Co., 1910, pp. 5-9.

Holland, Francis Ross, Jr. *America's Lighthouses: Their Illustrated History since 1716.* Brattleboro, VT: Stephen Greene Press, 1972, pp. 14-21.

The Illustrated Coast Pilot. The Atlantic and Gulf Coasts. Boston, MA: N.L. Stebbins, 1896.

The Illustrated Coast Pilot with Sailing Directions. The Coast of New England from New York, to Eastport, Maine. Boston, MA: N.L. Stebbins, 1891.

Johnson, Arnold Burges. *The Modern Lighthouse Service.* Washington, DC: Government Printing Office, 1890.

McCurdy, James G. *Concrete Superceding Wood in Lighthouse Construction. Concrete-Cement Age.* April 1915, p. 198.

Meyer, Richard; Smith, Edward; Templeton, Dorothy B. *Historic Sites Survey, Inventory and Analysis of Aids to Navigation in the State of Connecticut.* Appendix A, B, C. Prepared for the United States Coast Guard, Third District, Governor's Island, New York 10004. West Chester, PA: John Milner Associates, Inc., May 1986.

National Archives, Washington, DC: Record Group 26, U.S. Coast Guard records.

National Archives, Washington, DC. Still Picture Branch, Lighthouse photographs.

Putnam, George Rockwell. *Lighthouses and Lightships of the United States.* Boston: Houghton, Mifflin and Co., 1917, pp. 34-38, 202.

Rattray, Jeannette Edwards. *Ship Ashore! A Record of Maritime Disasters Off Montauk and Eastern Long Island.* 1640-1955. New York: Coward-McCann, Inc., 1955.

Snow, Edward Rowe. *Famous Lighthouses of America.* New York: Dodd, Mead & Co., 1955.

U.S. Bureau of Lighthouses. *Annual Report.* Washington, DC: Government Printing Office, 1913, p. 16.

United States Light House Board. *Annual Report.* Washington, DC: Government Printing Office, 1877, *et seq.* Title varies.

Weiss, George. *The Lighthouse Service: Its History, Activities and Organizations.* Baltimore, MD: The Johns Hopkins Community Press, 1926, pp. 2, 8-10.

Chapter 1. Throg's Neck Light (1827)
"Lights to Sail By," *The Lookout.* New York: Seaman's Church Institute., July 1956, p. 4.

"An Old Lighthouse. The Ancient Tower at Throgg's Neck to be Pulled Down. 1883. Newspaper article.

Wilensky, Julius M. *Where to Go, What to Do, How to Do It on Long Island Sound.* Stamford, CT: Snug Harbor Publishing Co., 1968, p. 14.

Chapter 2. Stepping Stones Light (1877)

Annual Report of the Light-House Board. 1874, 1876, 1877. Washington, DC: National Archives.

Jenkins, Stephen. *The Story of the Bronx.* New York: The Knickerbocker Press, 1912, pp. 414-416.

"Lights to Sail By," *The Lookout.* New York: Seaman's Church Institute, July 1956, p. 2.

Microfilm Drawings, Civil Engineering Section, United States Coast Guard, Third District, Governor's Island, New York 10004.

"Stepping Stones Lighthouse." *National Register of Historic Places Inventory— Nomination Form.* Prepared for the United States Coast Guard, Third District, Governor's Island, New York 10004. Hartford, CT: Historic Resource Consultants, April 20, 1983.

"The Stepping Stones Light." *Boating Digest.* Spring 1965, pp. 37, 38.

Chapter 3. Execution Rocks Light (1850)

"Execution Rocks Lighthouse." *National Register of Historic Places Inventory— Nomination Form.* Prepared for the United States Coast Guard, Third District, Governor's Island, New York 10004. Hartford, CT: Historic Resources Consultants, May 20, 1983.

Putnam, George Rockwell. *Sentinels of the Coasts: The Log of a Lighthouse Engineer.* New York: W.W. Norton & Co., Inc., 1937.

"Report of the Secretary of the Treasury in Relation to the Delay in Erection of a Lighthouse on Execution Rocks." Washington, DC, 1848. National Archives.

Whitney, Dudley. *The Lighthouse.* Boston, MA: New York Graphic Society, 1975.

Chapter 4. Sands Point Light (1809)

Bahn, Jaqueline K. and Williams, George L. Introductory Paragraph by Joan G. Kent. "The Sands Point Lighthouse." *The Sketchbook of Historic Homes on Cow Neck Peninsula.* Port Washington, NY: Cow Neck Peninsula Historical Society, 1982, p. 10.

Brierly, J. Ernest. "Long Ago on Long Island." *Long Island Press,* May 26, 1963.

Cagney, W. Oakley. "Lighthouse Guided Pilots of Long Island Sound." *Long Island Press,* April 18, 1971.

"Echoes on the Sound." Sands Point, NY: Sands Point Civic Association, 1985. Videotape.

"Fabulous Sands Point Estate With Historic Lighthouse Sold Again." *Newsday.* December 13, 1943.

Gleason, Gene. "Sands Point, Community with More Acres Than People." *New York Herald Tribune,* November 7, 1965, pp. 1-5.

Kassner, Robert George. "Noah Mason and Sands Point Lighthouse." *Long Island Forum,* January 1982, pp. 9-10.

Marshall, Virginia D. *Port Recalled.* Port Washington, NY: Port Printing Service, 1967.

"Old Port Picture." *Port Mail-Reporter,* August 5, 1971.

"Old Sands Point Lighthouse Meant Much to Mariners." *North Shore Daily Journal,* April 19, 1935.

Sands Point. Sands Point, NY: Sands Point Civic Association, 1979.

Scheidell, Cathy. "Beacon Shines on 140-Year Service." *Newsday*, July 16, 1949.

Simon, Ernest. "Port Remembered." *Port Washington News*, September 24, 1970.

Chapter 5. Great Captain Island Light (1829)

Before and After 1776: A Second Edition of the Comprehensive Chronology of the Town of Greenwich 1640-1978.

Collins, Libby. "Lonely Lighthouse." *The Greenwich Review*, March 1976, p. 17.

Cutler, Jaqueline. "Keepers of the Island." *Greenwich Time*, March 19, 1984.

"Lighthouse's Repair Bids To Be Opened." *Greenwich Time*, October 7, 1974.

"Lights to Sail By," *The Lookout.* New York: Seaman's Church Institute, July 1956, pp. 3-4.

Stevens, John W. "Greenwich Sees the Ghost of 1656." *New York Times*, August 1, 1956.

Webster, Gretchen. "A Sanctum on the Sound." *Greenwich Time*, August 1, 1982, Section B.

Chapter 6. Ledge Obstruction (Chatham Rock) Light (1882)

Anderson, David. "Stamford Light, Scene of Murder and Romance, Faces Destruction." *New York Times*, June 16, 1953.

Crabill, Steven. "Flash: Lighthouse goes for $230,000." *Stamford Advocate*, December 15, 1984.

Day, Llyod N. and Scofield, Edward Candee. "The Stamford Lighthouse, 1882-1953." Stamford, CT: Stamford Historical Society, Inc., 1953.

DeMarco, Jerry. "Lighthouse for sale: Pvt. rms, harbor vu." *Fairpress*, November 30, 1983, pp. A1, A2.

"High Bid Wins It." *Yankee*, May 1984, pp. 142-146.

Janis, Chris. "Harbor Beacon." *Stamford Advocate.* September 21, 1983.

Koller, Patty. "Stamford Lighthouse sold to bidder." *Soundings*, Section II, February 1985, pp. 1, 60.

"Light Housekeeping? For Sale" *New York Times*, December 18, 1983.

"Lighthouse Sold Near Stamford." *New York Times.* October 15, 1967, pp. 1, 7.

Chapter 7. Lloyd Harbor Light (1912)

Bleyer, Bill. "Refueling a Dying Harbor Light." *Newsday*, June 5, 1985.

"Preservationists Bound to Rescue Lighthouse." *Newsday*, November 11, 1985.

"Dimming Lighthouse Here Evokes Protest." *Long Islander.* September 7, 1967, pp. 1-2.

Documents Relating to Lighthouses 1789-1871, p. 221. Washington, DC: National Archives.

Humeston, Reverend E.J. "Lighthouse Marked Sandspit For Sailships Since 1847." *The Long Islander.* November 20, 1947, p. 1; Section 3, p. 1.

"Huntington Remembered." *The Long Islander*, March 31, 1983.

Kongelbeck, Bertha. "In Our Town." *Long Islander*, October 29, 1964.

"Lloyd Harbor Lighthouse." *National Register of Historic Places Inventory—Nomination Form.* Prepared for the United States Coast Guard, Third District, Governor's Island, New York 10004. Hartford, CT: Historic Resource Consultants, May 20, 1983.

May, Clifford D. "L.I. Group Works to Save Lighthouse from Ruin." *New York Times*, Sunday, February 16, 1986, p. 54.

"Placing a Floating Concrete Crib for a Lighthouse." *Engineering Record* 62, No. 21 (November 19, 1910): pp, 571-572.

United States Commissioner of Lighthouses. *Annual Report . . .* 1912. Washington: United States Government Printing Office, 1912.

Chapter 8. Greens Ledge Light (1902)

"Greens Ledge Lighthouse." *National Register of Historic Places Inventory—Nomination Form.* Prepared for the United States Coast Guard, Third District, Governor's Island, New York 10004. West Chester, PA.: John Milner Associates, Inc., May 1986.

Log Books. Greens Ledge Light Station, Rowayton, CT, 1939-1943.

"Older Lighthouses Blinking Out." *Sunday News*, March 21, 1971, p. W34.

One Artist; one subject; endless variations . . ." *North Light*, November/December, 1972, pp. 16-21.

United States Coast Pilot 2, Atlantic Coast: Cape Cod to Sandy Hook, 19th Edition. Washington, D.C.: National Ocean Service, January 1984, p. 197.

United States Lighthouse Board. *Annual Report of the Lighthouse Board, 1896-1902.* Washington: National Archives.

Chapter 9. Peck Ledge Light (1906)

"Peck Ledge Lighthouse." *National Register of Historic Places Inventory—Nomination Form.* Prepared for the United States Coast Guard, Third District, Governor's Island, New York 10004. West Chester, PA.: John Milner Associates, Inc., October 22, 1985.

Tulin, Bud. "Norwalk Islands, Our National Heritage." *Norwalk Star*, May 14, 1981.

United States Lighthouse Board. *Annual Report of the Lighthouse Board, 1896-1902, 1905-1907. 1909.* Washington, DC: National Archives.

Williams, Dick. *The Historic Norwalk Islands.* Darien, CT: Pictorial Associates, 1978.

Chapter 10. Sheffield Island Light (1868)

"Barge may have dragged down tugboat that sank, killing 6." *Staten Island Advance*, November 23, 1984.

"Co-owner says sunken barge was good for '4 or 5 years.' " *Staten Island Advance*, December 4, 1984.

"Did overload sink tugboat?" Staten Island Advance, November 28, 1984.

"Holes found in sunken barge." *Staten Island Advance*, November 30, 1984, p. A10.

Kerr, Peter, "Tug Disappears With 6 Aboard; Search Pressed," *New York Times*, November 19, 1984, Section B, 4:6.

Lacy-Pendleton, Stevie. "Islander's body found in tug." *Staten Island Advance*, November 21, 1984.

"Four bodies pulled from tug." *Staten Island Advance,* November 20, 1984.

Law, Richard. "Collector's Office, Proposals . . ." *Norwalk Gazette*, August 15, 1826.

McFadden, Robert D. "Tug sinks; 4 Bodies Recovered." *New York Times*, November 20, 1984, 1:1, B10:1.

Messing, Philip and Rosensohn, Sam. "3 Bodies Recovered From Sunken Tug." *New York Post*, November 20, 1984, p. 22.

"M/V *Celtic*—Freight Barge *Cape Race*—Investigation into the Sinking of with Subsequent Loss of Life on 17 November 1984, Action by the Commandant." A final Report of the Commanding Officer, U.S. Coast Guard, Marine Inspection Office, Battery Park Building, New York, NY 10004, May 20, 1986, 40 pp.

"Tug Inquiry Told About Leak." *New York Times*, November 22, 1984, Section B 4:6.

"Tug 'shipshape' at start of trip." *Staten Island Advance*, November 29, 1984.

"2 More Bodies Found in Tug." *New York Times*, November 21, 1984, Section B 4:6.

Williams, Dick. *The Historic Norwalk Islands*. Darien, CT: Pictorial Associates, 1978, pp. 6-9.

"Wood from barge shown at hearing in tugboat sinking." *Staten Island Advance*, November 27, 1984.

Chapter 11. Eatons Neck Light (1799)

"Eaton's Neck Lighthouse." *Historic Survey and Inventory of Selected Real Property Facilities*. Prepared for the United States Coast Guard, Third District, Governor's Island, New York 10004. The Ehrenkrantz Group, July 1983.

"Focus: Eaton's Neck Station U.S. Coast Guard." *Soundings*, June 1964.

Knowles, Howard N. *A Lighthouse of Stone*. Northport, NY: Northport Historical Society, 1978. Monograph.

"Notes on Eaton's Neck Lifeboat Station, Northport, L.I." Governor's Island, NY: Public Information Office, Third Coast Guard District, April 1968.

Chapter 12. Old Field Point Light (1824)

Documents Relating to Light- Houses, 1789-1871, p. 217. Washington, DC: National Archives.

Klein, Howard. *Three Village Guidebook*. 1976.

"The Lighthouse, Old Field Point, Old Field." n.d. Unknown source.

"Old Field Lighthouse." Extract from private journal of the Daughter of the American Revolution, n.d.

Snow, Edward Row. *The Lighthouses of New England*. New York: Dodd, Mead & Company, 1945, pp. 331-340.

United States Coast Pilot 2. Atlantic Coast: Cape Cod to Sandy Hook. 19th Edition. Washington, DC: National Ocean Survey, January 1984, p. 210.

Chapter 13. Penfield Reef Light (1874)

Baldor, Lolita C. "Memories haunt Penfield Lighthouse." *Fairfield Citizen-News*, July 22, 1983, pp. 3, 12-13.

Coles, Matthew A. "Fight to Preserve Penfield Lighthouse Being Pressed by Weicker, McKinney." *Bridgeport Telegram*. July 4, 1970.

Decerbo, Frank W. "Inside Penfield Lighthouse." *Bridgeport Sunday Post*, April 6, 1958, pp. 3-5.

Descriptive List of Light Stations, Penfield Reef, 1880. National Archives Record Group 26.

"McKinney's Plea: 'Save Lighthouse!' " *The Town Crier*, January 14, 1970.

"96-Year-Old Lighthouse Wins Demolition Stay." *Town Crier*, January 17, 1970.

"Officials Modify Lighthouse Plan." *The Town Crier*, January 23, 1970.

"Penfield Reef Lighthouse." *National Register of Historic Places—Nomination Form*. Prepared for the United States Coast Guard, Third District, Governor's Island, New York 10004. West Chester, PA.: John Milner Associates, Inc., October 22, 1985.

"Penfield Lighthouse to Go 'Automatic' on Saturday." *Bridgeport Post*, September 2, 1971.

"Smith, Francis Hopkinson." *The Twentieth Century Biographical Dictionary of Notable Americans*, Vol. IX. Boston: The Biographical Society, 1904.

"Tradition Wins Out." *The Town Crier*, March 31, 1970.

United States Coast Pilot 2. Atlantic Coast: Cape Cod to Sandy Hook, 19th Edition. Washington: National Ocean Service, 1984, p. 195.

U.S. Lighthouse Board. *Annual Report of the Light-House Board*, 1868-1875, 1877-1883, 1887-1889, 1892, 1894, 1898-1899, 1901-1902. Washington, DC: National Archives.

Chapter 14. Black Rock Harbor Light (1809)

Bishop Collection. Bridgeport Public Library, Bridgeport, CT.

"Board tries to save lighthouse." *Bridgeport Post*, Tuesday, January 22, 1980.

Brilvitch, Charles. *Walking Through History; the Seaports of Black Rock and Southport*. Fairfield, CT: Fairfield Historical Society, 1977, pp. 1-11.

Roth, Matthew. "Fayerweather Island Light." *An Inventory of Historic Engineering and Industrial Sites*. Hartford, CT: Society for Industrial Archeology, 1981, p. 24.

"U.S. Light House Establishment." Unpublished and undated U.S. Coast Guard document.

Chapter 15. Tongue Point Light (1894)

"A New Lighthouse." *Bridgeport Standard*, January 16, 1891.

"Tongue Point Lighthouse." *Historic Sites Survey, Inventory, and Analysis of Aids to Navigation in the State of Connecticut*. Prepared for the United States Coast Guard, Third District, Governor's Island, New York 10004. West Chester, PA.: John Milner Associates, Inc., May 1986.

United States Lighthouse Board. *Annual Report of the Lighthouse Board*, 1892, 1894-1900, 1905. Washington, DC: National Archives.

Chapter 16. Stratford Shoal (Middleground) Light (1837)

Bache, Lieutenant George M. "The Middleground floating light, November 22, 1893." *Documents Relating to Light-houses, 1789-1871*. Washington, DC: National Archives, p. 216.

"A Beacon to Mariners for 133 Years, Middleground Light Now Automated." *Bridgeport Sunday Post*, March 27, 1977, p. A-4.

List of Light-houses, Lighted Beacons, and Floating Lights on the Altantic Gulf and Pacific Coasts of the United States. Washington, DC: Government Printing Office, 1879, p. 38.

"Stratford Shoal Lighthouse." *National Register of Historic Places Inventory—Nomination Form*. Prepared for the United States Coast Guard, Third District, Governor's Island, New York 10004. West Chester, PA.: John Milner Associates, Inc., October 22, 1985.

U.S. Lighthouse Board. *Annual Report of the Light-House Board*, 1873, 1878. Washington, DC: National Archives.

U.S. Lighthouse Board. *Inspection Reports of Light Stations*. Washington: National Achives, Record Group 26.

U.S. Lighthouse Board. *Journal*, Volume 5 (1873). Washington: National Archives.

Chapter 17. Stratford Point Light (1822)

"Stratford Point," 1887. *Descriptive List of Light Stations*. Washington, DC: National Archives, Record Group 26.

"Stratford Point Lighthouse." *National Register of Historic Places Inventory— Nomination Form*. Prepared for the United States Coast Guard, Third District, Governor's Island, New York 10004. West Chester, PA.: John Milner Associates, Inc., May 1986.

U.S. Lighthouse Board. *Annual Report of the Light-House Board*, 1867-1881, 1883, 1888-1890, 1895-1896, 1899, 1910. Washington, DC: National Archives.

Wilcoxson, W. Howard. "Stratford Point." *Excerpts from History of Stratford, 1639-1939*. Stratford, CT: Stratford Tercentenary Commission, 1939, Chapter 42.

Chapter 18. New Haven Harbor Light (1805)

"Lighthouse Gets First Paint In 20 Years." *New Haven Evening Register*, Wednesday, May 25, 1949.

"Lighthouse Opening Set For May 28." *New Haven Evening Register*, 8, 1949.

Lynne, Frank. "New Haven Harbor - Lighthouse." *Saturday Chronicle*, n.d., p.8.

Townsend, Charles H. "The Old New Haven Lighthouse." *New Haven Old and New*, n.d., pp. 12-18.

Chapter 19. Southwest Ledge Light (1877)

Barnard, J.G. "Lighthouse Engineering as Displayed at the Centennial Exhibition." *American Society of Civil Engineers Transactions*, Volume 8 (March 1879): pp. 55-94.

Johnson, Arnold Burges. "Light-Houses on Tubular Foundations. Southwest Ledge." *The Modern Light-House Service*. Washington, DC: Government Printing Office, 1890, pp. 35-36.

Lynne, Frank. "New Haven Harbor - Lighthouse." *Saturday Chronicle*, n.d., p. 8.

Osterweis, Rollin. *Three Centuries of New Haven*. New Haven, CT: New Haven Colony Historical Society, 1952.

"Southwest Ledge Lighthouse." *National Register of Historic Places Inventory— Nomination Form*. Prepared for the United States Coast Guard, Third District, Governor's Island, New York 10004. West Chester, Pa.: John Milner Associates, Inc., May 1986.

United States Lighthouse Board. "Southwest Ledge lightstation, Conn." *Annual Report of the Light House Board*, 1872, 1874-1881, 1883-1884, 1887-1889, 1892, 1894-1899, 1902, 1907. Washington, D.C.: National Archives.

Chapter 20. Falkner Island Light (1802)

Brughardt, Dee. "Faulkner's Island, Landmark for Sailors and Landlubbers." *Shore Line Times*, August 4, 1960.

"Captain Brooks Passes Away." *Shore Line Times*, January 9, 1913, pp. 151-152.

Dale, Mabel. "Fire devastates Faulkner's." *Shore Line Times*, March 18, 1976.

Dix, John. "Faulkner's Island; from farming to lifesaving." *Shore Line Times*, January 24, 1984, pp. 1, 8.

"Faulkner Island Lighthouse." *National Register of Historic Places Inventory— Nomination Form*. Prepared for the United States Coast Guard, Third District, Governor's Island, New York 10004. West Chester, PA.: John Milner Associations, Inc., May 1986.

Floherty, John J. *Sentries of the Sea*. New York: J.B. Lippincott Co., 1942, p. 136.

Hopkins, D. Scott and Spendelow, Jeffrey A. "The 1983 Falkner Island Tern Project." Guilford, CT: Little Harbor Laboratory, Inc., 1983.

"Isle Lighthouse Razed By Fire." *New Haven Register*, March 18, 1976, p. 7.

Steiner, Bernard C. "Falcon or Faulkner's Island." *History of the Plantation of Menunkatuck*. Baltimore, MD: The Friedenwald Co., 1897, pp. 202-203. Reprinted 1975 by The Guilford Free Library, CT.

United States Coast Pilot 2. Atlantic Coast: Cape Cod to Sandy Hook. 19th Edition. Washington: National Ocean Service, January 1984, p. 177.

"Wreck of the Moses Webb," *Shore Line Times*, January 23, 1913, pp. 87-89.

Chapter 21. Horton Point Light (1857)

Neugebauer, William. "A town steeped in tradition." *Daily News*, February 25, 1979.

Rattray, Jeannette Edwards. *Ship Ashore! A Record of Maritime Disasters off Montauk and Eastern Long Island, 1640-1955*. New York: Coward-McCann, 1955, p. 40.

Wegner, Frances. "Original Light Returning to Horton's Point."*The Suffolk Times*, July 14, 1977.

Wilensky, Julius M. *Where to Go, What to Do, How to Do It on Long Island Sound*. Stamford, CT: Snug Harbor Publishing Company, 1968, p. 161.

United States Coast Pilot 2. Atlantic Coast: Cape Cod to Sandy Hook. 19th Edition. Washington, DC: U.S. Department of Commerce, National Oceanic and Atmospheric Administration, National Ocean Service, 1984, p. 186.

Chapter 22. Lynde Point Light (1803)

Carse, Robert. *Keepers of the Lights: A History of American Lighthouses*. New York: Charles Scribner's Sons, 1968, pp. 61-63.

Floherty, John J. *Sentries of the Sea*. New York: J.B. Lippincott Co., 1942, pp. 32-26.

Grant, Marion Hepburn. "The Lighthouses." *The Fenwick Story*. Old Saybrook, CT: Cardavon Press, 1974, pp. 50-54. Privately printed.

"In All Weather, the Lights Must Beam." *The Middletown Press*, August 16, 1963, pp. 5, 8-9.

"Lynde Point Lighthouse." *National Register of Historic Places Inventory—Nomination Form*. Prepared for the United States Coast Guard, Third District, Governor's Island, New York 10004. West Chester, PA: John Milner Associates, Inc., October 22, 1985.

Chapter 23. Saybrook Breakwater Light (1886)

Adamson, Hans Christian. *Keepers of the Lights*. New York: Greenberg, Publisher, 1955, pp. 136-137.

Grant, Marion Hepburn. "The Lighthouses." *The Fenwick Story*. Old Saybrook, CT: Cardovan Press, 1974, p. 51. Privately printed.

The Light-House Board. *Annual Report of the Light-House Board*, 1889, 1891. Washington: National Archives.

"Saybrook Breakwater Light." *National Register of Historic Places Inventory—Nomination Form*. Prepared for the United States Coast Guard, Third District, Governor's Island, New York 10004. West Chester, PA: John Milner Associates, Inc., October 22, 1985.

Chapter 24. Plum Island Island (1827)

Documents Relating to Light Houses, 1789-1871. Washington: National Archives.

The Light-House Board. *Annual Report of the Light-House Board*, 1868, 1878. Washington. DC: National Archives.

Plows, Diane. "P.I. Light To Go Dark." *Suffolk Times*, March 23, 1978.

The Plum Island Animal Disease Center. Washington, DC: United States Department of Agriculture, Agricultural Research Service, Northeastern Region, Plum Island Animal Disease Center, 1982, pp. 20-21, 38-39.

United States Coast Pilot 2. Atlantic Coast: Cape Cod to Sandy Hook. 19th Edition. Washington: National Ocean Service, January 1984, p. 152.

Chapter 25. Orient Point Light (1899)

Dorman, Barbara. "Coast Guard Begins Restoring Orient Point Light." *Soundings*, November 1973.

The Light-House Board. *Annual Report of the Light-House Board*, 1896-1898, 1899. Washington. DC: National Archives.

Long Island Press, October 4, 1970.

"Orient Point Lighthouse." *National Register of Historic Places Inventory—Nomination Form.* Prepared for the United States Coast Guard, Third District, Governor's Island, New York 10004. Hartford, CT: Historic Resource Consultants, April 20, 1983.

Reports of the Commissioner of Lighthouses, 1896-1898. Washington, DC: National Archives.

Suffolk Times, January 29, 1971.

Chapter 26. Cedar Island Light (1839)

Diamond, Stuart. "Gutted Landmark Was Uninsured." *Newsday*, January 13, 1974, p. 6.

Keeler, Bob. "Lighthouse Gets a Quick Fix-Up." *Newsday*, July 20, 1974. p. 10.

The New York Times. Rotogravure Picture Section, Sunday, February 28, 1937.

Rattray, Everett T. *The South Fork.* New York: Random House Inc., 1979, p. 168.

Rattray, Jeanette Edwards. *Ship Ashore!* New York: Coward-McCann, Inc., 1955, p. 39.

United States Coast Pilot 2. Atlantic Coast: Cape Cod to Sandy Hook. 19th Edition. Washington: National Ocean Survey, January 1984, p. 154.

"Up at Auction: One Lighthouse 97 Years Old." *New York Herald Tribune,* Sunday, December 13, 1936.

Chapter 27. Montauk Point Light (1797)

Clennan, Noel. "Keepers of the Light Replaced by a Computer," *The Whale*, Sept. 19, 1986, p. 10.

Goldstein, Marilyn. "She Holds the Patent on Tenacity." *Newsday*, October 1984, p. 19.

Ketcham, Diane. "Montauk's Lighthouse: On the Edge of Disaster." *New York Times* (Long Island Edition), Section 11, Sunday, September 22, 1985, pp. 1, 10.

Makay, Marion P. "Montauk Light, 'Sentry of Sea,' Attracts Legions of Auto Tourists." *New York Herald*, Sunday, August 31, 1932.

Rattiner, Dan. "Is the Montauk Light Saved?" *The Montauk Pioneer*, Volume XXV, Number 19, September 18, 1985, pp. 1-4.

"The Ceremony at the Montauk Lighthouse," *Dan's Papers*, Vol. XXI, Number 24, September 18, 1986, pp. 1, 3.

Rattray, Jeannette Edwards. *Ship Ashore!* New York: Coward-McCann, 1955, pp. 20-21, 24, 26-28, 100.

Reid, Giorgina. "Reed-Trench Terracing," Patent 3,412,561. Washington, DC: United States Patent Office, November 26, 1968. *How to Hold up a Bank.* New York: A.S. Barnes, 1969. "Holding Up the Shoreline." *Newsday*, Tuesday, April 3, 1973. "Giorgina Reid's Progress Report—February 1980." *Montauk Almanac IV*, pp. 11-12.

Snow, Edward Rowe. *Famous Lighthouses of America.* New York: Dodd, Mead & Co., 1955, p. 106.

"U.S. Gives up Lighthouses after 189 Years," *The Southampton Press,* September 18, 1976.

Watkins, T.H. "A Heritage Preserved." *American Heritage,* Volume 32, Number 4, June/July 1981, pp. 28-29.

Whitney, Dudley. *The Lighthouse.* Boston: New York Society, 1975, pp. 186-187.

Chapter 28. Block Island Southeast Light (1875)

Adamson, Hans Christian. *Keepers of the Lights.* New York: Greenberg, Publisher, 1955, p. 116.

Collins, Francis A. *Sentinels Along Our Coast.* New York: The Century Co., 1922, pp. 88-90.

Pettee, Edward. *Block Island Illustrated.* Boston, MA: 1884, pp. 64-65.

Reports to the Commissioner of Lighthouses, 1872-1875. Washington, DC: National Archives.

Willoughby, Malcolm F. *Lighthouses of New England.* Boston: T.O. Metcalf Co., 1929, pp. 210-211.

Chapter 29. Block Island North Light (1829)

"Block Island North Light." *National Register of Historic Places Inventory—Nomination Form*. Prepared for the United States Coast Guard, Third District, Governor's Island, New York 10004. Providence, RI: Rhode Island Historical Preservation Commission, March 1974.

"Island is Given Granite Lighthouse." *The Sun,* Westerly R.I., Wednesday, November 21, 1984.

The Lighthouse Board. *Annual Report of the Light-House Board to the Secretary of the Treasury of the Year 1875.* Washington, DC: Government Printing Office, 1875, pp. 11, 27, 32-33, 107-108, 110, 113. 1877, p. 22. 1891, p. 248. 1896, p. 25.

Pratt, Karson Eugene and Downie, Robert M. *A Brief History of the North Light originally known as Sandy Point Light.* New Shoreham, RI: North Light Commission, 1974.

"Probably 150 Lost in Wreck." *The New York Times,* Wednesday, February 13, 1907, pp. 1-2.

Report of Lieutenant George M. Bache, U.S. N., Washington City, November 22, 1838." *Documents Relating to Light Houses, 1789-1871,* p. 20. Washington, DC: National Archives.

Willoughby, Malcolm. F. *Lighthouses of New England.* Boston, MA: T.O. Metcalf Co., 1929, pp. 210-211.

Chapter 30. New London Harbor Light (1760)

"New London Harbor Light." *National Register of Historic Places Inventory— Nomination Form.* Prepared for the United States Coast Guard, Third District, Governor's Island, New York 10004. West Chester, PA.: John Milner Associates, Inc., October 22, 1985.

"New London Harbor Lighthouse." *Historically Famous Lighthouses,* CG-232. Washington, D.C.: Department of Transportation, U.S. Coast Guard, Public Information Division, 1972, pp. 9, 10.

Snow, Edward Rowe. *Famous Lighthouses of America.* New York: Dodd, Mead & Company, 1955, pp. 88-92.

Whitney, Dudley. *The Lighthouse.* Boston, MA: New York Graphic Society, 1975, p. 189.

Chapter 31. New London Ledge Light (1908)

Collins, David. "Automation may close an unusual house at sea." *The Day,* April 30, 1984, pp. 1, 4.

Gaby, Stan. *The Orient Point Passage.* Published privately, 1984, pp. 12-13.

"New London Ledge Light." *National Register of Historic Places Inventory— Nomination Form.* Prepared for the United States Coast Guard, Third District, Governor's Island, New York 10004. West Chester, PA: John Milner Associates, Inc., October 22, 1985.

Plummer, Dale S. "New London Ledge Lighthouse." *Historic Resources Inventory, Buildings and Structures.* Hartford, CT: Connecticut Historical Commission, September 10, 1980.

Report of the Commission of Lighthouses, 1912, pp. 91-92. Washington, DC: National Archives.

St. Clair, Tim. "They'll leave 'The Ledge' come June." *Soundings,* February 1979, p. 1.

Chapter 32. Little Gull Island Light (1806)

"Little Gull Island." *National Register of Historic Places Inventory—Nomination Form.* Prepared for the United States Coast Guard, Third District, Governor's Island, New York 10004. Hartford, CT: Historic Resource Consultants, April 20, 1983.

Snow, Edward Rowe. *Famous Lighthouses of America.* New York: Dodd, Mead & Co., 1955, pp. 92, 93.

Station Log Books. Little Gull Island Light Station, 1944-1947.

Chapter 33. Race Rock Light (1878)

Adamson, Hans Christian. *Keepers of the Lights.* New York: Greenberg, Publisher, 1955, pp. 138-179.

"American Lighthouses." *Scientific American,* November 15, 1873, p. 306.

"Capt. Thomas A. Scott." *Genealogical and Biographical Record of New London County, Conn.* Chicago, IL: J.H. Beers & Co., 1905.

Decher, Robert O. "T.A. Scott Company." *The Whaling City.* New London: New London County Historical Society, 1976.

Floherty, John J. *Sentries of the Sea.* New York: J.B. Lippincott Co., 1942, pp. 110-122.

Lewiton, Nina. *Lighthouses of America.* Eau Claire, WI: E.M. Hale & Co.., 1964, pp. 61-64.

The Light-House Board. *Annual Report of the Light-House Board,* 1878. Washington, DC: National Archives.

"Race Rock Lighthouse." *Boating Digest.* Winter 1966, pp. 57-58.

"Race Rock Lighthouse." *Historically Famous Lighthouses,* CG-232. Washington, DC: Department of Transportation, U.S. Coast Guard, Public Information Division, 1972, pp. 67-68.

"Race Rock Lighthouse." *National Register of Historic Places Inventory— Nomination Form.* Prepared for the United States Coast Guard, Third District, Governor's Island, New York 10004. Hartford, CT: Historic Resource Consultants, April 20, 1983.

"Smith, Francis Hopkinson." *Dictionary of American Biography, Volume XVII.* New York: Charles Scribner's Sons, 1935, pp. 265-267.

Smith, F. Hopkinson. *Captain Thomas A. Scott, Master Diver.* Boston, MA: American Unitarian Association, 1908. *Caleb West, Master Diver.* Boston, MA: Houghton Mifflin Co., 1898.

Snow, Edward Rowe. *Famous Lighthouses of America.* New York: Dodd, Mead & Co., 1955.

Whitney, Dudley. *The Lighthouse.* Boston, MA: New York Graphic Society, 1975.

Willoughby, Malcolm F. "Race Rock Light Station." *Lighthouses of New England.* Boston, MA: T.O. Metcalf Co., 1929, pp. 212-220.

Chapter 34. North Dumpling Light (1849)

Colby, Bob. "Lighthouse getting face lift," *Soundings,* November 1980.

De Wire, Elinor. "The Dogs of the Lighthouses," *Dog Fancy,* December 1983, pp. 20-22.

"Isle He Purchased A 4-Acre Headache." *Herald Tribune,* March 2, 1962.

Snow, Edward Rowe. *Famous Lighthouses of America.* New York: Dodd, Mead & Co., 1955, p. vii. *Famous Lighthouses of New England.* New York: Dodd Mead & Co., 1945, pp. 155-156.

Chapter 35. Latimer Reef Light (1884)

"Latimer Reef Lighthouse." *National Register of Historic Places Inventory— Nomination Form.* Prepared for the United States Coast Guard, Third District, Governor's Island, New York 10004. Hartford, CT: Historic Resource Consultants, April 20, 1983.

The Light-House Board. *Annual Report of the Light-House Board 1884.* Washington, DC: National Archives.

Light List, Third District, Long Island Sound and Tributaries. Washington, DC: Government Printing Office, June 30, 1900, p. 56.

U.S. Coast Pilot, Atlantic Coast, Part IV, Long Island Sound with approaches and adjacent waters. Washington, DC: Government Printing Office, 1971, p. 120. Fifteenth Edition, 1980, p. 152. Nineteenth Edition, 1984, p. 159.

Chapter 36. Morgan Point Light (1831)

Noank Historical Society *Newsletter,* Volume II, Number 2, June 1968, pp. 3, 4.

"Noank National Register District." *National Register of Historic Places Inventory—Nomination Form.* Washington, DC: U.S. Department of Interior, National Park Service, 1974, pp. 23, 33-36.

Chapter 37. Stonington Light (1823)

Haynes, William. *The Stonington Chronology, 1547-1949.* Stonington, CT: Pequot Press, 1949.

Johnson, Arnold B. *The Modern Lighthouse Service*. Washington, DC: Government Printing Office, 1890.

Palmer, Henry R. *Stonington by the Sea*. Stonington, CT: Palmer Press, 1913.

"Stonington Harbor Lighthouse." *National Register of Historic Places Inventory—Nomination Form*. Prepared for the United States Coast Guard, Third District, Governor's Island, New York 10004. Hartford, CT: Historic Resource Consultants, July 8, 1975.

U.S. Light-House Board. *Annual Reports*, 1852-1889. Washington, DC: National Archives. *Documents Relating to Light-Houses*, 1789-1871. Washington, DC: Government Printing Office, 1871.

U.S. Treasury Department Fifth Auditor. *List of Lighthouses, Beacons and Floating Lights*. Washington, DC: C. Alexander, 1848.

Chapter 38. Watch Hill Light (1807)

Ben-Itzak, Paul. "Lighthouse Enters Age of Automation." *The Day* (New London, CT), September 2, 1986, pp. D1, B9.

Best, Mary Agnes. "The Town that Saved a State—Westerly." 1943, p. 191.

Cole, J.R. *History of Washington and Kent Counties, R.I.* Volume 2. New York: W.W. Preston & Co., 1889, p. 271.

Coy, Sallie E. "Watch Hill B.C. and A.D." Unpublished manuscript, n.d.

The Light-House Board. *Annual Report of the Light-House Board*, 1855, 1876. Washington, DC: National Archives.

"Lighthouse Decommissioned" (Photo), *The Sun* (Westerly, RI), September 2, 1986, p. 6.

Light-House Laws and Appropriations, 1789-1855, p. 44. Washington, DC: National Archives.

National Archives, Record Group #26, papers, clippings, and other documents from Watch Hill Light file.

Pendleton, Albert P. "The Watch Hill Road—past and present—buildings and tenants." 1916, pp. 30-31.

Perlstein, Steven M. "A New Era for Watch Hill Lighthouse." *The Providence Journal-Bulletin,* September 1, 1986, p. A-03.

Shreenan, Fanny Clark. "Brief History of Watch Hill Light Station." Unpublished manuscript, n.d., Westerly (RI) Public Library.

"Watch Hill Light Station." *National Register of Historic Places Inventory—Nomination Form*. Prepared for the United States Coast Guard, Third District, Governor's Island, New York 10004. Providence, RI: Rhode Island Historical Preservation Commission, February 1983.

Chapter 39. Point Judith Light (1810)

Bonham, Julia C. and Kulik, Gary. "Point Judith Lighthouse." *Rhode Island, An Inventory of Historic Engineering and Industrial Sites.* Washington, DC: United States Department of the Interior, Heritage Conservation and Recreation Service, Office of Archeology and Historic Preservation, Historic Engineering Record, 1978, pp. 111-112.

"A Century on Guard." *The Providence Sunday Journal,* Fifth Section. January 2, 1916, p. 1.

Cole, J.K. *History of Washington and Kent Counties, Rhode Island,* Volume 2. New York: W.W. Preston & Co., 1889, pp. 622-623.

Documents Relating to Light-Houses, 1789-1871, p. 202. Washington, DC: National Archives.

The Light-House Board. *Annual Report of the Light-House Board to the Secretary of the Treasury, 1867-1923*. Washington, DC: Government Printing Office, 1923, pp. 17-19.

"Point Judith Lighthouse." *Inventory Form*. Prepared for the United States Coast Guard, First District, Boston, MA 02114. Stonington, CT: Eugene Wick York, consultant in Historic Preservation and Building Restoration, June 1985.

United States Coast Pilot 2. Atlantic Coast: Cape Cod to Sandy Hook. 19th Edition. Washington, DC: United States Department of Commerce, National Oceanic and Atmospheric Administration, National Ocean Service, January 1984, p. 147.

Ward, John. "Sentinels Along The Shore." *Providence Sunday Journal*, November 10, 1963, pp. 12-14.

Willoughby, Malcolm F. *Lighthouses of New England*. Boston: T.O. Metcalf Co., 1929, pp. 206-207.

Chapter 40. Automation of the Lights

Bastian, Richard E. "Automation Turns Over Lighthouse to the 'Ghosts.' " *The New Haven Register*, Sunday, December 10, 1978, p. B5.

The Lighthouse Board

United States Coast Guard. *The Coast Guard at War, Aids to Navigation XV*. Washington, DC: United States Government Printing Office, July 1, 1949, pp. 1-2.

Keepers of the Light

"Lights to Sail By." *The Lookout*. New York: Seaman's Church Institute, July 1956, pp. 4-5.

Phillips, Wendell. "They Light Up Your Life!" *Water Boating*, July 1980, p. 41.

Early Lighthouses

"Lights to Sail by." *The Lookout*. New York: Seaman's Church Institute, July 1956, pp. 2-3.

De Wire, Elinor. "The old tower." *Sea Frontiers*, July-August 1984, pp. 223, 226-227.

The Structure of Lighthouses

Chapman, Charles F. "Structures," *Piloting, Seamanship and Small Boat Handling*. 51st Edition. New York: The Hearst Corporation, 1974, pp. 317, 320.

Wave-Swept Lighthouses

Collins, Francis A. *Sentinels Along Our Coast*. New York: The Century Co., 1922, pp. 42-51, 58-61.

Chapter 41. Lenses

Carse, Robert. *Keepers of the Light: A History of American Lighthouses*. New York: Charles Scribner's Sons, 1968, pp. 61-63, 66-67.

Floherty, John J. *Sentries of the Sea*. New York: J.B. Lippincott Co., 1942, pp. 32-36.

Phillips, Wendell. "They Light Up Your Life!" *Western Boating*, July 1980, p. 41.

United States Coast Guard. *Aids to Navigation Manual* (CG-222). Washington, DC: United States Government Printing Office, January 1953, pp. 29-4 to 29-6.

Aids to Navigation Manual, Amendment 4. Washington, DC: United States Government Printing Office, June 1956, p. 23-2.

Aids to Navigation - Technical Manual (M16500.3). Washington, DC: United States Government Printing Office, 11 September 1979, pp. 6-82 to 6-84.

Aids to Navigation - Technical Manual (M16500.3). Washington, DC: United States Government Printing Office, 29 August 1986, pp. 6-56 to 6-88.

Wheeler, Wayne. "The Fresnel Lens," *Keeper's Log 1* (Winter 1985): pp. 12-13.

Witney, Dudley. *The Lighthouse*. Boston: New York Graphic Society, 1975.

Chapter 42. Forms of Illuminant in Lighthouses

United States Coast Guard. "Forms of Illuminant," *Aids to Navigation Manual, Amendment 4*. Washington, DC: United States Government Printing Office, June 1956, pp. 23-2, 23-3.

Light Characteristics

Chapman, Charles F. "Light Characteristics," *Piloting, Seamanship, and Small Boat Handling*. 51st Edition. New York: The Hearst Corporation, 1974, pp. 320-321.

United States Coast Guard. "Characteristics of Fixed Structures," *Aids to Navigation Manual, Amendment 1*, Washington, DC: United States Government Printing Office, March 1953, pp. 6-3, 6-6, 6-7.

Types of Lights

Floherty, John J. *Sentries of the Sea*. New York: J.B. Lippincott Co., 1942, pp. 34-36.

Types of Light Beams

United States Coast Guard. "Types of Light Beams," *Aids to Navigation Manual, Amendment 4*. Washington, DC: United States Government Printing Office, June 1956, p. 23-9.

The Colors of Lights

United States Coast Guard. "Primary and Secondary Lights," *Aids to Navigation Manual, Amendment 1*, Washington, DC: United States Government Printing Office, March 1953, p. 6-6.

The Visibility of Lights

Chapman, Charles F. "The Visibility of Lights," *Piloting, Seamanship and Small Boat Handling*. New York: The Hearst Corporation, 1974, pp. 321-322.

The Range of Lights

Carse, Robert. *Keepers of the Light: A History of American Lighthouses*. New York: Charles Scribner's Sons, 1968, pp. 68-69.

Miscellaneous

Richard, Robert G. "Sentinels on the Sound." *Connecticut Magazine,* July 1984, pp. 60-63.

Bleyer, Bill. "Beautiful Beacons. The Lighthouses of Long Island." *The Newsday Magazine,* May 25, 1986, pp. 10-17, 30-33.

Cox, Rachel and Bowker, Michael. "The Lighthouse: Endangered Species?" *Historic Preservation,* Volume 37, Number 6, December 1985, pp. 52-59.

Description of Light Stations. Form 60, Third Light House District. Washington, DC: Department of Commerce and Labor, January 15, 1935.

Light Keepers, 1848-1906. Washington, DC: National Archives.

Light List, Volume I. Atlantic Coast: St. Croix River, Maine to Little River, South Carolina. CG-158, Department of Transportation, Coast Guard, Washington, DC: U.S. Government Printing Office, 1984.

"List of Historical Societies and Museums, Historic Coast Guard Lighthouses, Third District." Appendix 4. Washington, DC: U.S. Department of Transportation, June 1982.

List of Light-Houses, Lighted Beacons, and Floating Lights of the Atlantic, Gulf, and Pacific Coasts of the United States. Washington, DC: Government Printing Office, 1872.

The 1985 IMS/AYER Directory of Publications. Port Washington, PA: IMS Press, 1985.

Scheina, Robert L. *United States Coast Guard Annotated Bibliography, Aids to Navigation (Lighthouses and Lightships).* Washington, DC: U.S. Department of Transportation, June 1982.

United States Coast Pilot, Atlantic Coast, Part IV. From Point Judith to New York. Second Edition. Washington, DC: Government Printing Office, 1892.

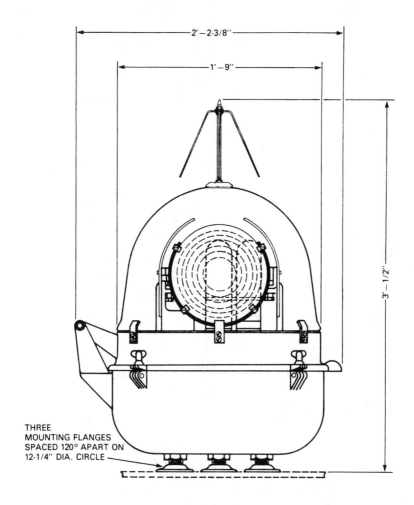

2′ − 2-3/8″

1′ − 9″

3′ − 1/2″

THREE
MOUNTING FLANGES
SPACED 120° APART ON
12-1/4″ DIA. CIRCLE

Dimensions of the DCB-10 Lantern.
Old Field Point Light (Chapter 12) has one of these. See also page 255

Courtesy U.S. Coast Guard

INDEX

278

279

280

281

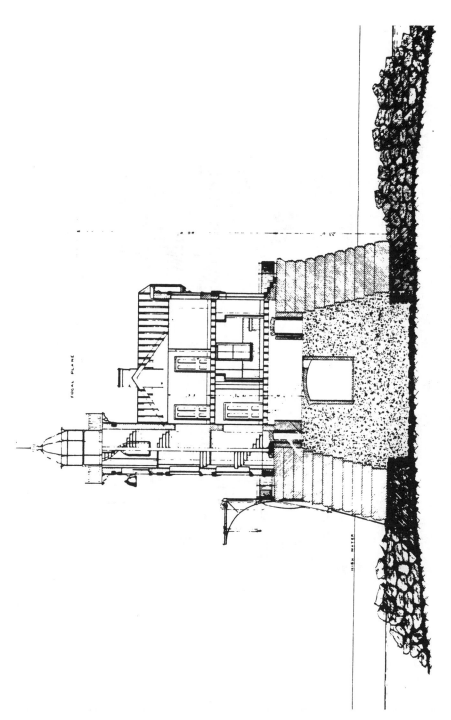

Elevation from plans for Stratford Shoal Light drawn March 24, 1878. Chapter 16

Courtesy U.S. Coast Guard

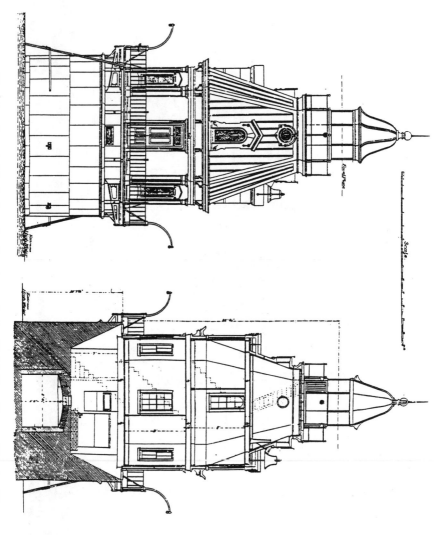

Elevation from original plans for Southwest Ledge Light, New Haven. Chapter 19

Courtesy U.S. Coast Guard

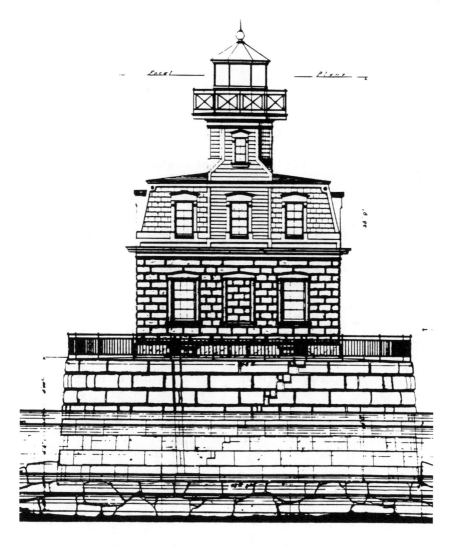

Elevation from original plans drawn for Penfield Reef Lighthouse. Chapter 13

Courtesy U.S. Coast Guard

Other Cruising Guides and books published by
Wescott Cove Publishing Co., Box 130, Stamford, CT 06904

Cruising Guide to Maine - Volume I, Kittery to Rockland
by Don Johnson

Cruising Guide to Maine - Volume II, Rockport to Eastport
by Don Johnson

Yachtsman's Guide to the Windward Islands
by Julius M. Wilensky

Cruising Guide to the Abacos and Northern Bahamas
by Julius M. Wilensky

Cruising Guide to the Bay Islands of Honduras
by Julius M. Wilensky

Cruising Guide to Tahiti and the French Society Islands
by Marcia Davock

I Don't Do Portholes! a compendium of useful boatkeeping tips
by Gladys H. Walker and Iris Lorimer. Illustrated by Peter Wells